ZBrush® Studio Projects

REALISTIC GAME CHARACTERS

ZBrush® Studio Projects

REALISTIC GAME CHARACTERS

RYAN KINGSLIEN

WILEY

Wiley Publishing, Inc.

Acquisitions Editor: Mariann Barsolo
Development Editor: Stephanie Barton
Technical Editors: Paul Gaboury
Production Editor: Christine O'Connor
Copy Editors: Judy Flynn and Elizabeth Welch
Editorial Manager: Pete Gaughan
Production Manager: Tim Tate
Vice President and Executive Group Publisher: Richard Swadley
Vice President and Publisher: Neil Edde
Assistant Project Manager: Jenny Swisher
Associate Producer: Josh Frank
Quality Assurance: Doug Kuhn
Book Designer: Caryl Gorska
Compositor: Kate Kaminski, Happenstance Type-O-Rama
Proofreader: Publication Services, Inc.
Indexer: Robert Swanson
Project Coordinator, Cover: Katherine Crocker
Cover Designer: Ryan Sneed

Library of Congress Cataloging-in-Publication Data
Kingslien, Ryan, 1973-
  ZBrush studio projects : realistic game characters / Ryan Kingslien.
    p. cm.
  ISBN 978-0-470-87256-7 (pbk.)
        978-1-118-06762-8 (ebk.)
        978-1-118-06772-7 (ebk.)
        978-1-118-06763-5 (ebk.)

  1. Computer games—Design. 2. Video game characters. 3. ZBrush. I. Title.
  QA76.76.C672K56 2011
  794.8'1536—dc22

                              2010054034

Dear Reader,

Thank you for choosing *ZBrush Studio Projects: Realistic Game Characters*. This book is part of a family of premium-quality Sybex books, all of which are written by outstanding authors who combine practical experience with a gift for teaching.

Sybex was founded in 1976. More than 30 years later, we're still committed to producing consistently exceptional books. With each of our titles, we're working hard to set a new standard for the industry. From the paper we print on, to the authors we work with, our goal is to bring you the best books available.

I hope you see all that reflected in these pages. I'd be very interested to hear your comments and get your feedback on how we're doing. Feel free to let me know what you think about this or any other Sybex book by sending me an email at nedde@wiley.com. If you think you've found a technical error in this book, please visit http://sybex.custhelp.com. Customer feedback is critical to our efforts at Sybex.

Best regards,

Neil Edde
Vice President and Publisher
Sybex, an Imprint of Wiley

To the craft of figurative sculpting and those who keep it alive.

Acknowledgments

The single most important person in shaping the ideas and approach of this book is Al Gury, chair of the Painting Department at the Pennsylvania Academy of the Fine Arts (PAFA), who gave me the tools I needed when I was a student at PAFA. ■ The single most important person in making this book possible is Ofer Alon, founder of Pixologic. Ofer brought me into Pixologic based on a review I wrote many years ago. Since then Ofer has taught me how to understand the technology of an artist in a way I never thought possible, and his trust and kindness have been a guiding light for me. ■ Jaime Labelle, COO of Pixologic, is the glue that binds all things ZBrush together and is the best boss I ever had. Today, he is ZBrushWorkshops' most tireless supporter and a great friend. ■ I would also like to thank Marianne Barsolo, Stephanie Barton, Christine O'Connor and all the great people at Wiley Publishing for their work on this book. Paul Gaboury, my tech editor, offered suggestions and kept me honest. ■ Tomas Babinec, at 3D.sk, has helped create one of the most important resources for 3D artists and is always supportive. Travis Bourbeau, at the Gnomon Workshop, has been a tireless supporter and always has encouraging words. Andrew Cawrse and Grace Fua at Anatomy Tools provided models, kindness and reference. ■ Finally, I would like to thank my wife for her support and encouragement during the long hours it took to create a book like this.

About the Author

Ryan Kingslien is the founder of www.zbrushworkshops.com.
He attended the Pennsylvania Academy of Fine Art and the Gnomon School
of Visual Effects. He was the first product manager for ZBrush at Pixologic,
where he combined the efforts of programmers and artists to help create some
of the revolutionary tools in ZBrush. He also created the first industry-
standard curriculum and documentation that helped bring ZBrush to companies such as Industrial Light & Magic (ILM), Sony Pictures Imageworks,
and Electronic Arts (EA).

CONTENTS AT A GLANCE

Introduction ■ **xv**

Chapter 1 ■ Sculpting Tools and Workflow **1**

Chapter 2 ■ Sculpting the Body **21**

Chapter 3 ■ The Head and the Face **65**

Chapter 4 ■ Texturing the Head **95**

Chapter 5 ■ Suiting Up with Clothes **129**

Chapter 6 ■ Building Weapons **175**

Chapter 7 ■ Getting It Into the Game **215**

Chapter 8 ■ Posing and Rendering in ZBrush **247**

Appendix ■ About the Companion DVD **279**

Index ■ **283**

Contents

Introduction   xv

Chapter 1 ■ Sculpting Tools and Workflow   1

The Problem of Sculpting   1

Our Sculpting Toolkit   3

Unpacking Our Toolkit   9

The Road Ahead   18

Chapter 2 ■ Sculpting the Body   21

Proportions   21

Project 1: Modeling Base Mesh in Maya   22

Project 2: Bony Landmarks   34

Project 3: Volume and Massing   38

Project 4: Painting in the Anatomy   45

Project 5: Filling in the Anatomy   52

Chapter 3 ■ The Head and the Face   65

Proportions   66

Project: Establishing the Foundation   66

Project: Establishing the Eye   73

Project: Establishing the Nose   79

Project: Establishing the Mouth   82

Project: Creating New Topology   87

Summary   93

Chapter 4 ■ Texturing the Head   95

Project: Texture Painting by Hand   96

Project: Texture Painting Approach #2 ZAppLink   113

Summary   127

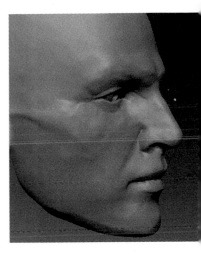

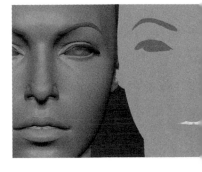

Chapter 5 ▪ Suiting Up with Clothes   **129**

    Creating a Jacket   130

    Summary   172

Chapter 6 ▪ Building Weapons   **175**

    The Anatomy of the Weapon   175

    Anatomy of the Holster   195

    Texturing   210

    Summary   213

Chapter 7 ▪ Getting It Into the Game   **215**

    The Topology Spectrum   215

    Project: Topology - Removing
Interior Polygons   216

    Project: Topology - Combining Parts   218

    Project: Adding the Holster   221

    Project: Topology - Decimation Master
& Polypainting   223

    Project: In-Game Hair   224

    Project: Create UVs using UV Master   227

    Project: UVs, Topology, and the Platform   228

    Project: Creating Maps   230

    Project: Setting Up Model in Maya   232

    Assessing Your Topology   233

    Project: Importing Jacket's
Reflowed Topology   237

    Project: Getting Model into Marmoset   238

    Summary   245

Chapter 8 ▪ Posing and Rendering in ZBrush   **247**

    Project: Finding the Pose with Mannequins   247

    Project: Establishing the Pose for the Body   250

    Project: Posing Multiple Objects   254

    Project: Creating the Base   260

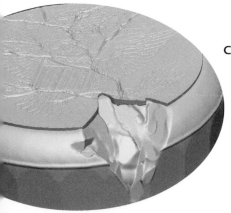

Project: Damaging the Base   265

Project: Shadows and Ambient Occlusion   267

Project: Using Render Passes   269

Project: Plastic Maquette Material   270

Project: Adding Some SSS   273

Project: Timeline Turntable   274

Project: XPose   275

Project: Exporting a Movie   276

Summary   278

Appendix ▪ About the Companion DVD   **279**

What You'll Find on the DVD   279

System Requirements   280

Using the DVD   281

Troubleshooting   282

Customer Care   282

Index   **283**

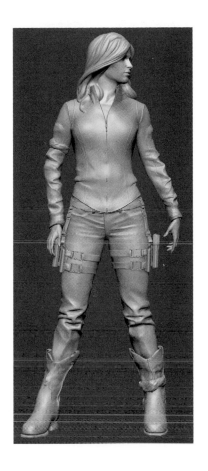

Introduction

Sculpting is hard work. It's not like painting or drawing or making pretty pictures. It's just plain old hard work. You don't need to know how to draw to do it. I've known several incredible sculptors who can't draw. You don't need to understand color theory. You just need to be able to apply a certain amount of willpower to overcome obstacles and accomplish the task, and trust me, there will be obstacles.

I want to tell you about a place where I've spent a lot of my professional life. It's called "the Valley of the Suck." It's not a nice place to be. In fact, it absolutely sucks to be there, but it's a necessary place to be. It's an essential place to be. You simply cannot get to be a better sculptor unless you walk through the Valley of the Suck and walk through it often.

It is the one place where your weaknesses are absolutely and completely obvious for anyone to see. It's that place you go to when you sculpt the wrists and you just don't quite understand them. It's that place you go to when you muddle through the anatomy of the back.

There is one good thing about the Valley of the Suck: it's just a valley and it's not the entire planet, so you can eventually find your way out of it. Of all the skills that help you find your way out of the valley the most, I find a stubborn, willful disregard for failure to be the most important.

Who Should Buy This Book

Sculpting is one of those unique actions, like dancing, that fuse our senses with a way of seeing the world. When you're a sculptor, you just see things differently. You see the zygomatic process under the skin. You look for the lacrimal bone in the corner of someone's eyes.

This book is for sculptors—traditional or digital. For me, it's all the same. I sculpt in Roma Plastilena and in ZBrush. ZBrush is simply one medium in which I work. It has its technical difficulties, just like clay, and it has its specific working properties, just like clay.

This book is suitable for everyone from beginners to advanced artists. In some sections you will need to have a certain comfort level with ZBrush. These sections are pushed to the end, though, to give beginners a chance to catch up. If you're very new to this world of digital sculpting, I recommend reviewing the "Introduction to Sculpting" workshop included with this book on the accompanying DVD.

If your goal is to work in the game industry or simply master digital sculpting, this book is one of the essential steps along the way. My goal with this book is to fuse traditional learning with the digital nature of ZBrush while preparing you for the real world of production sculpting. When you sculpt a character for production you will not paint its anatomy. However, once you have painted the anatomy onto your model, you are much better prepared to sculpt the figure without it.

What You Need

To follow the techniques this book, you will need a Wacom tablet, a copy of ZBrush 4, a computer, and willpower strong enough to eat through titanium.

Sculpting in ZBrush with a mouse is like painting with a brick. It's just not going to work. Sculpting with a Wacom tablet is the only way to go. If you can at all afford it, though, I highly recommend the 21″ Cintiq from Wacom. There is no other way to get more closely connected to your sculpt than by using a Cintiq monitor.

You'll also need Maya or a similar 3D application. "Why include Maya?" you might ask. Maya is what they call a *hub* application. It's the main application that everyone in a production pipeline plugs into.

Digital sculptors, in the game industry, will work in ZBrush, but they still need to get the model along with the normal map in Maya or another 3D application for export to the game engine.

Anatomy Resources

The first resource you should have on your desk is Anatomy Tools' Male and Female Anatomy figure. You might balk at the price and wonder if it's worth it, but I urge you to look at that money as a down payment on the skills that will land you a job and take your sculpting to the next level. For me, it is more important to get this anatomy figure than it is to get any other book. As sculptors we need the thing in 3D, not as 2D on a page.

Regarding books, I highly recommend Gottfried Bammes' *Die Gestalt des Menschen* (Urania Verlag, 2002) and Eliot Goldfinger's *Human Anatomy for Artists* (Oxford University Press, 1991).

What's Inside

Here's a peek at what each chapter covers:

Chapter 1: Sculpting Tools and Workflow This chapter focuses on the stuff under the hood of ZBrush. Although this is a highly technical chapter, it holds the key to understanding how ZBrush's brush system works.

Chapter 2: Sculpting the Body This chapter takes you through the process of sculpting the body. It is not possible to discuss everything we need to cover in one chapter, though, and this chapter is best viewed as a crash course.

Chapter 3: The Head and the Face Sculpting realistic game characters is more about sculpting realistic faces than anything else. This chapter focuses on the anatomy that you need to know that no one else is teaching. Learn it well and you'll be creating realistic faces in no time.

Chapter 4: Texturing the Head Texturing means two things. It means texture painting and it also means sculpting details like pores and wrinkles. In this chapter we look at both concepts.

Chapter 5: Suiting Up with Clothes Clothing is an essential part of sculpting the character. This chapter is a crash course on creating the base mesh and sculpting the wrinkles that will make your character believable.

Chapter 6: Building Weapons Sculpting hard surfaces in ZBrush is a real treat if you know how to use the tools. This chapter helps you understand them and create a pistol entirely in ZBrush using the new Clip brushes.

Chapter 7: Getting It Into the Game Once you are done with the model, it's time to put it in a game. This chapter teaches you to work with your topology and the new Multi Map Exporter to get everything ready in Maya.

Chapter 8: Posing and Rendering in ZBrush Posing the character adds that next bit of life that is essential for a great presentation. This chapter teaches you how to use Transpose to pose your models and how to get the most out of ZBrush's Best Preview Rendering system.

Companion DVD

The companion DVD includes a few of the resources you'll use in the book. It also includes some extra tutorials from ZBrushWorkshops to help you get the most out of your reading time.

For those just starting with ZBrush, I've included one of our first workshops, "Introduction to Sculpting." This workshop is over 90 minutes of training that takes you through learning to use the interface to learning how to get control over your sculpting.

The DVD also includes resource files for each chapter and may include the final sculpts done to demonstrate each project.

How to Contact the Author

If you are looking for more training, the best way to reach me is at my training site, www.ZBrushWorkshops.com. At ZBrushWorkshops we train artists to sculpt in ZBrush. We focus on specific problem areas like sculpting skin and scales or hard surfaces, and provide the tools you need to master ZBrush.

We also provide custom training for companies and count Electronic Arts (EA), Industrial Light & Magic (ILM), and many others in our list of clients.

You can also visit my personal site at www.ryankingslien.com where I keep you up-to-date on my sculpting activities.

Please also check the book's website at www.sybex.com/go/zsprealisticgame, where we'll post updates to this book as needed.

ZBrush® Studio Projects

REALISTIC GAME CHARACTERS

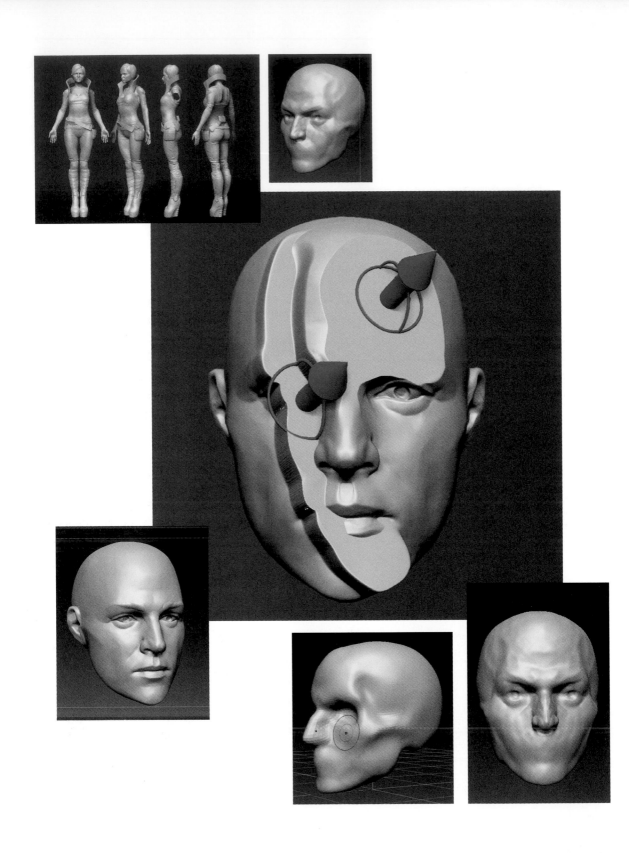

CHAPTER 1

Sculpting Tools and Workflow

You face two core issues when you create realistic game characters: technology and artistic ability. Five years ago the biggest problem was technology. We simply couldn't put enough polygons on the screen to get true realism. Today, artistic ability is the biggest factor limiting a 3D modeler's growth in the game industry.

The demand for realism increases with technological advances. Today, it is your ability to sculpt a face, but in two years' time realism may depend on understanding what happens to the palpebral ligament when your character is frightened.

Your artistic ability is the one constant in the equation of creating realistic characters, whether you are painting in Photoshop or sculpting in ZBrush.

The Problem of Sculpting

The central problem of sculpting, in my view, revolves around understanding the hierarchy of planes. In a life model, we are confronted with thousands of planes all calling for attention. How do we know which planes to focus on and which to ignore, at least for the moment? Figure 1.1 shows a sculpture by Jean-Baptiste Carpeaux of a woman smiling. Even with its smooth, beautiful surface, the underlying planes of its construction still shine through.

Figure 1.1

Planes define the sculpture by Carpeaux.

The key to working with planes is to move from the largest to the smallest. You, the artist, must create inside of your own brain a 3D model that has multiple levels of resolution. On level 1, it should have the most basic and simplistic planes. On level 5, it might have planes small enough to describe the caruncula of the eye.

The sculpture by Carpeaux reveals that the side of the nose is a plane, the lips have several planes, and even the round surface of the eye can be distilled into a few essential planes. As we get more detailed with our model, though, we focus on smaller and smaller planes. In Figure 1.2 you see Anatomy Tool's artist busts, which helps break down the different stages of sculpting a face into easy-to-digest forms. The human body is simply too complex to tackle everything at once. Creating a hierarchy of planes will help you solve only the problems you need to at each stage of your sculpt.

Finding these planes and organizing them is, unfortunately, a task through which I can only guide you. You must enter the dark woods by yourself and find your own way through the endless variations of form that come before you. I will do my best to provide a map, arm you with the necessary tools, and send you on your way with my best advice.

Figure 1.2
**Anatomy Tool's
artist busts**

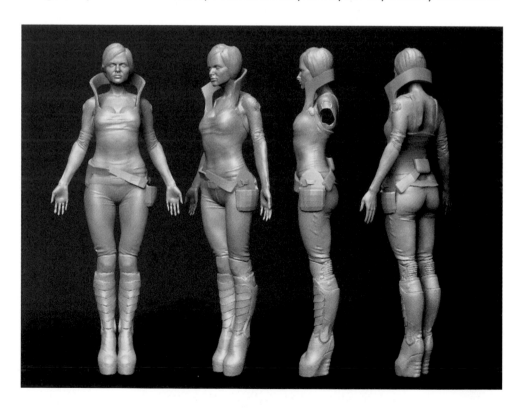

Our Sculpting Toolkit

There are many features in ZBrush and many ways to work with the application. The goal of this book is to guide you in creating realistic game characters, and so in this section, I will present what I consider to be a sculptor's workflow. This workflow should help you organize complexity, create your own hierarchy of planes, and sculpt realistic characters faster than ever before.

Project: Sculpting a Human Face

To really get a sense of how tools work together, we will look at them in the context of a project. In this case, we will sculpt a human face and look at each tool in its turn:

1. Our first goal is to establish the overall shape of a head with the *Move brush* so that we can use other brushes to create the internal forms. Start with a PolySphere on the canvas (see Figure 1.3). Make sure Symmetry is on.

2. Set Draw Size to 200 to increase the size of your brush. Click on the bottom half of the PolySphere and drag downward to form the jaw and lower face.

   Lower your Draw Size to somewhere around 50 and pull the nose outward and to the left. Then push the eye socket inward toward the right. Note the S-shaped curve in Figure 1.4.

Figure 1.3

A PolySphere on the canvas

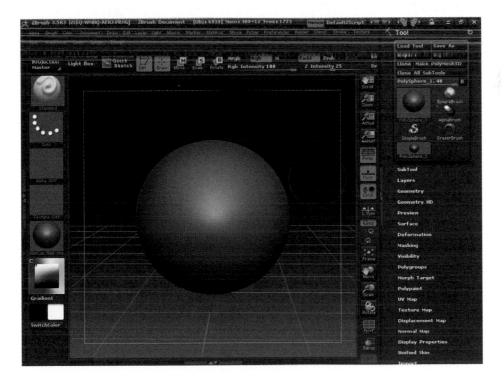

Figure 1.4

Side view with
the S curve of
the side of face

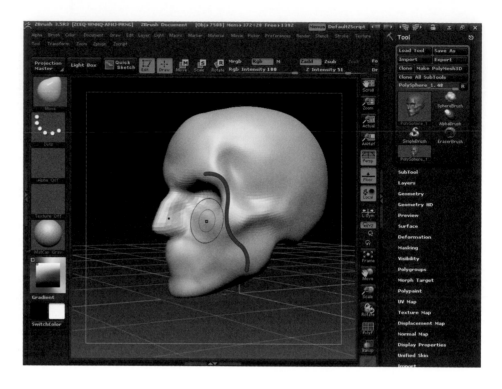

Rotate the model to a front view. Set your Draw Size to 256 and pull the sides inward to flatten them. Continue working over the surface of your model. At a certain point you will suffer diminishing returns and form will be harder to create. When that happens to you, it's time to switch brushes.

3. Once you have your "digital clay" roughly in the shape of the head, it is time to sculpt some of the internal forms, such as the cheeks, forehead, eye area, and mouth area. We'll start this process with the *Clay brush*. Click the Brush icon in the far left tray and select the Clay brush.

Press Alt and dig into the eye area to create the eye cavities. Continue sculpting into the side of the nose, top of the nose, and down into the mouth. Release Alt when you want to build the form back up.

Add a little bit of clay in the mouth area, but stay away from defining the lips. At this point, you should be more focused on sculpting the barrel shape of the teeth. When done, your model should look like Figure 1.5. Don't try to take it much further than that, as we will use other tools to refine the surface. The Clay brush is used mostly to add volume and roughly sketch in form.

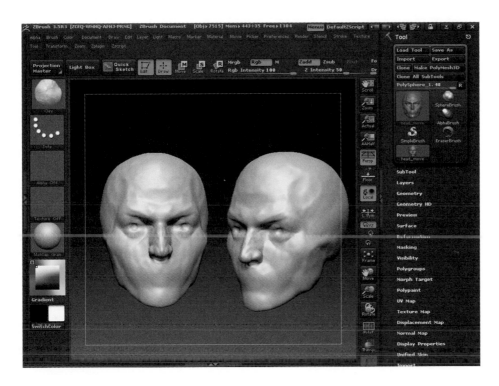

Figure 1.5

Results after using the Clay brush

The Clay brush is an important part of our sculpting workflow because of its unique algorithm. ZBrush 4 has added newer brushes that build upon this and give us greater control, but the Clay brush remains an important part of the process in the early stages.

4. Make sure to add geometry to your model as needed by choosing Tool → Geometry → Divide. In fact, with the newer topology-independent brushes such as Clay, we can begin to increase our polygon count earlier in the sculpting process without worrying about muddy form.

5. Eventually, your sculpt will have a lot of the form you want, but it will be a little messy. This is where **Trim Dynamic** comes in. Select Trim Dynamic from the Brush palette and use it the same way you use the Clay brush. Notice how the form it creates is very clean and planar.

Continue developing the form, switching between the Clay brush and Trim Dynamic. When you need to add more form, use the Clay brush. Then immediately switch to Trim Dynamic and create the necessary planes. Figure 1.6 shows you how far you should take your work with Trim Dynamic. Again, don't take your model too far. We will keep looking at new tools for each stage.

Figure 1.6

Results after using the Trim Dynamic brush

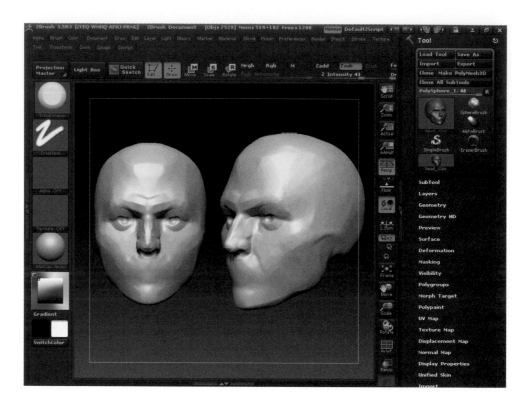

Figure 1.6

Results after using the Trim Dynamic brush

Trim Dynamic is an extension of the Clay brush. Its algorithm goes further than the Clay brush, however, and allows you to build up planes with a loose freehand stroke that cannot be achieved any other way. It is an essential tool in your toolkit.

6. To create precise forms, we will need a sculpting knife. We can use the *Standard brush* for this. Set Draw Size to somewhere around 10 and press Alt while you carve into the model.

   When you do this, it's important to proceed with caution and maybe even to use multiple strokes to carve in the surface. As always, it's very important to smooth out any irregularities as soon as you see them. When you are finished, your model should resemble Figure 1.7.

The Standard brush is one of the oldest brushes in ZBrush and still considered by many artists to be the workhorse of all the brushes. You can also try a variation of the Standard brush called the Dam_Standard brush, named after the artist who created it, Damien Canderle. You can access the Dam_Standard brush from Lightbox.

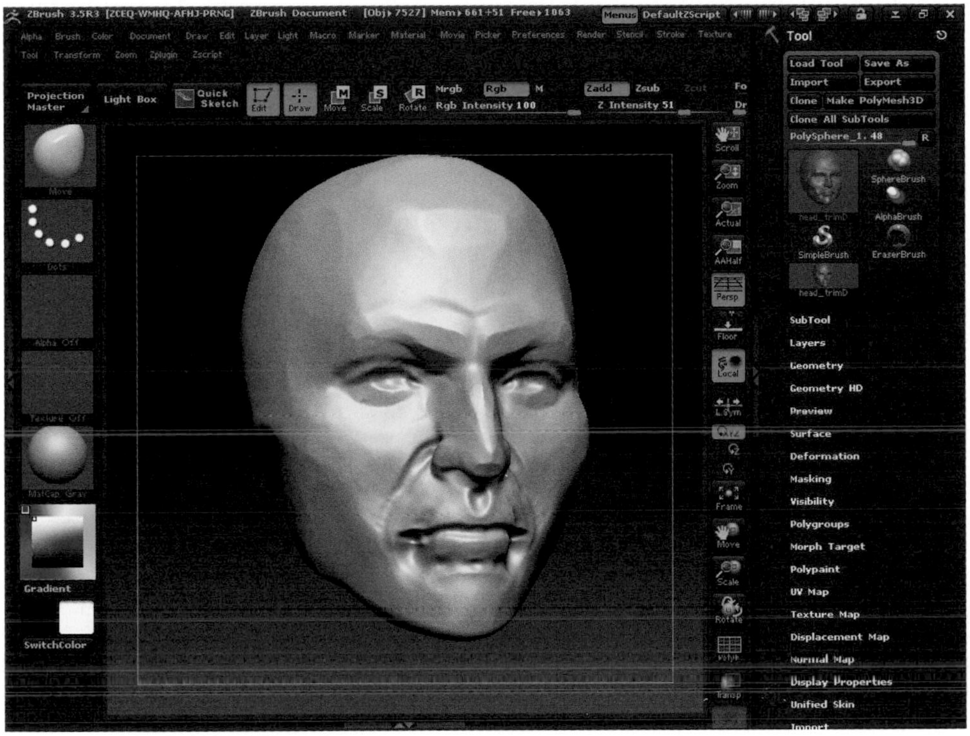

Figure 1.7

Results after using the Standard brush

7. Now we should have a fairly good approximation of the face. We should have clear planes, but the separation of planes may not be very precise. All in all, our model should look like a blurry but planar version of what we want.

   To create more precise breaks in the form, we use *Trim Adaptive*. Click on the side plane of the nose and use Trim Adaptive to create a consistent plane. With Trim Adaptive you have to be careful where you start your brush stroke. The brush will take the orientation of the first place you click and extend that orientation through your model.

   To get the most out of Trim Adaptive, repeat the stroke while pressing Alt, and the brush will lift areas of the surface as well. Using Trim Adaptive and Trim Dynamic and experimenting with Trim Front should get your sculpt to the level of Figure 1.8.

8. Masks allow us to isolate one part of the model and keep it safe from our brush.

   Press and hold Ctrl and brush on the general shape of the ear. Then choose Tool → Masking → Inverse to invert this mask. Using the Move brush, pull out the backs of the ear and set up the simple planes as shown in Figure 1.9.

Figure 1.8

Results after
using various Trim
brushes

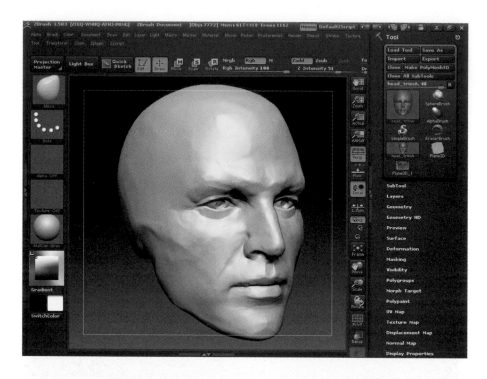

Figure 1.9

Using masks to
establish the ear

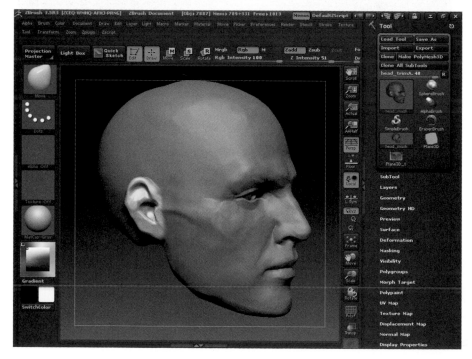

9. After you have worked the surface of your model, you may want to smooth out some areas and refine the surface. The Polish brushes are great tools to do this.

I like to use H_Polish because it respects hard edges very well. This allows me to be looser and more freehand without worrying about messing up the clean edge work I created earlier. Consider H_Polish a finishing tool. The form has to be in place for this brush to do its job right. Use Figure 1.10 as your guide.

> Polish brushes are similar to the Flatten brushes. They are the finishing tools of ZBrush. You can smooth out surfaces with a bit more control than you can with the Smooth brush, as well as grind areas down as though you're using sandpaper.

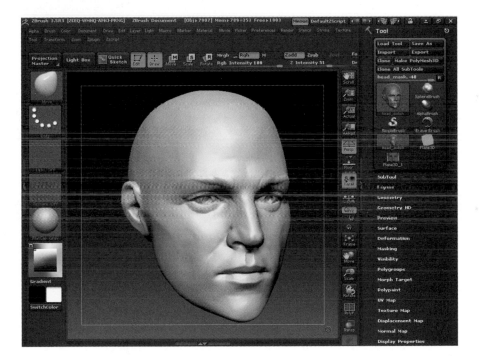

Figure 1.10

Results after using the Polish brush

Unpacking Our Toolkit

Let's review our toolkit and make sure that you understand what is in it and what each tool is good for. This section is the largest lecture-based section of the book. There will be a lot of reference-style descriptions. Use this section as you would any reference book and come back to it when you need an explanation of things like ZBrush's Depth setting.

Move brush Our first tool; it creates the largest planes and biggest form changes.

Clay brush Blocks in areas of the model and adds "clay" to the model that you will refine with other brushes.

Trim Dynamic Creates the primary planes of your model and keeps the surface clean and structured.

Trim Adaptive Creates and extends planes. It is the wooden sculpting tool you would use to enforce a strong plane, and you may even cut into the model with it.

Dam_Standard and Standard brushes These are great knives. By setting DrawSize low, you can cut thin lines into the model.

Masks Isolate areas of the model to help you when you are making large changes or even small adjustments. In ZBrush 4, you have several different masking options: To change your masking type, simply select it in the Brush pop-up.

The Polish brushes Create refined surfaces and blend structured planes into each other.

The Sculpting Spectrum

The entire brush system in ZBrush can be divided into four zones (see Figure 1.11). These zones correspond to your approach toward sculpting and what you are actually sculpting. Are you sculpting loosely or do you need more refined control? Are you sculpting soft forms or hard forms?

Figure 1.11

Brush system spectrum

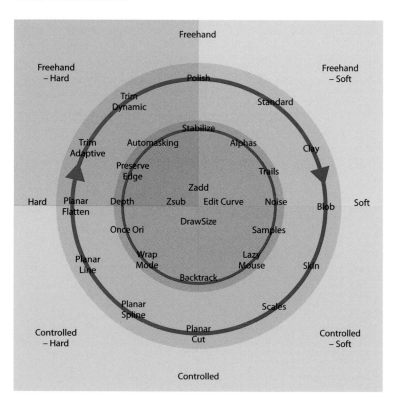

Along the outside of this spectrum are the brush types. Every brush was created to fit a specific need. Some brushes, like the Blob brush, can create amazingly random concrete surfaces with just a few simple modifications. Other brushes, like the Planar brushes, create hard-edged and mechanical details but require some complicated brush modifications to work. Some brushes blend magically between these two opposites and, with only a few modifications, can create both hard and soft forms. The Clay brush is a good example of this.

At the center of these two axes are core features of the sculpting system, features like Zadd/Zsub, DrawSize, and Z Intensity. These features are the same no matter what you are sculpting.

Between the brush types and the core features are all the brush modifiers, which are as basic as Alphas and Stroke Type and as specific as BackTrack, Samples, Depth Imbed, and Tablet Pressure. These modifiers can have a profound effect on your brush and completely alter its behavior. As we look at each part of the brush system, try to place each feature somewhere in the spectrum.

The Brush Algorithm

At the core of every brush is the algorithm that it uses to affect the surface. The algorithm is the 1s and 0s, the very foundation of a brush's behavior, and Pixologic excels in finding and exploiting new algorithms. We call this algorithm the brush type.

ZBrush contains close to a hundred brushes, but most of them are derivatives of other brushes. For example, the Polish brushes appear to be derived from the Flatten brush. Some brushes are different by just a few settings. Some brushes are a variation on the algorithm of the brush type itself.

The Magnify and the Inflate brushes are good examples of variations on an algorithm, while brushes like the Rake brush use the same algorithm but have preset modifications that alter its behavior.

First, we'll unpack the Clay brush and see what makes this brush so special for blocking in form.

Clay Brush

The Clay brush was definitely created to work with soft surfaces in a freehand way. However, with a little finesse it can also block out harder surface objects.

The algorithm of the Clay brush was an important step toward sculpting brushes that are topology independent; that is, they behave the same regardless of whether your model is an organized mesh or decimated scan data. Its specific behavior is such that it fills up the lowest areas of the surface before it affects the higher areas of the surface. This allows you to quickly build up form without worrying about all the interpenetration and artifacting that the Standard brush might introduce.

An important part of the Clay brush is the Depth:Imbed setting. Let's take a good look at Depth to be sure you have a solid understanding of how to use it.

Depth

The Depth feature was introduced in ZBrush 3.5r3. It is located in the Brush → Depth sub-palette (see Figure 1.12) and is a change from ZBrush 3.1, where Brush → Brush Modifier was sometimes used for this purpose. Now Depth is a major new feature that affects the entire spectrum of your brush's behavior.

What does Depth do? To understand it better, you should be clear that a brush in ZBrush is a 3D sphere. The red circle that encompasses your brush shows the brush size, but it doesn't indicate the real spherical nature of a brush. All the variations and modifications of the brush take place within this sphere of activity. As you brush along the model, this sphere is dragged along the surface. In thin areas of your model it will affect the other side as well.

Figure 1.12

The Depth subpalette

Depth either raises this sphere above or lowers it below the surface of your model, as shown in Figure 1.13. Now, I know what you are thinking. You're thinking, "Isn't that what Z Intensity does? Doesn't Z Intensity decide how far up or down my brush pushes the surface of the model?" Well, in short, no. Z Intensity is something else entirely!

Think about it this way. Depth + DrawSize defines the outer limits of your brush's intensity. DrawSize defines how large an area your brush will affect. Depth defines where, along the normal that area will intersect with your model, as well as the maximum distance the brush will push or pull the form.

Figure 1.13

The effects of Depth

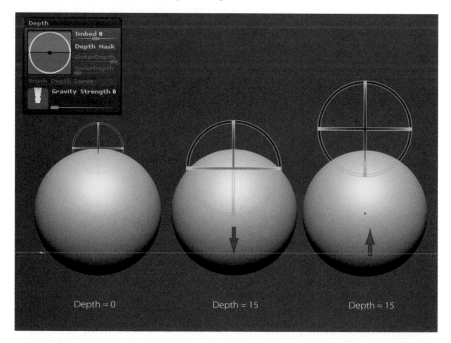

Z Intensity controls how fast you will reach those limits. If you set Z Intensity to 100, then your brush will be at full intensity right from the start. If you set Z Intensity to 5, then it will take some time to reach full intensity, and you can be more subtle about it.

A lot of other factors determine the maximum distance the brush will push or pull the form, such as Alphas, Tablet Pressure, Zadd, Zsub, Samples, and Stroke Type. Depth, though, could be considered über-Depth. It controls where the center of your brush's power is coming from.

A good example of the use of Depth is in the Skin brush. Its depth is set to –74. In combination with the Alpha and small circular strokes, the Skin brush will lay down an amazingly detailed skin texture without destroying your form or adding too much new volume. Try lowering and raising the Depth value to understand the effect better.

If Depth is über-Depth, Depth Mask is the squash and stretch of your brush's outer limits. While DrawSize controls the circumference of your brush, Depth Mask allows you to narrow in on a specific slice of the sphere for your brush to take effect.

A great example of Depth Mask is the PlanarCutThin brush. Try setting Depth to 14 and turning off MRGB to get some interesting results. This brush also does wonders for creating rock striations when used with the Spray stroke.

So how does Depth relate to the Clay brush? It determines how far outward or inward the Clay brush will push form. To see it in action, set Brush → Depth → Imbed to 100 and make one stroke. Set it to 3 and make another stroke.

In general, I leave Imbed at default settings unless I am creating softer forms. In that case, I set Imbed to 3. If you feel the need to increase it above 10, consider using the Move brush instead.

Figure 1.14

Depth Mask limits your effect to a cross section of your model.

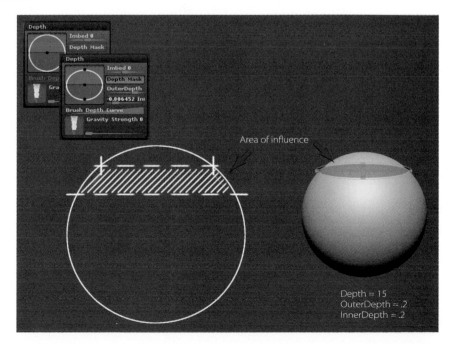

Trim Dynamic

Trim Dynamic is an extension of the Clay brush's algorithm; it allows you to work free-hand while creating both hard and soft surfaces. To create softer surfaces, you must lower the DrawSize and make smaller and smaller plane changes. To work with hard surfaces, you can use this brush to establish broad strokes and major planes and then switch over to Trim Adaptive for more localized control.

The Trim Dynamic brush gives you an opportunity to understand how ZBrush responds to the surface of your model. By default, most brushes are designed to feel light and snappy in your hands. Yes, designed. The experience each brush gives you when you brush along the surface of your model is something that is as designed as the car you drive.

Figure 1.15

Samples subpalette

Samples

Speaking of cars, if the brush system is a car, Samples is part of the suspension mechanism. Samples control how your brush responds to the surface of your model (see Figure 1.15). Think about your model's surface as if it were a road. Driving through Kansas, there isn't much need for a robust suspension system. Except for the occasional pot hole, it's a pretty flat state. However, going four-wheeling in Moab, Utah, is a whole different story.

Figure 1.16

The sampled area

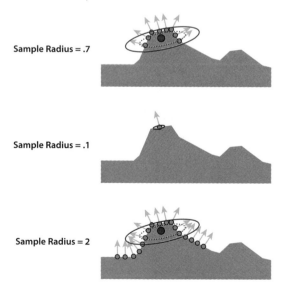

Sample Radius = .7

Sample Radius = .1

Sample Radius = 2

The heart of Samples is Sample Radius (see Figure 1.16). This is the shock absorber of the entire system. In simple terms, Sample Radius determines whether your brush's response to the road is light and snappy to the road or whether it bulldozes through any surface variation.

In more specific terms, Sample Radius determines how much of the area within your brush's sphere of influence will be used to calculate the orientation of your brush. By default, Sample Radius should be set to provide a quick but not hypersensitive response to your surface. Think Porsche. For most brushes this is .75, but this does vary.

As you decrease this number, ZBrush considers a smaller and smaller percentage of the surface area. This makes it much more responsive to changes in the surface direction and makes for a very bumpy ride.

Another way to think about this is with a boat analogy. A smaller boat has a smaller area of the water's surface to sample from, so it is more sensitive to waves and swells. A cruise ship, on the other hand, has a vastly larger area of the water's surface to sample from and is therefore much more stable. However, a cruise ship can't be turned on a dime as a smaller boat can. The trade-off is the same in ZBrush: stability for maneuverability.

The other features that influence the brush's stability and maneuvering are as follows:

- Stabilize Orientation
- Stabilize Direction
- Constant Sample
- OnSurface
- Preserve Edge
- Buildup

All these features work together to give you the ride you need for the form you are trying to create. When adjusting them, it is useful to keep in mind that Sample Radius is the main influence. Everything else works to help Sample Radius do its job.

Trim Adaptive

Trim Adaptive is built to give us a more controlled experience. If used freehand style, it can get a little too aggressive. If used in a controlled manner, though, it creates clean planes that would be very hard to create any other way. At the core of its control is a feature in ZBrush that hasn't received a lot of attention: orientation.

Orientation

Orientation is the steering system in ZBrush. Often you aren't even aware of it, and that's the way it should be. We don't think about the steering column once we are in our car. We just put the key in and go.

Sometimes, though, we need to take full control of our steering wheel and we do this in the Picker palette. The three buttons that we are concerned about in the Picker palette are as follows:

- Once Ori
- Cont Ori
- Select Orientation

To understand what these features do, we should back up a bit and return to the sphere of influence from the Depth section. When you click on the surface of the model, ZBrush samples the polygons within its sphere of influence. It then determines the orientation of that sphere by averaging out the surface normal within its sampled radius. However, the job is not done there. ZBrush has a choice. It can either continually resample the orientation or lock it down and drag that through your model. Figure 1.17 illustrates the effect of each option.

Figure 1.17

The effect of the Picker palette options

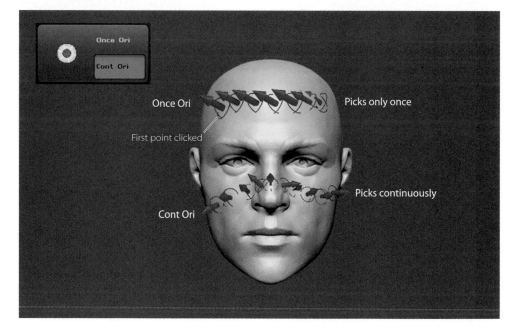

The Once Ori option (see Figure 1.18) will lock down the orientation to the area of the model on which you first clicked. The selected angle will be used for the rest of your brush stroke. The Trim Adaptive brush uses this feature to great effect.

In fact, Trim Dynamic and Trim Adaptive provide the clearest example of the steering differences. Once Ori is the defining characteristic of the Trim Adaptive brush. Set Cont Ori on and you essentially have the Trim Dynamic brush.

Figure 1.18

The Once Ori option

Selected Orientation is different. In this feature, you have to click the arrow in the center and move it around to the angle you want to enforce. You can also click the arrow and drag it to a specific area of your model to choose exactly that orientation. The effects of this brush are the defining characteristic of the Trim Front brush. Figure 1.19 illustrates the effect of the front brush used at several points along the model.

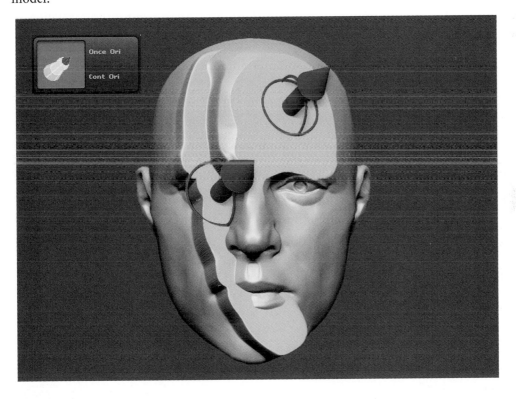

Figure 1.19

The effects of Selected Ori

Dam_Standard Brush and Brush Modifier

The Dam_Standard brush is amazingly smooth and cuts through your model as if it were butter! The secret of its power comes in the Brush → Modifiers → Brush Modifier slider. This slider behaves differently for each brush, but for the Standard brush it works to combine either the Pinch brush or the Magnify brush. The Dam_Standard brush combines the Pinch brush with the Standard brush by setting the slider to 32. The effect is to bring

Figure 1.20

Interface: BrushMod

more polygons into the valley while you are sculpting it and create smoother, cleaner lines. Figure 1.20 illustrates the location of this feature in the Brush palette.

H_Polish Brush and Preserve Edge

The H_Polish brush makes great use of the new Preserve Edge feature in the Brush → Samples palette, shown in Figure 1.21. The goal of Preserve Edge is to do exactly what it says: preserve edges. A great way to see the difference is to run the M_Polish brush over an

Figure 1.21

Preserve Edge

edge and then repeat that same stroke with the H_Polish brush. H_Polish will work to keep hard edges while still smoothing out the other areas of the model.

Working with Masks

Masks are essential for controlling effect on specific areas of your model. You can work with masks through the Tool →Masking subpalette or by using the hotkeys as follows:

- To create a mask, press Ctrl+LMB and click and drag on the surface.
- To erase part of a mask, press Ctrl+Alt+LMB and click and drag on the surface.
- To clear a mask, press Ctrl+LMB and click and drag outside of the model.
- To invert a mask, press Ctrl+LMB and click outside of the model
- To blur a mask, press Ctrl+LMB and click on the model.

If you want to make a lasso selection of a mask or drag out a selection rectangle to mask off an area, then just select the MaskLasso or the MaskRect brush in the Brush pop-up.

The Road Ahead

While unpacking our toolkit, we have looked at a few features that I want to keep on your radar as we continue learning about ZBrush. Once you understand how ZBrush's brush system works, you can create your own Rake brush, custom stitch brushes, and a whole host of other customized tools.

It's important to keep in mind that learning an art form is a lot like learning a new language. You cannot rush it. Your brain will change only so fast, and you can retain only so much information. Be patient with yourself. Learn to turn frustration into success, not by overcoming it but by outlasting it. Frustration is part of the learning process. Whatever you do, though, don't give in.

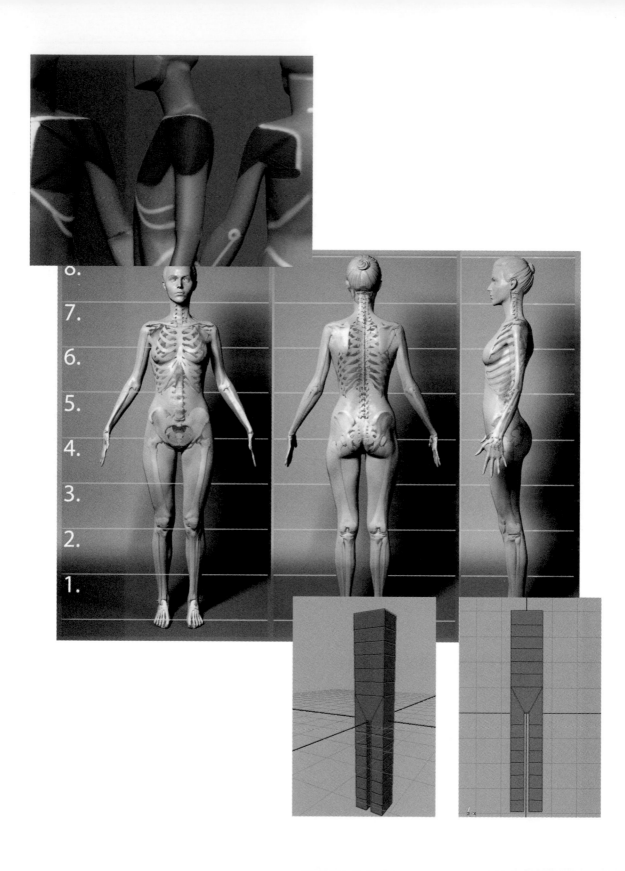

CHAPTER 2

Sculpting the Body

A digital sculptor is not that different from a traditional sculptor. In both cases, the brain must understand form in 3D and learn various tricks to plot the landscape of the body.

A digital sculptor, however, works in a virtual environment, which is a blessing and a curse. Traditional sculptors move around the model and use their entire body. A digital sculptor uses small movements of the wrist on a Wacom pad or a Cintiq. As digital sculptors, we do not get to move around and all that jazz, but we have undo!

In this chapter, I give you an overview of my method for teaching digital sculpting in ZBrush. This method is a volume-centric approach to sculpting and focuses on muscular anatomy only during the last 25 percent of the journey. Note that in the finished sculpt at the end of the chapter, the head is not sculpted yet. We sculpt the head in Chapter 3 and spend more time talking about the specific anatomy of the face.

Proportions

Proportion and gesture are the first battle we need to face. We will use the head as our primary unit of measurement. The total character height will be 8 heads, which gives our character a distinctly graceful yet powerful look. It also makes measurements much easier than using a more natural 7.5 head tall figure.

Figure 2.1 is our proportional chart. Our primary concerns here are accurate measurements for each major part of the model, accurate alignment of the form, and nailing the natural gesture of the human body. Pay attention to the following parts of the model:

Head	Thigh
Neck	Knee
Shoulder	Calf
Waist	Ankle
Hip	Foot

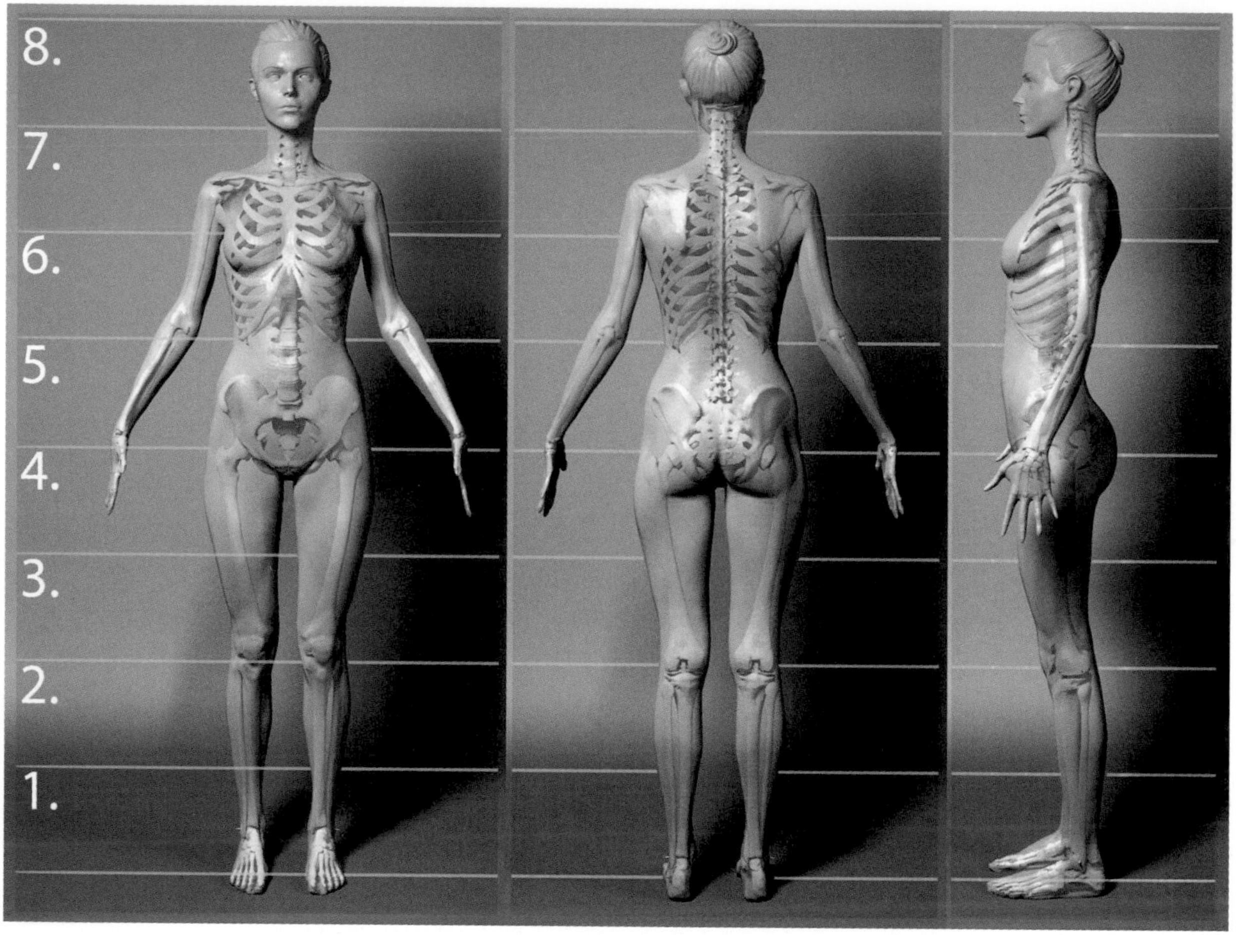

Figure 2.1
Proportion chart

Project 1: Modeling Base Mesh in Maya

If you are not familiar with Maya or any other polygon modeler you can skip this section and use the mesh titled 8HeadBaseMesh.obj in the accompanying DVD.

We start our process in Maya, but you can work in any 3D modeling application. I am using Maya instead of ZBrush because many production artists find this a more comfortable place to begin and an understanding of working in another application such as Maya is essential for working in the game or film industry.

When I work on my own meshes, I typically start in ZBrush and stay there until the end. Either way, the goal is the same, and we can take advantage of Maya's polygon modeling toolset to help us optimize our base mesh and create a few happy accidents along the way.

Proportions and Gesture

Follow these steps to begin:

1. We begin with the front view in Maya and a PolyCube. Raise the PolyCube so that it sits on the ground plane. Increase its X Scale to 1.25. Select the top face and extrude upward one-half unit (See Figure 2.2). Repeat this extrusion every half unit until you have extruded upward 3 units in Y.

2. Select the bottom face and scale it down along the x-axis until its width is very small. Make sure to only scale it along the x-axis. Then select the faces of both sides and choose Edit Mesh → Extrude. Immediately press **W** to enter Move mode and pull downward one-half a head unit.

   Press **R** to enter Scale mode and drag the top scale manipulator into the center. This will flatten the face as much as possible and help create even topology later.

   Press **G** to repeat the extrude, immediately press **W** to enter Move, and drag down another half-head unit. Repeat this process until you have legs that are 4 heads tall, as in Figure 2.3.

Figure 2.2

Starting the torso

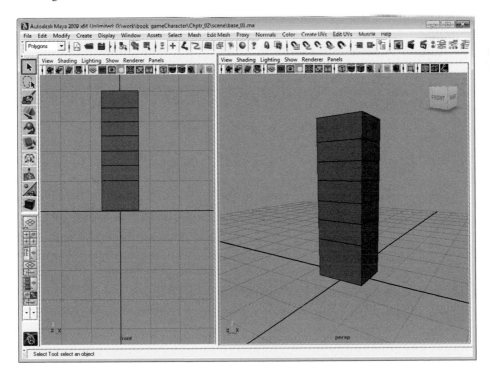

Figure 2.3

Adding the legs

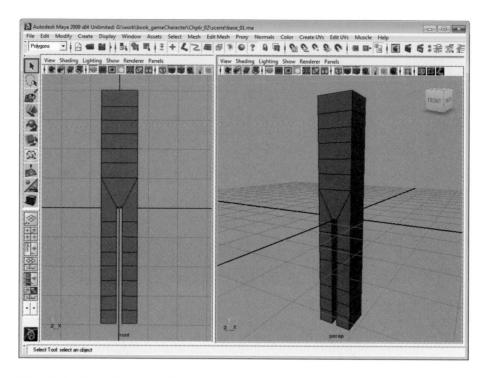

3. Now, let's adjust the shape of our model and make it more human. Turn Reflection on by pressing **W** and then clicking and dragging upward to the Reflection marking menu. Make the following adjustment (refer to Figure 2.4).

   - First, move the line that will be the pit of the neck (7.5 heads from the ground) upward so that it is one-third of a head from the chin.

   - Make sure the head is .75 units wide.

   - Move the line at 5 heads downward until it is 4.75 heads off the ground. This line will represent the anterior-superior iliac crest.

   - Move the line at 5.5 heads down to 5 heads off the ground and scale it inward to become the waist.

   - Move the outer vertices at line 3.5 heads upward so that it describes the hips at the 4 head mark.

   Your model should now look like Figure 2.4.

4. Select the faces on the side of the model that represent the shoulder area. These will be directly below the neck. Choose Edit Mesh → Extrude and pull the faces outward one-half unit until they touch the next grid line. Select the vertices along the bottom and scale them inward.

   Once the faces are scaled inward, you can select them along the side and choose Edit Mesh → Extrude. Click the tiny circle in the upper right section of the manipulator to switch to World Space and drag downward. Scale as you did the legs. Continue extruding the arms and hands downward. Remember to extrude downward in half-head units. Use Figure 2.5 as your guide.

Figure 2.4

Adjusting the shape

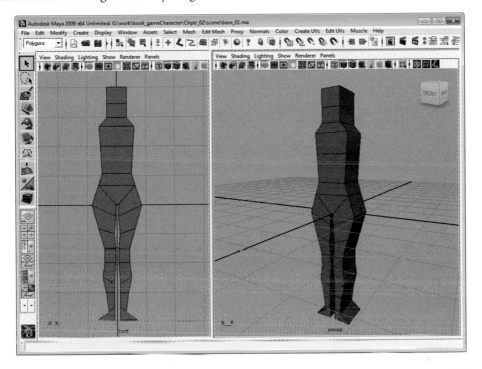

Figure 2.5

Adding the arms

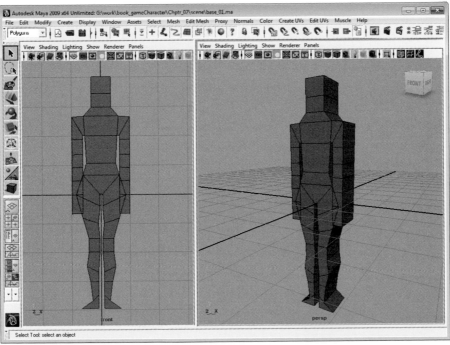

5. Adjust the shape of the arms to match Figure 2.6. It's important to pay attention to the high points on the inside and the outside. In fact, nothing could be more important at this stage. Let me say that again: there is no more important item at this particular moment than for you to get the high points of the arm and the rest of the body exactly as I have them.

Figure 2.6

Shape of arms

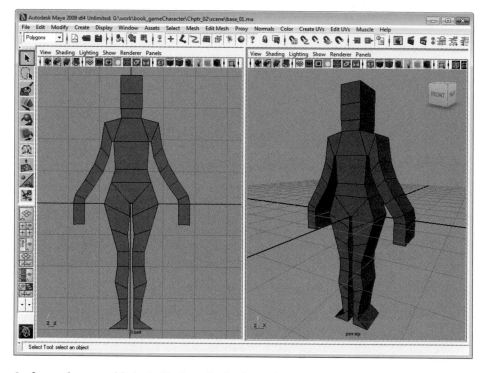

So far, we have established all of our limbs from the front view. However, the side view shows us that we still have some work to do. We are making great progress though, and our base mesh is already shaping up into the perfect armature to sculpt upon.

I can't stress enough how important it is to take time while making your base mesh to get the natural gesture and correct proportions as accurate as you can.

Refining the Shape from the Side View

Now it's time to work on the side view. Before we go further, though, I want to point out the two major conceptual hurdles to getting the side view working correctly:

- The placement of the knee
- The placement of the shoulder

Students are invariably placing the shoulders and the knees too far forward. Also, the deltoid often inflates and becomes one with the pectoralis muscle.

Follow these steps to continue:

1. Select each of the following sets of vertices and move them backward to the center line (refer to Figure 2.7).

   - Pit of neck
   - Front of shoulder
   - Knee
   - Front of lower leg

2. Adjust the front and back vertices as shown in Figure 2.08. Here is a checklist of the modifications to make:

   - Thin the chest and stomach area slightly.
   - Extrude the feet.
   - Bring the calf muscle back slightly.
   - Adjust the alignment of the neck and shoulder area.
   - Define the bottom of the cranium.

3. Select just the back and butt vertices seen in Figure 2.09 and move them backward a tiny bit. It's important not to select any of the arm faces in this process. Then press **3** to see how you are doing. Looking pretty good, huh? Press **1** to get back into low poly mode.

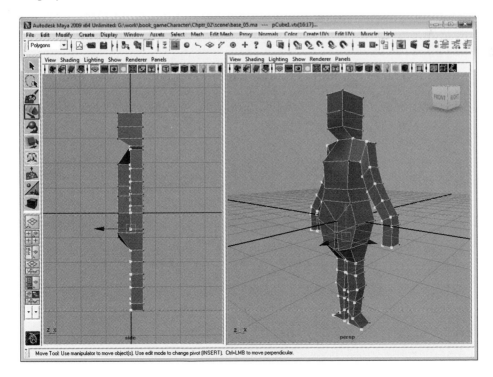

Figure 2.7

Creating center of balance

Figure 2.8

Refining the form

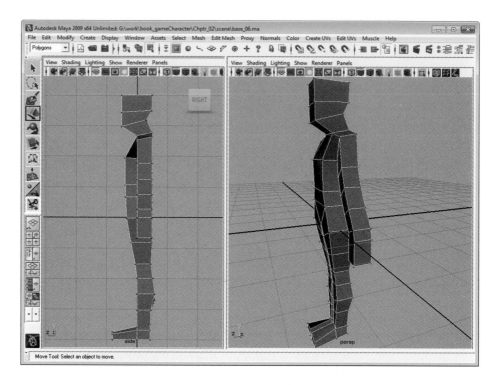

Figure 2.9

Refining further

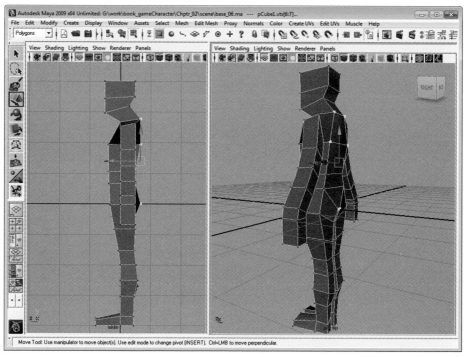

4. Next, we need to give the arm its natural gesture, as in Figure 2.10. If you followed all of the preceding steps, the gesture should already be accurate from the front.

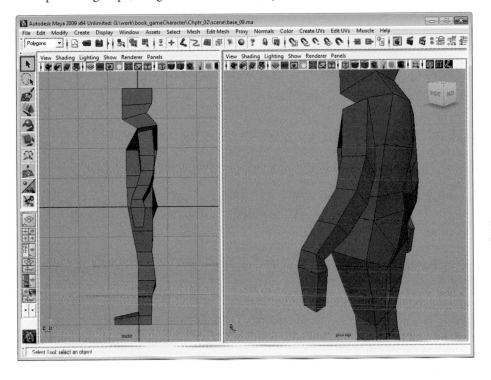

Figure 2.10

Rounding the arm

Creating Hands

Adding hands requires a little polygon finesse. This is the one area where ZSpheres falter, in my opinion. I usually find it better to create them in Maya, but they require a lot of geometry to describe all five fingers. Luckily, if you follow the steps I lay out it will be relatively painless:

1. First add one edge loop directly down the center as in Figure 2.11.

2. Then select the faces on either side of both hands and extrude outward as shown in Figure 2.12. At this point the hands are much too big, but that is easy to fix once you have the geometry all set up.

3. Extrude all four fingers. Make sure to turn off Keep Faces Together in the channel box. Extrude three segments so the fingers will have the natural setup of your own fingers, as in Figure 2.13.

4. To extrude the thumb, we will have to first insert an edge loop around the hand and then extrude the face above the edge loop as seen in Figure 2.14. At this point, we will not be working on both sides of the model and will mirror the other half before sending it over to ZBrush.

Figure 2.11

Splitting the arm

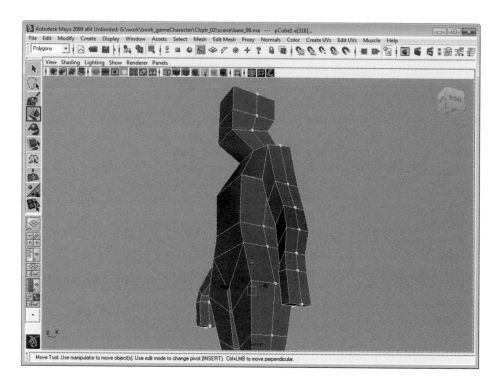

Figure 2.12

Extruding the palm

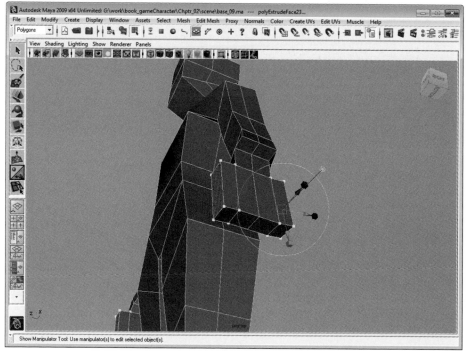

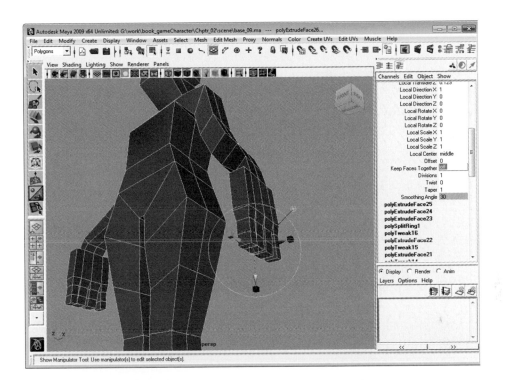

Figure 2.13

Extruding the fingers

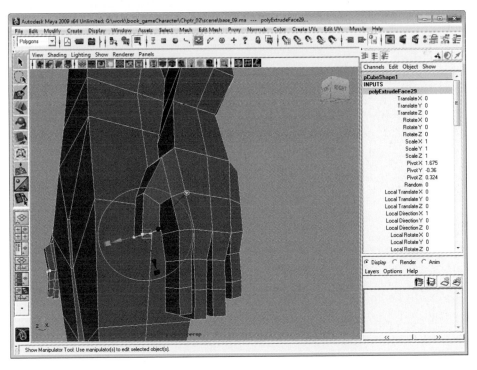

Figure 2.14

Extruding the thumb

Mirroring and Finishing the Model

Part of the job of our base mesh is to put polygons where we will need them most, so our last step before mirroring over our topology is to insert edge loops as needed:

1. Use Figure 2.15 as a guide for where to add edge loops. In general, you want to make sure you have enough polygons in the chest area, elbow area, knee area, and shoulder area.

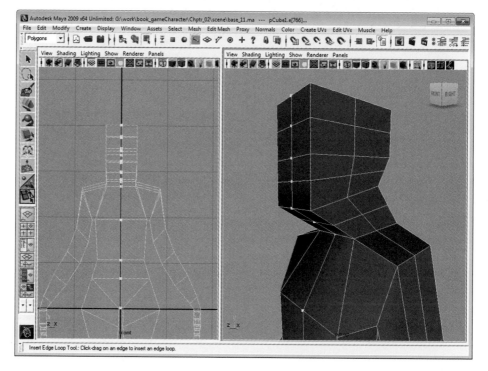

Figure 2.15

Splitting the model

2. Now, delete the half of the model that does not have a thumb. Select the half with the thumb and duplicate it by choosing Edit → Duplicate. Set its X scale to -1.25 so that it mirrors the other side, as seen in Figure 2.16.

3. Select both and choose Mesh → Combine. Select the vertices along the center and scale them inward toward each other. Choose Edit Mesh→ Merge Vertices to merge them into one mesh. Press **3** to check the mesh and to make sure everything merged correctly. Make sure to fix any problems you see before moving on. Your base mesh must be in perfect working order before you start sculpting.

4. Finally, in my model I rounded some forms in the arms and the head, but otherwise, the model is unchanged from our process. Figure 2.17 is as far as you should take the base mesh. The rest of the work will be sculpted in ZBrush.

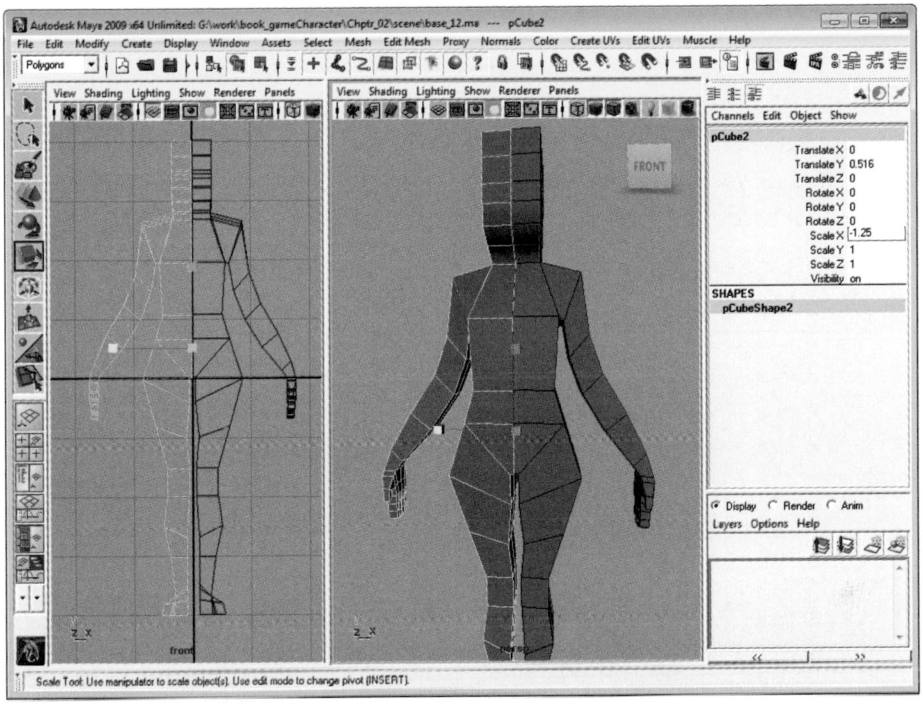

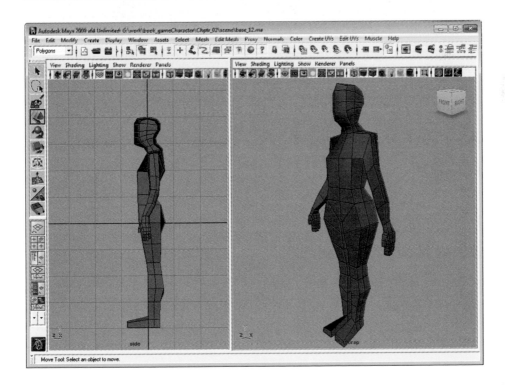

Figure 2.16
Mirroring the model

Figure 2.17
Final result of
base mesh

You may have noticed that we have not edge-looped the eyes, mouth, or nose in any way yet. We have enough to worry about when sculpting without throwing topology into the mix. We'll look at retopologizing the head in the next chapter.

Project 2: Bony Landmarks

The bony landmarks are the foundation of our sculpting. They are our first road map into the human body. Most of our sculpting will reference a bony landmark at one stage or another, so it is very important to establish them first, as shown in Figure 2.18.

Figure 2.18

Establishing bony landmarks

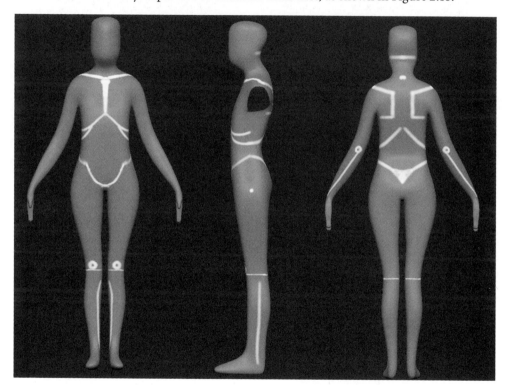

Follow these steps:

1. Divide the model until it is around 1 million polygons by choosing Tool → Geometry → Divide a few times.

2. Set the RGB sliders all to 128 in the color palette and choose Color → Fill Object.

3. Select the Standard brush, turn RGB on, turn Zadd off, and set the color swatch to white. Start by placing the *pit of the neck*. Use the topology as your placement guide, as shown in Figure 2.19.

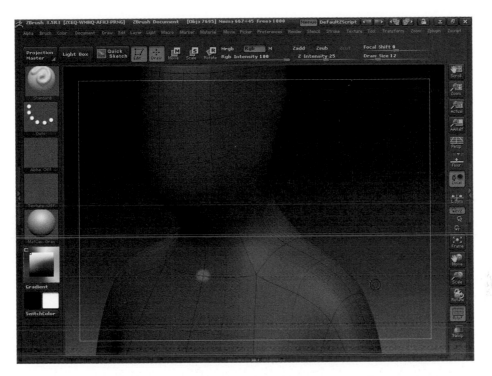

Figure 2.19

Placing the pit of the neck

4. Next, place the *acromion process*. To get this landmark accurate, it's important to keep in mind that the clavicle is .75 heads in length. To measure this out, we use Transpose.

    Press **W** or Move in the shelf. Click on the pit of the neck and drag toward the shoulder. Keep your eye on the Dist3D button in the status line until it reads .75, as shown in Figure 2.20. It's not important to be 100 percent accurate but just to get it in the ball park.

5. Then draw an S-curve to connect the points as shown in Figure 2.21. Notice how the acromion process is toward the back of the figure.

6. Pay particular attention to how the clavicle connects to the spine of the scapula and the square shape of the acromion process, as shown in Figure 2.22.

7. When you draw out the *sternum*, make sure to make it .75 heads long, as shown in Figure 2.23.

8. Continue painting in the rest of the bony landmarks using Transpose to keep the measurements accurate. As you work, try to take advantage of the topology. A good place to see where the topology really helps you find bony landmarks is in the knee. Figure 2.24 shows you how the patella fits neatly above one row of polygons.

Figure 2.20
Using Transpose

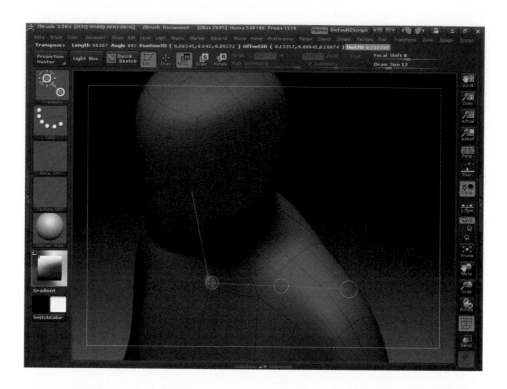

Figure 2.20
Using Transpose

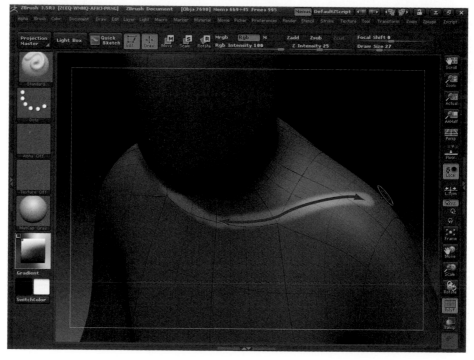

Figure 2.21
Defining the clavicle

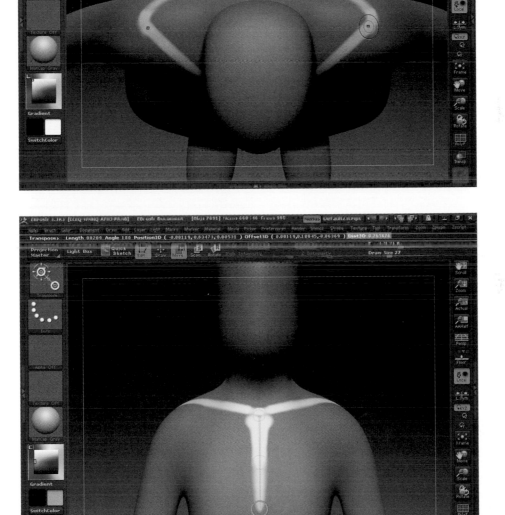

Figure 2.22

The clavicle and spine of scapula

Figure 2.23

Defining the sternum

Figure 2.24

Creating the patella

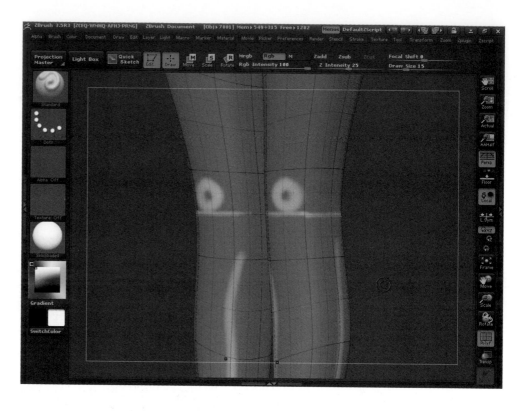

Project 3: Volume and Massing

When you hear the word *anatomy*, you likely think about muscles. Muscles, though, are only half of the equation. You must also be very mindful of the bones when you are sculpting. My friend Cesar Dacol, Jr., points out that "muscles literally hang from some part of the skeleton."

Either way, focusing on muscles alone will not give you the results you need. Instead, it can lead you to overemphasize every single muscle at the cost of every shred of reality your model had. To avoid this sort of distortion, you must always remember the actual volume of the part you are sculpting.

In Figure 2.25, you can see how our base mesh fits into the first stage of volume. Notice how all the volumes fit neatly into what we did in Maya and into the concept for our character's body.

1. To get the volume of the head correct, you must correctly place the neck area. So we will tackle the neck first. The key is to sculpt a cylinder, not a neck. If you are thinking "neck" when you sculpt, then you automatically start sculpting things like the trapezius and the sternocleidomastoid. This is an example of putting the cart before the horse. If, instead, you think "cylinder" when sculpting, then you will set yourself up for success when it is time to sculpt the muscles of the neck later.

To sculpt the neck, I use a combination of the Clay brush, Standard brush, and Smooth. You will have to cut in the bottom and the top of the cylinder with the Standard brush and then use the Clay brush to build up the edges, as in Figure 2.26.

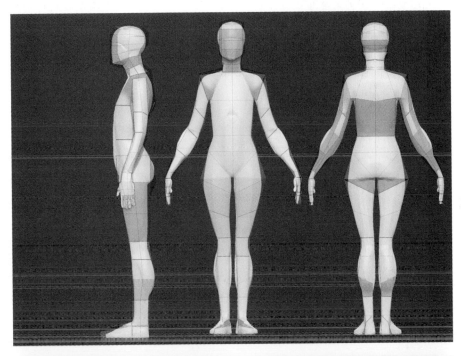

Figure 2.25

Volume and base mesh

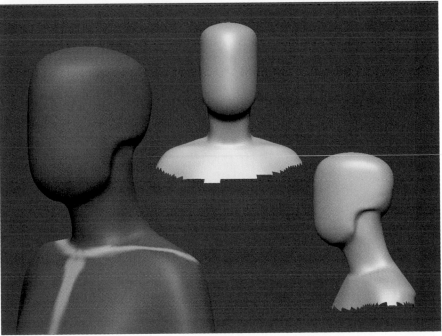

Figure 2.26

Creating the neck cylinder

2. Having placed the neck, it's time to establish the volume of the head. The best way to visualize the head is with a sphere and a wedge. The sphere takes up the cranial mass and the wedge forms the front plane of the face, as in Figure 2.27.

Figure 2.27

Establishing basic head volume

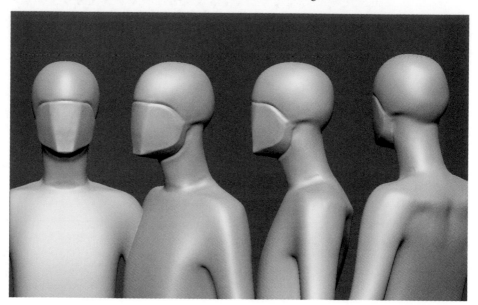

The trick to building the front plane of the face is to press Alt while using Trim Front and drag from the brow down to the chin. Then use Trim Dynamic with Alt pressed to integrate it with the side of the faces.

3. To mass-in the rib cage, we will use Trim Dynamic and simply round the hard edges. If you need to switch to the Clay brush, be careful not to add too much volume. This should be a subtle adjustment. Use Figure 2.28 as your guide.

   Remember, our goal is not perfection. Our goal is simply to set the basic planes of the rib cage: front, side, back, and the transition planes between the front and the side and between the side and the back.

4. To quickly block in the hip, grab the anterior-superior iliac crest and drag it toward the back of the model just the tiniest bit. This will create a slight offset between the iliac crest and the profile of the stomach.

   Then use the Clay brush to build the butterfly shape of the buttocks. Take a swipe with Trim Dynamic to separate the buttocks from the upper leg and you are done. Figure 2.29 illustrates these steps for you.

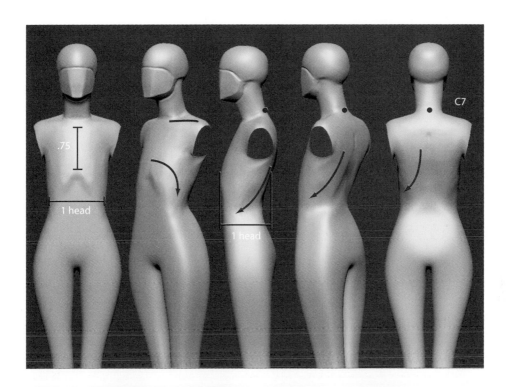

Figure 2.28
Creating the volume
of the rib cage

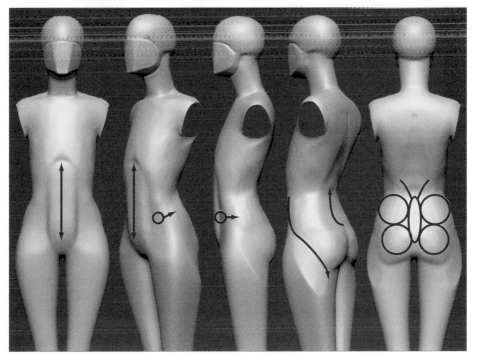

Figure 2.29
Creating abdominal
and hip muscless

5. The upper leg and the knee can be massed in with a few complex curves. Pay particular attention to the curve along the side that flows from the back of the ribs to the iliac crest and then back again to the side of the leg. Another important plane to create is the back of the upper leg. This is the area the hamstrings will occupy later, but for now use Trim Front to create their flat plane. Use Figure 2.30 as a guide.

Figure 2.30

Creating leg volume and planes

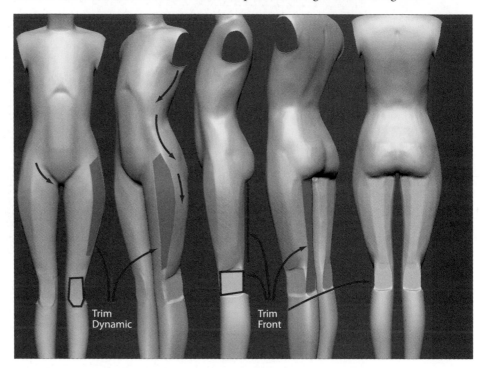

6. The lower leg can be treated as two separate volumes just as we did for the head. The upper half contains a spherical mass while a thin rectangle runs from the knee to the ankle. Figure 2.31 illustrates this concept. It is not important to sculpt this exact volume. It is important to have in your own mind a concept that is equivalent to this.

7. The foot should look like a wedge with a few extra inches along the bottom. Make sure it flattens as it ends in the toes and that it tapers toward the ankle as shown in Figure 2.32.

8. Now, let's take a look at the arms and hands. The upper arm will remain largely the cylinder it already is. Use the Trim Dynamic brush to round the edges as needed.

    The lower arm, otherwise known as the forearm, is a bit more complex. We divide it into two parts as we did with the lower leg. The lower half is almost all bone and is easily represented by a long thin box. The upper half is still fairly flat but is wider along the sides. Use Figure 2.33 as your guide. Your results should look similar to Figure 2.34.

Watch me block out the hand in the hand.mov file on the companion DVD.

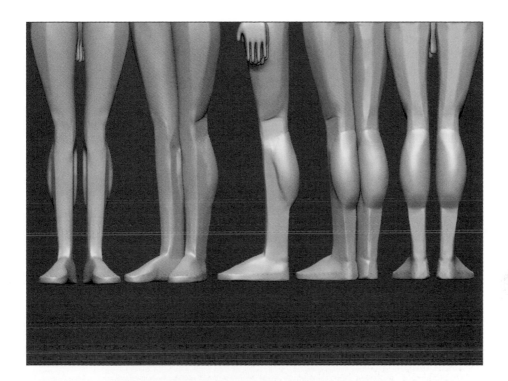

Figure 2.31

Defining the knee block

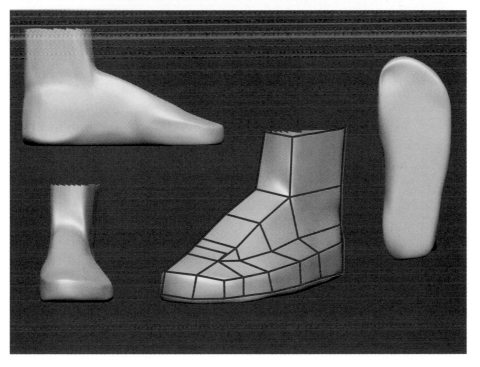

Figure 2.32

Creating the foot

Figure 2.33

Creating the upper and lower arm

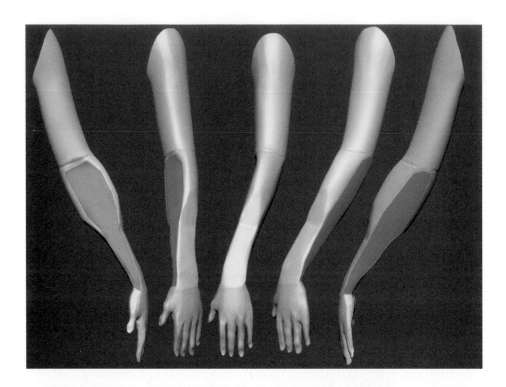

Figure 2.34

Final version of the volume sculpt

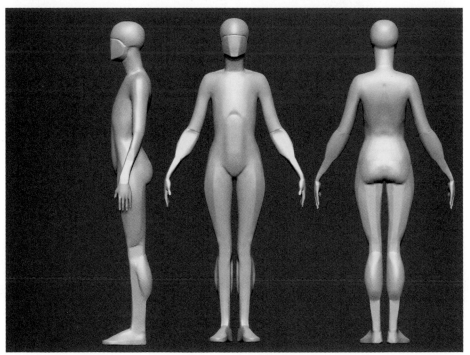

Project 4: Painting in the Anatomy

I do not paint the anatomy in every time I start a model. I do, however, paint the anatomy in every time I get lost or can't figure out what the anatomy is doing. So, in this project our goal will be to practice our understanding of the anatomy by painting it before we commit to actually sculpting it. Figure 2.35 shows the result we'll get from our efforts, so let's get started.

As you go through this project, I highly recommend that you keep an anatomy book open next to you. A great book to use is Eliot Goldfinger's *Human Anatomy for Artists* (Oxford University Press, 1991). A better resource than any book, though, is Anatomy Tools's Male Anatomy Figure.

When you encounter an anatomical term you don't know, stop and check your book. Spend a moment and try to describe that anatomical part in common language before you move on. At first terms like *lateral epicondyle* will seem completely inaccessible, but as soon as you learn to put the term *lateral epicondyle* into some form of common language such as "the bony area on the outside of the elbow," it will be much easier to remember.

Figure 2.35

Finished muscle painting

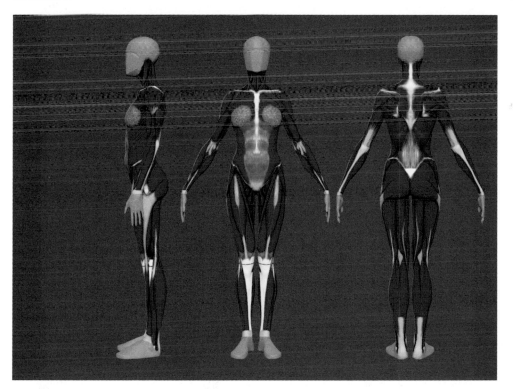

To begin painting the anatomy onto the model, follow the steps below:

1. Load the Ecorche_muscle brush and the Ecorche_tendon brush from the accompanying DVD by choosing Brush → Load Brush and navigating to their location on the DVD.

2. Choose MatCap_Gray from the Material pop-up to make it easier to see the paint. You can also use SkinShade4 or any other material that works for you other than MatCap Red Wax. Red Wax is just too intense for this kind of painting.

3. Start with the chest muscle group: the pectoralis and the deltoid. Draw along the direction of the muscle fiber. Try to be as precise as possible. Remember that the pectoralis muscle has three origins that all head toward the humerus and cross along the way. Figure 2.36 illustrates this concept.

Figure 2.36

Painting the pectoral muscles

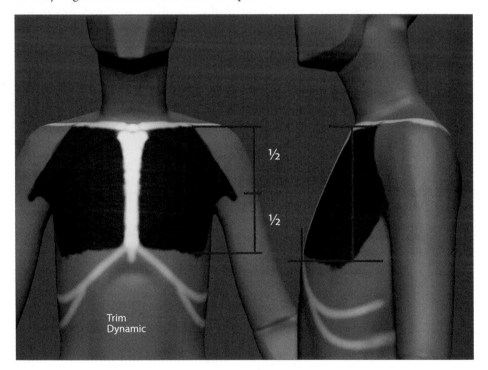

4. Create the deltoid muscle; it originates along the last one-third of the clavicle, the acromion process, and the last third of the spine of the scapula. This creates the three main heads of the deltoid, and each of these three heads inserts into the humerus, as shown in Figure 2.37.

5. Before we leave the back, make sure you understand the relationship between the scapular muscles and the triceps. This is an area of much confusion. The key to understanding it is remembering that the teres major attaches to the front of the humerus bone, as shown in Figure 2.38.

Figure 2.37
**Defining the deltoid
muscle**

Pectoralis

Deltoid

Teres minor

Infraspinatus

Teres major

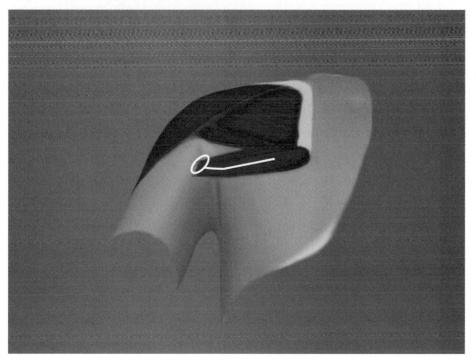

Figure 2.38
**Defining the
scapula muscles**

Figure 2.39

The scapula muscles with the long head of the tricep

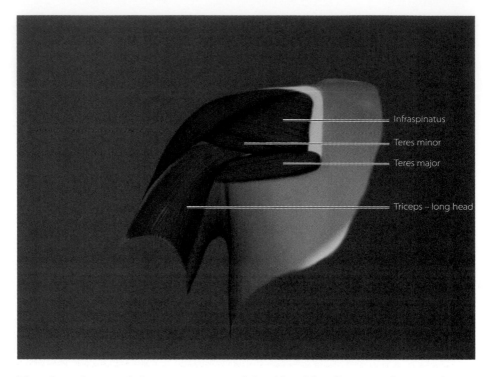

Infraspinatus

Teres minor

Teres major

Triceps – long head

Therefore, the scapula has to wrap around the side of the rib cage and pass underneath the long head of the triceps, as shown in Figure 2.39.

Once you have the long head of the triceps overlapping the teres major, you can overlap the long head of the triceps with the teres minor! Confused yet? Don't worry, that's all there is to it. It's just important to remember that the long head of the triceps threads its way between the teres major and teres minor.

6. We can now move on to the rest of the torso muscles, illustrated in Figure 2.40. We want to get the external oblique, the latissimus dorsi, and the abs.

   Use Figure 2.40 to help you gauge the muscle direction. Notice how the external oblique changes direction when it encounters the rib cage. Look for other changes in direction.

7. When we get to the arm muscles, you need to pay special attention to organizing the muscles in the forearm. There are three muscle groups that you will need to focus on:

   · Extensors

   · Flexors

   · Ridge Muscles

Figure 2.40

Creating the torso muscles

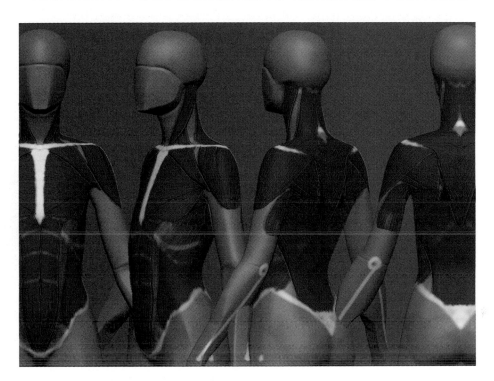

From the lateral, or outside, epicondyle, you can pull the extensor muscle group all the way down to the back of the hand. The extensors are fairly thin muscles, with the bulk of their body in the upper half. Note that this is true of all forearm muscles because the lower half of the forearm is mostly influenced by the bones.

From the medial, or inside, epicondyle, you can pull the flexor muscles all the way down to the palm of the hand. The flexors are larger muscles than the extensors and create a fuller body.

The ridge muscles as a concept come from Eliot Goldfinger's incomparable book *Human Anatomy for Artists*. The ridge muscles comprise two muscles: the brachioradialis and the extensor carpi radialis longus. Together, they are an important part of the shape characteristic of the forearm. They begin on the lower third of the humerus and descend to the wrist.

Figure 2.41

Forearm muscle groups

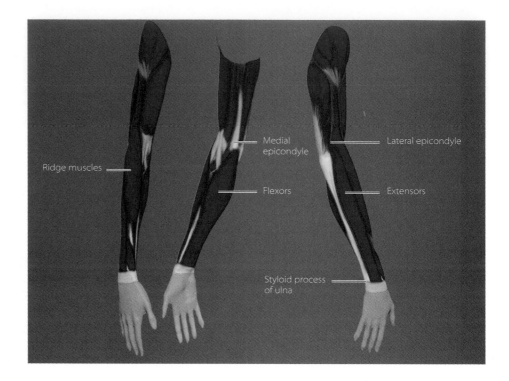

Figure 2.41 illustrates these muscle groups. I have found that the key is to place the epicondyles of the humerus first. Once they are placed, I draw the line of the ulna bone all the way to the styloid process. This is the bump on the outside of your wrist. I then draw another line from the bicep to the thumb. These two lines effectively distribute the muscles. As shown in Figure 2.42, the muscles to the inside of the biceps-wrist line are the flexors. The muscles from the back to outside of the elbow-wrist line are the extensors.

These lines provide a major advantage when you pronate the forearm. If you keep these lines in mind, you can redraw the muscle group no matter what the wrist is doing (see Figure 2.42).

Figure 2.42

**Distribution of
forearm muscles**

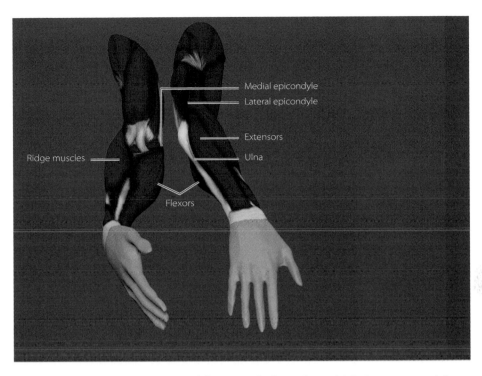

8. We will now skip the upper leg and focus on the lower leg, which deserves special attention. It is composed of six muscles that you need to be aware of:

- Tibialis
- Gastrocnemius
- Soleus
- Fibularis
- Fibularis brevis
- Extensor digitorum longus

As with the elbow, it is important to place a few bony landmarks in the knee before tackling the lower leg. You will need to know where the head of the fibula, the tibial tuberosity, and the line of the tibia are. Once you have placed them, you can paint the rest of the muscles in as shown in Figure 2.43.

Figure 2.43

Painting the lower leg

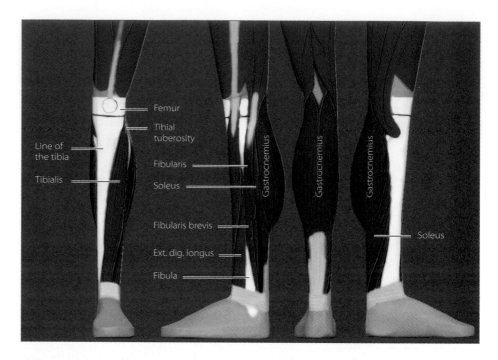

9. Double-check your muscles with Figure 2.43 and make sure that they are as accurate as possible. Of course, there will be some problems as you progress, and you might have missed a few areas, but this process gets easier the more you do it. If necessary, go over the separation of the muscle masses with the Pen Sketch brush.

10. We have skipped the upper arm and the upper leg. Using your own resources, try to get those as accurately placed as possible. Google is a great place to look, as is Gold-finger's *Human Anatomy for Artists*, but again, I highly recommend grabbing the *Male Anatomy Figure* from Anatomy Tools.

Project 5: Filling in the Anatomy

My approach for this book has come from years of watching students struggle with anatomy as well as my own lifelong struggle with it. Over these years, the overarching observation I've made is that volume and realistic form are often the first thing out the door when we focus on muscular anatomy. Instead, we become enamored with muscles. We see muscles everywhere. Every bump and swerve in the form is a new muscle for us to discover.

Muscles can be learned quite easily. They all have a beginning and an ending, a defined shape, and a specific mechanical function that we can commit to memory.

It is important to know which muscle goes where, but that is only the first stage of the struggle to understand how the human body is put together. Our real task is to get at the specific shape characteristics of the body and understand how specific muscles work within the volume of a generic figure to create a character.

It is not within the scope of this book to go over each muscle, but I will highlight significant areas of interest and special problem areas that I have observed over the years of teaching sculpting. For your reference, the final blocking is shown in Figure 2.44.

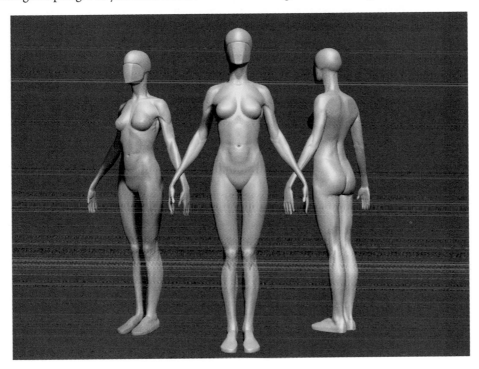

Figure 2.44
Our finished sculpt

To begin sculpting the forms follow the steps below:

1. Lower your resolution until the model is around 100,000 polygons. To reduce the brightness of your Polypainting, you can set your color swatch to white, set RGB Intensity to 40, and choose Color→ Fill Object. Then select the Standard brush and turn RGB off. Finally, turn RGB off for the Smooth brush by pressing and holding the Shift button and clicking RGB off.

2. Our first target is the clavicle and the spine of the scapula. Once we lock these down, we can build the trapezius and deltoid from them. The key to these bones is to look at them from a top view and get the relationship in Figure 2.45 as correct as possible, as well as the side and back view.

Figure 2.45

**Defining the clavicle
and spine of the
scapula**

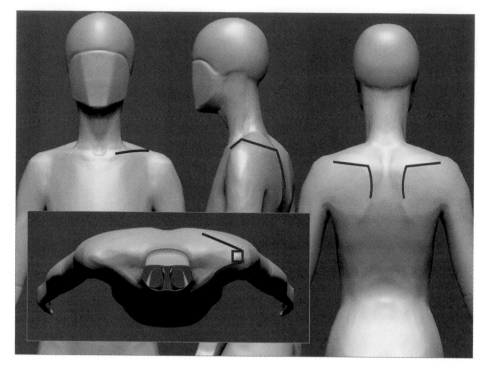

3. Once the bones are placed correctly, we can lock in the muscles of the shoulder region. We will focus our attention on two of them:

   • Trapezius

   • Deltoid

   The trapezius is the first muscle that I want to map out. It has several important shape characteristics. An important but often missed element is the separation between its upper mass and its lower mass. Figure 2.46 illustrates the basic volume and landscape of this muscle. As always, it's imperative to locate the bony landmarks and chart your way out from them.

   The deltoid has one important characteristic that is often misunderstood. It takes a step back from the pectoralis muscle. Often when we think of the deltoid connecting to the pectoralis muscle we begin to fuse the muscles and improperly combine them into one mega muscle. Figure 2.47 shows both the step down and the separation. I find that to get this form right, I have to focus on each muscle separately and just let the connection take care of itself. Remember to turn Polypaint on to check your muscles.

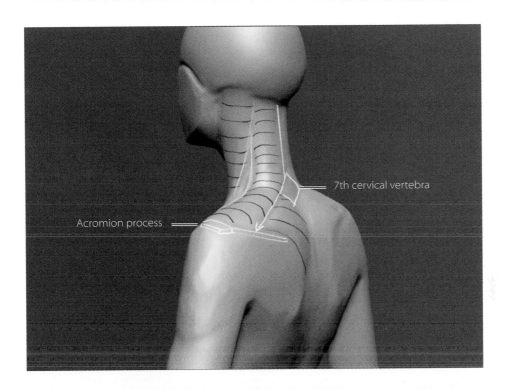

Figure 2.46
Creating the landscape of the trapezius

7th cervical vertebra

Acromion process

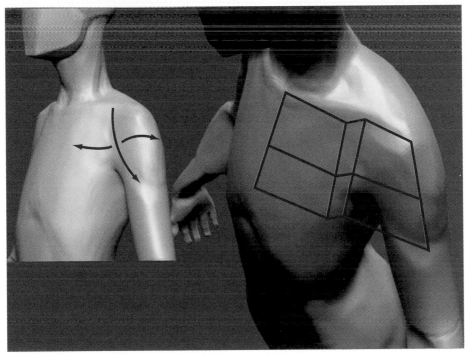

Figure 2.47
The deltoid steps backward

4. We will explore these muscles in more depth later, but for now we want to establish the general shape of the pectoralis and the external oblique. Think of the pectoralis as a rectangle and set its mass as though it sits on top of the rib cage.

Block in the latissimus dorsi by cutting across the bottom edge of the scapula and focusing on the triangle from the armpit to the bottom of the scapula to about the eighth rib.

It's also important to note that I do not sculpt the breasts until the very end. Figure 2.48 shows our progress on the chest muscles.

Figure 2.48

Creating the chest sculpt

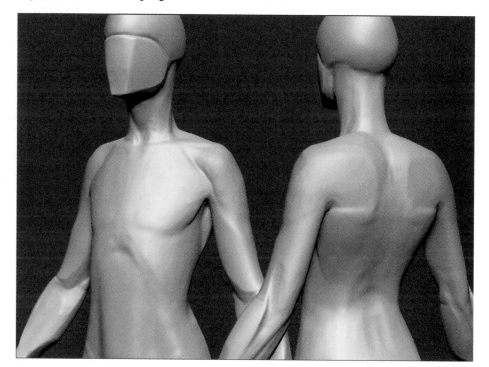

5. Now, in order to get the rest of the upper arm right we must get the elbow clearly delineated. We have already located most of the important elements, but now we want to establish the specific shape characteristics of the elbow. Figure 2.49 shows you the simple cut we make from the front view. Figure 2.50 shows you the more complex cut we make from the back where our job is to separate the ulna from the epicondyles and to place the line of the ulna.

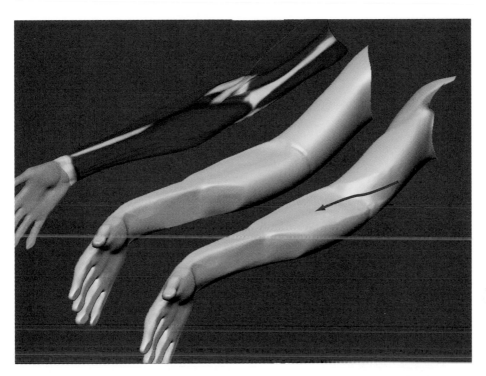

Figure 2.49
Blocking in the fore-arm from the front

6. The finished arms, as shown in Figure 2.51, show the subtle work you can do with the Clay, Trim Dynamic, and Standard brush. However, that subtle work is not easy to explain in text. Make sure you take a look at forearm.mov in the accompanying DVD to see how those brushes can be combined.

7. Moving on to the torso muscles, I like to switch my material to MatCap_GreenClay. This helps me see the flat areas better than I can with MatCap_Gray. Figure 2.52 shows the rough sculpt of the torso at this stage. The abdominal muscles are sketched in and the pelvic region is sculpted. It's important to note that the abdominal muscles overlap the rib cage—as you saw in the paintover—and that the belly button is roughly 5 heads up from the floor.

When sculpting the external oblique, work with your reference to get the exact curve as it reaches back to the line of the rib. Notice how it thins and try to get the triangle that separates it from the latissimus dorsi, as in Figure 2.53. Of course, fat will fill some of this region, but it will help us, in the beginning, to see the anatomy first.

Figure 2.50

Blocking in the fore-
arm from the back

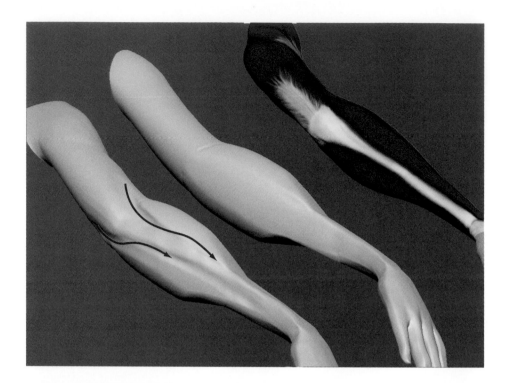

Figure 2.51

Creating the
forearm

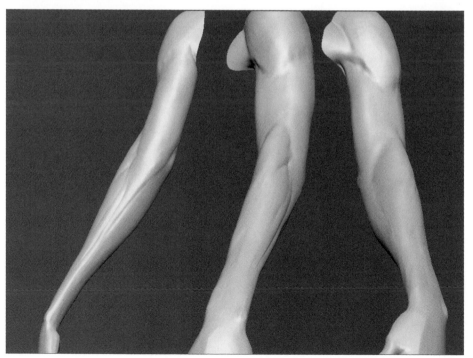

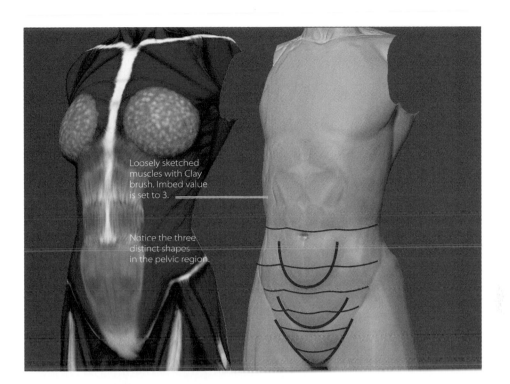

Loosely sketched muscles with Clay brush. Imbed value is set to 3.

Notice the three distinct shapes in the pelvic region.

Figure 2.52
Developing the abdomen

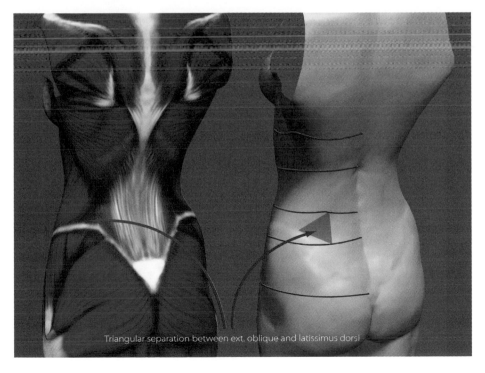

Triangular separation between ext. oblique and latissimus dorsi

Figure 2.53
Sculpting the external oblique

8. When we move to the leg we should clearly delineate each muscle using the Standard brush, as shown in Figure 2.54. Our goal here is to lay the groundwork for us to push and pull the muscles as we did for the forearm. Getting the overlap of muscle over muscle can be a difficult task and absolutely requires patience and technique.

Using a combination of the Clay, Trim Dynamic, and Standard brushes, we can soften the forms and create the necessary peaks and valleys of the leg. Remember to smooth your strokes often. That is a necessary requirement of getting the form to look natural. Figure 2.55 shows the final stage of the legs and torso muscles.

Figure 2.54

Sketching in the anatomy

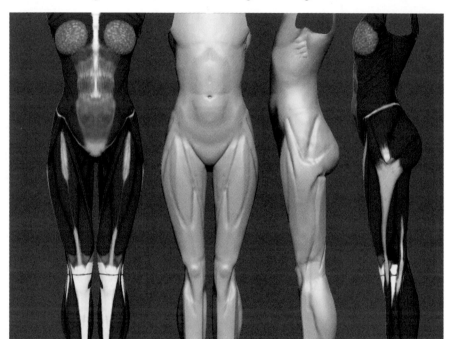

Figure 2.55

The final stages of sculpting the legs

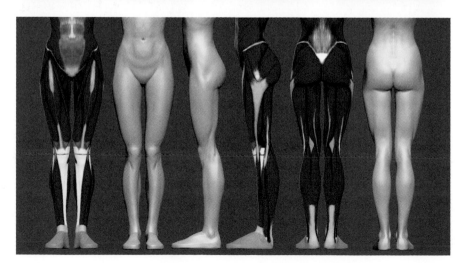

If we take a closer look at the leg, we should pay some attention to the volume of the quadriceps and hamstring muscles, as shown in Figure 2.56 and Figure 2.57.

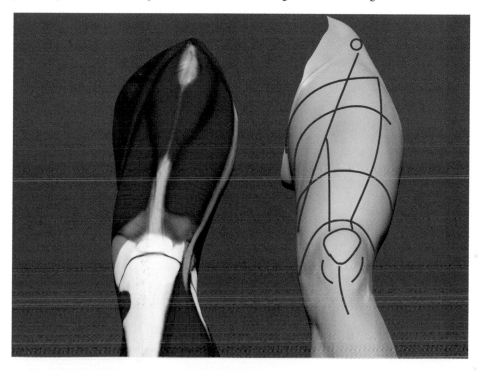

Figure 2.56
Creating quadriceps

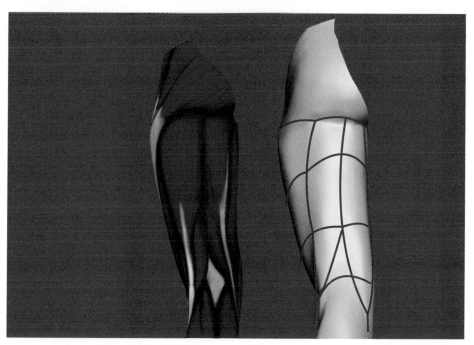

Figure 2.57
Creating hamstrings

When I sculpt the lower leg, the first thing I block in is the line of the tibia. This is a crucial line to get right and deserves as much study as you can give it. Once I have that, I find the tendon lines of the vastus lateralis and the biceps femoris. Both of these lines can be continued all the way down the lower leg. Figure 2.58 shows you the rhythm of these lines as they move down to the foot.

Figure 2.58

Creating the lower leg

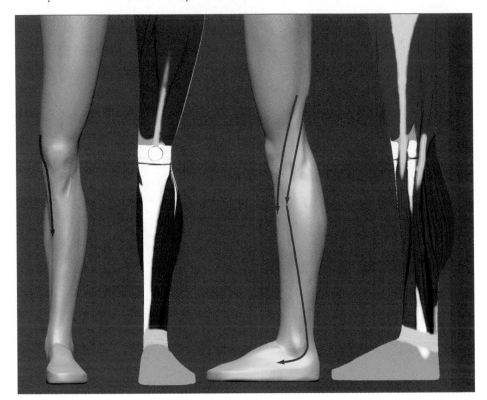

9. The breasts can be confusing. They sit on top of the rib cage and the pectoralis muscles, and if we are not mindful of this, they can lead our sculpting astray. I find it helpful to use SubTools to create the breasts. This allows me to treat them separately from the rest of the anatomy. Figure 2.59 illustrates what they would look like as SubTools. It also illustrates one of the elements you want to check as soon as you put in the breasts: the pectoralis muscle. In the case of Figure 2.59, the pectoralis is too bulky. The red line indicates where it should be.

10. Once you have the breasts sculpted out of spheres, you can use ZProject to integrate them with your sculpt and work on their connection with the rest of the chest.

Figure 2.59
Defining the breasts

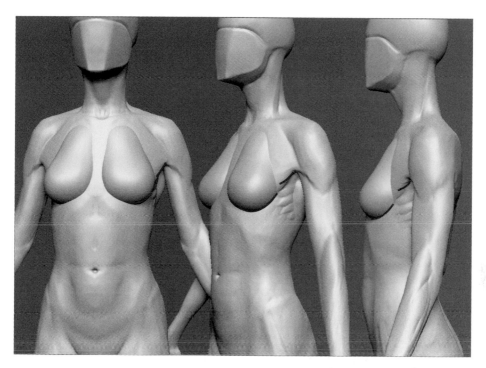

We have covered a lot of ground in this chapter. We have created a base mesh in Maya. We painted the anatomy on our model and we sculpted that anatomy. This should be one of the longest chapters for you and one that you continually come back to.

I have left a few things for you to figure out on your own. I have complete confidence that you will succeed. Google is a good friend to you, but Anatomy Tools's Male Anatomy Figure is your best friend and Goldfinger's *Human Anatomy for the Artist* should be like a brother. Good luck with your sculpting!

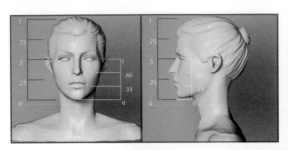

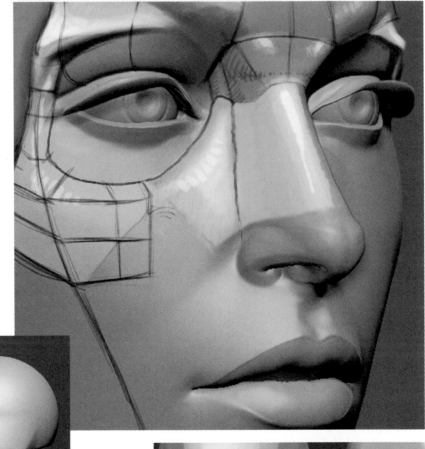

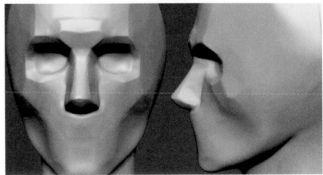

CHAPTER 3

The Head and the Face

You would think the human face would be easy to sculpt because we have looked at it our entire life. But we haven't looked at it from a trained sculptor's viewpoint. Instead, we have looked for clues to people's emotions, their motivations, and their personality. Is this girl really into me? How is dad taking the news that I'm failing PE class?

We have looked to understand expressions, but not structure. As sculptors, we must understand the form in three dimensions to be able to create something realistic.

In this chapter, we will first study the human face in broad strokes. After we cover the broad strokes, we will explore each area of the face in structural detail.

Proportions

We start our approach toward the face with proportions. In my experience, it is not possible to absorb everything about proportions in 1, 2, or even 20 sittings. Proportion is something you have to revisit for the rest of your life.

In that sense, a picture is worth a thousand words. Come back to the image in Figure 3.1 when you start a project. Come back to this image during the middle of your project. Come back to this image at the end of your project. Whatever, you do, just come back and check that your model matches these proportions. If it does not, make sure you know why it does not.

Figure 3.1

Proportions of the face

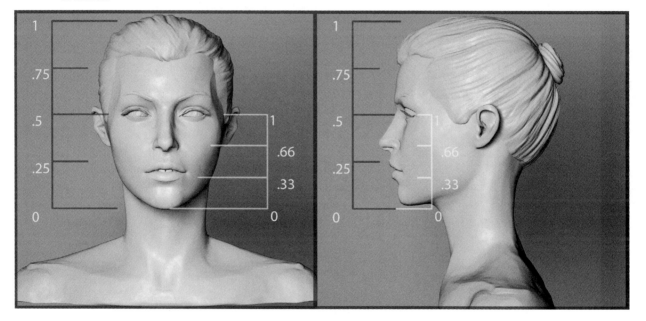

Project: Establishing the Foundation

Let's begin sculpting the foundation that we will use for the rest of this chapter. Notice that we are not working with the entire character. Instead, we are starting with a PolySphere. This will allow us to focus only on the problems at hand. In time, we will merge the face with the rest of the body, but for now, it's easier to limit our exposure to complications.

1. Start with a PolySphere on the canvas as in Figure 3.2. Perspective mode should be off for the next few steps.

Figure 3.2
**Starting with a
sphere**

2. Turn to the side view so that the symmetry points are on opposite sides of the model. Press Ctrl and click and drag out a mask around the lower-right area of the sphere, as shown in Figure 3.3.

The mask area absolutely must be only one quarter of the sphere's height and cover only the back half of the model. Every time I teach this workflow, there are artists who are careless about where they make this mask. Please do not be careless. If this step is done incorrectly, the rest of the sculpt will be incorrect.

3. Now invert the mask and use the Move brush to pull the area upward and into the sphere. You might also want to smooth this area out as well. Then clear the mask, as shown in Figure 3.4.

4. Create another mask. This time it must cover the lower-left quadrant of the sphere. Note that the mask should leave a little space between it and the area we just sculpted in the back of the head so that the jaw area will not be altered. Then invert this mask so your model looks like Figure 3.5.

5. Click Rotate in the shelf. Draw out an action line. Note that the action line must be dragged off the model as in Figure 3.6. Then click the red dot to the far right and drag downward and to the left. Be careful where you place the chin. I have found that it is best to angle it backward from the forehead slightly as shown.

Figure 3.3
Masking out the
back of the head

Figure 3.4
Using Move to lift
the area up

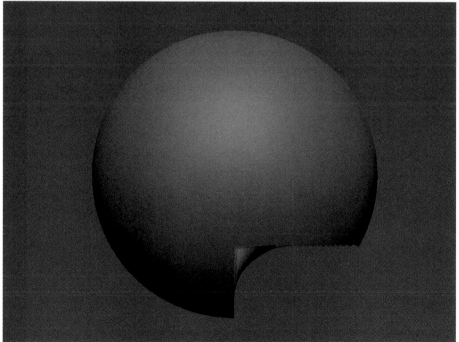

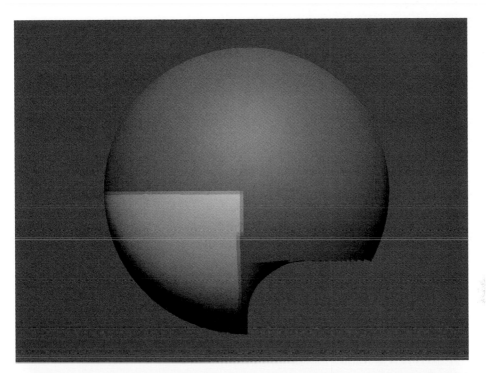

Figure 3.5
**Masking out the
front of the face**

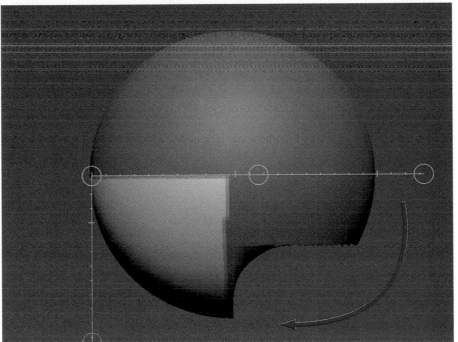

Figure 3.6
**Dragging out an
action line**

6. To resolve the polygon stretching underneath the chin, we use Tool → Geometry → Reproject Higher Subdiv. To do this, lower the geometry level a few notches and smooth the surface of the model. Then choose Tool → Geometry → Reproject Higher Subdiv. Figure 3.7 shows the before and after.

Figure 3.7

Before and after using Reproject Higher Subdiv

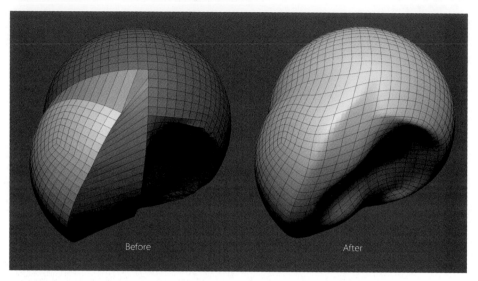

Before   After

7. Flatten the face at a lower subdivision level using the handy ol' Smooth brush as in Figure 3.8. Simply press Shift. Be careful not to lose the chin though. While you are here, you should also make sure to smooth out any artifacting that resulted from using Reproject Higher Subdiv.

8. Now, make sure that the width of the front of the face is three-quarters its height. I do this with the Move brush. My draw size is set to 256 and the model is usually taking up a third of the canvas area. Make sure to measure. "Measure twice; cut once," as the old carpenter saying goes. Figure 3.9 illustrates our progress on this.

9. Establish the side planes of the face using the Trim Dynamic brush. Note that these are different than the side planes of the head. You'll want to suggest the orbit of the eye at this stage as well and taper downward toward the chin. Figure 3.10 illustrates our progress here. Just a few strokes with Trim Dynamic will do the job. No need to belabor the point here.

10. Establish the eye socket with the Move brush. I usually orient the model in the side view and simply drag the brush backward into the model. Then, from the front view I press Alt, click on the inside area of the eye, and drag to the left to make sure the orbit of the eye is pushed all the way in. Your goal should be a simple spherical shape pushed into the model as in Figure 3.11.

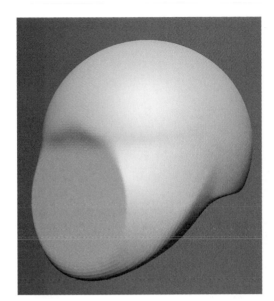

Figure 3.8
Flattening the front of the face

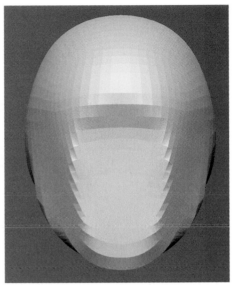

Figure 3.9
Front of the face

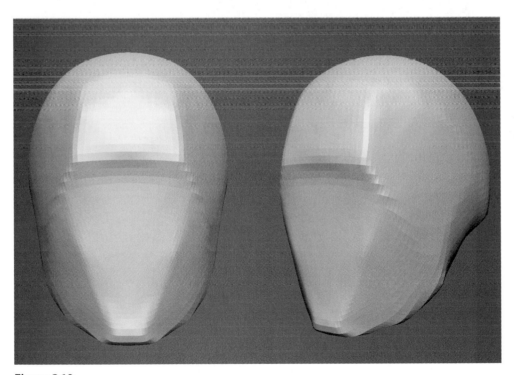

Figure 3.10
Planes of the facial area

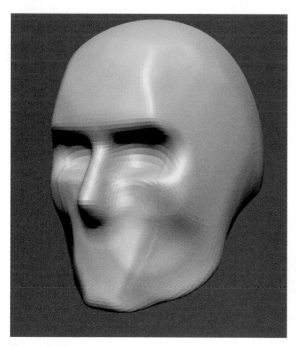

Figure 3.11

Orbit of the eye

11. From the side view, pull the nose outward. Then from a front view, make sure to pull the nose inward so that you keep the front of the face as shown in Figure 3.12. It is essential that you do not lose the front plane of the face when adding the nose and that you keep the planes of the nose clearly defined. I use Trim Dynamic to define the four main planes of the nose: left side, right side, front, and bottom.

12. Our final step is to establish a neck. Mask out a circular area on the bottom of the face. This should be centered toward the back and away from the chin. Invert the mask and then use the Move Elastic brush to pull the neck out. You want to create the entire length of the neck or it can be difficult later to judge whether or not the features are accurate. Figure 3.13 illustrates our neck.

Congratulations! You've now got a solid base to start with. If you did this part correctly, you will be in good shape for the rest of the chapter. If not, you'll have to come back to this stage in some form and fix it.

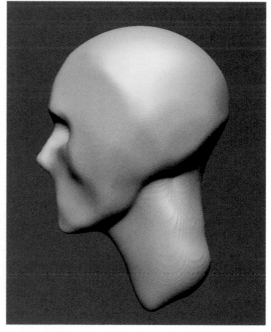

Figure 3.12

Blocking in the nose

Figure 3.13

Creating the neck

Project: Establishing the Eye

Most of the head is, actually, just the skull. The entire cranium is largely just skull and skin—and nothing else. This is especially true for the area around the eye. When I see sculptors having problems working with eyes, 99 percent of the problems are with the skull, not the eye itself.

Figure 3.14 lays out the landscape of the brow area. The list that follows contains the items you'll want to remember. Keep these items in mind as you look at your model and as you sculpt:

- Glabella
- Superciliary arch
- Supraorbital margin
- Frontosphenoidal process of the zygomatic
- Zygomatic bone
- Frontal process of the maxilla
- Nasal bone

To sculpt the brow, follow the steps below:

1. Using Figure 3.14 as a guide, start with the glabella. Why the glabella? Because it sits on top of the nose and joins the left and right brow in a T shape. It creates an anchor for us that we can use to establish the rest of the face. You can indicate the glabella with its classic wedge shape.

    It is also important to notice how the glabella serves as the end point for the infraorbital furrow, the side of the nose, and the frontal process of the maxilla. These are three distinct planes that all coalesce right underneath the glabella. When sculpting this yourself, try very hard to indicate each of these elements as a distinct plane.

Figure 3.14
The brow area

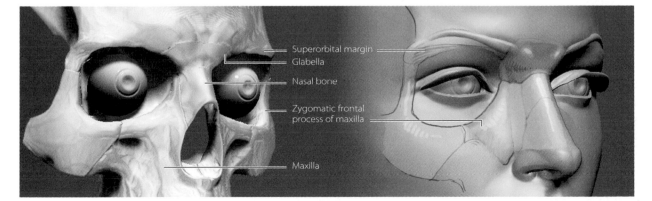

Superorbital margin
Glabella
Nasal bone
Zygomatic frontal process of maxilla
Maxilla

2. Continue the glabella by sculpting the superciliary arches that sit directly above them. They tend to be larger and more prominent in men than in women.

These arches share the same planar direction as the forehead, but they are lifted slightly above it. They are also lifted above the supraorbital margin. Notice, also, how they house the corrugator muscles, as shown in Figure 3.15, which are so important to creating emotion.

Figure 3.15

Inside corner of the brow

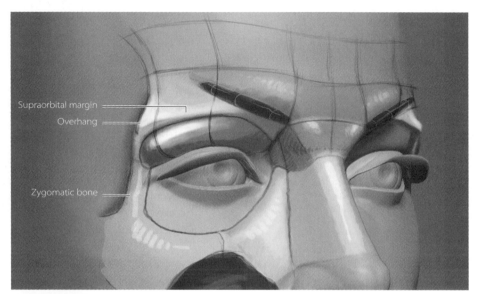

Supraorbital margin

Overhang

Zygomatic bone

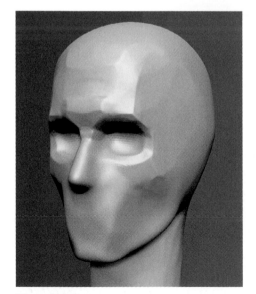

Figure 3.16

Sculpting the brow progress

3. The supraorbital margin is the next item to look at. Figure 3.16 illustrates our progress. Notice in Figure 3.15 how this margin creates an overhang over the eye and also how it slopes backward into the forehead. In terms of evolution, the supraorbital margin is designed to whisk the rain and elements away from our eyes. Knowing that, you can look at your model and ask yourself whether the brow will shield his eyes or not. Don't worry about the area under the eye just yet. We'll add that later.

4. The supraorbital margin sits on top of the zygomatic bone. The zygomatic bone frames the lower, outside corner of the eye. Figure 3.17 illustrates its influence on the planes of the face as well as its structural impact. For instance, notice how it is part of the front plane of the face and the side plane. For now, ignore the fat of the cheek and just sculpt the bony surface. If the bone is accurate, then the fat of the cheek will sit more naturally.

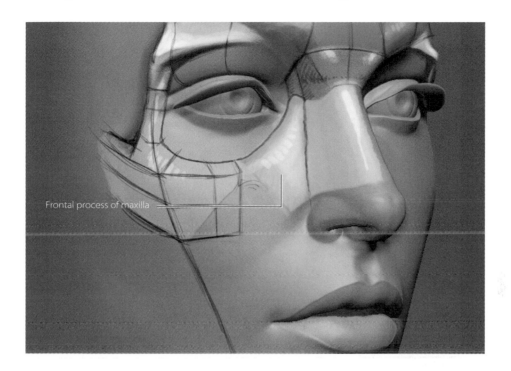

Figure 3.17
Zygomatic bone and the side of the face

Frontal process of maxilla

5. The frontal process of the maxilla closes our loop around the orbit of the eye. It is an incredibly important landmark for the face, and in my opinion, you cannot sculpt a realistic face without some understanding of the frontal process. The green area in Figure 3.17 illustrates how the frontal process of the maxilla connects with the nose and the glabella. You can clearly feel it by pressing in the area between your nose and your cheek.

Figure 3.18
Completing the brow

Our job is to indicate its slope and relative size. On some people it will be a smaller surface area because the fat of the cheek overcrowds it. In others it will be larger and more obvious. Figure 3.18 illustrates our progress.

6. To finish off the orbit of the eye, we need to establish the side plane of the nose and how it relates to the glabella and the frontal process of the maxilla. The side plane of the nose, indicated in yellow in Figure 3.17, makes a 60-degree plane change when it meets the frontal process of the maxilla. It makes about a 30-degree plane change when it reaches the glabella along the top. I prefer to keep the connection between these three planes as mechanical as possible for as long as possible. Blending should come last or you are more likely to lose the form. Figure 3.19 illustrates our progress.

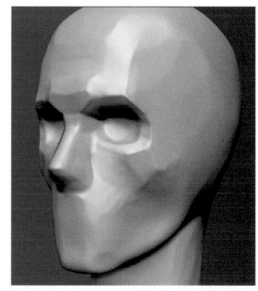

Figure 3.19

The planes of the nose

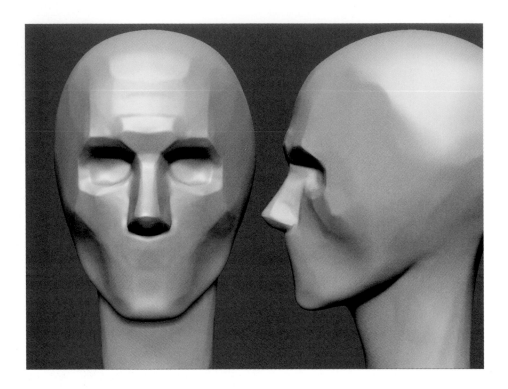

Have you ever heard of the lateral palpebral ligament? If not, you haven't been reading your *Gray's Anatomy*! Figure 3.20 illustrates the different areas of the orbicularis oculi that we will take a look at next.

Figure 3.20

Zones of the eye muscle

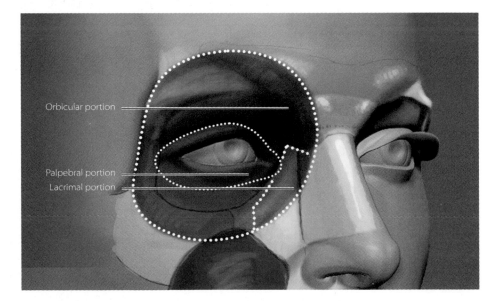

Orbicular portion

Palpebral portion
Lacrimal portion

Let's break down each of these sections:

- The palpebral section relates primarily to the eyelids. It provides a useful conceptual separation between the sphere of the eye and the column of the frontosphenoidal process of the zygomatic.

- The orbicular portion conforms to the shape of the skull all the way around. It is also much larger than we usually give it credit for. Note how much of the area around the eye it encompasses.

- The lacrimal part is involved when we squint our eye. Its action is to pull the corner of the eye upward and inward slightly while pulling the fibers of the orbicularis oculi toward our center.

7. To begin to sculpt the eye, you need to fill in the eye socket so that you have a small bump where the eyeball would be. Then add the eyelids, or palpebral section of the eye muscle. Make sure not to add the fat under the eyelid. You just want to sculpt the muscle here. Use the Clay brush to build up the form. Use the Standard brush to help define the edge of the eyelid and then use Trim Adaptive to create the clean plane change and hard edge of the eyelid. Figure 3.21 illustrates the progression.

8. If you are clear where the eyelids connect to the skull, then your sculpt will be clear. The inside corner of the eyelid is called the medial palpebral ligament, as shown in Figure 3.22. The medial palpebral ligament attaches to the frontal process of the maxilla.

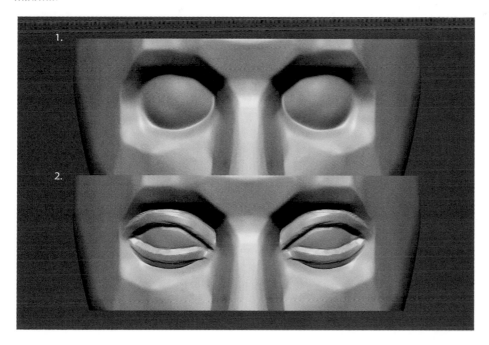

Figure 3.21

Progression of sculpting the eye

On the other side of the eye is the lateral palpebral raphe. The word *raphe* indicates the combination of two ridges of tissue. The lateral palpebral raphe is the union of the ridges of the upper and lower eyelids. It connects on the inside of the frontosphenoidal process of the zygomatic bone.

The frontosphenoidal process of the zygomatic defines the side of the eye. Figure 3.22 indicates its relationship with the eye as well as the palpebral ligaments.

I find that it is important to get the frontosphenoidal process properly indicated before connecting the lateral palpebral raphe. Also, it's important to connect the ligaments before establishing the fat under the eyebrow or the eye bag under the eyes.

Figure 3.22

Palpebral ligament and raphe

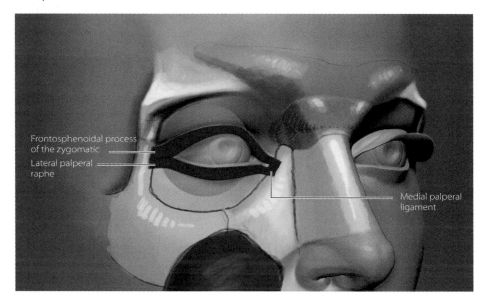

9. The fat of the eye appears both above the eye and below the eye. Above the eye, the oval of fat/skin runs directly beneath the supraorbital margin and terminates directly at the glabella. This can change with a person's particular shape, but it serves as a good rule of thumb to terminate it at the glabella. You can see this in Figure 3.23.

    The eye bag, under the eye, flows from the eyelid down to the infraorbital margin. In younger people this is a convex shape that conforms, mostly, to the shape of the eyeball itself. In older people this begins to sag and even overhang the infraorbital margin. Figure 3.24 indicates our final sculpt of the eyes.

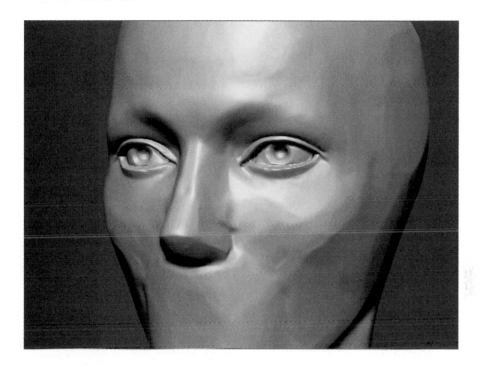

Figure 3.23

Final sculpt of the eyes

Project: Establishing the Nose

The nose is a fairly straightforward sculpt if you are mindful of a few structural elements. The elements that we want to consider in the nose area are illustrated in Figure 3.24. Figure 3.24 also illustrates the overall shape characteristics of each part. Notice the inset image that illustrates how the alar cartilage folds over itself.

The list that follows contains the items you'll want to remember. Keep these items in mind as you look at your model and as you sculpt:

- Alar cartilage
- Wings
- Lateral nasal cartilage
- Tip defining point
- Infratip lobule
- Supra-alar crease
- Alar lobule
- Alar-facial junction

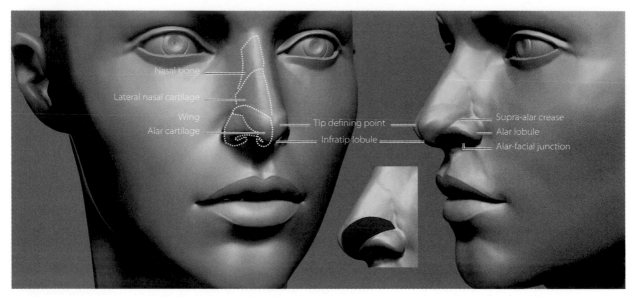

Figure 3.24

Areas of the nose

Follow these steps to sculpt the nose:

1. First, make sure you have the structure of the nose in place as in Figure 3.25. The key is to make sure you clearly indicate the side plane, front plane, and bottom plane and that you put them in proper relation to their surroundings.

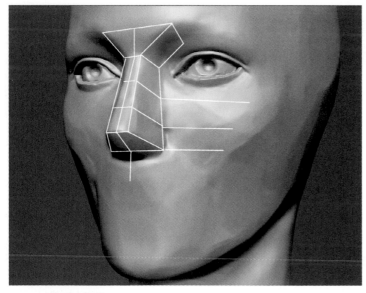

Figure 3.25

Planes of the nose

The side plane of the nose should take off at a 60-degree angle from the front plane of the face. The front plane of the nose should be clearly indicated, and the border between the front and the side should be clean. The down plane of the nose should be curved to indicate the alar cartilage that is to come.

Also, the bridge of the nose is defined by the plane break between the nasal bone and the lateral nasal cartilage. You'll want give some indication of this plane when you establish the basic planes of the nose.

2. Nostrils should be our next priority, but do not sculpt the nostrils. If you sculpt nostrils, you will likely sculpt huge mounds of malignant-looking flesh. Instead, cut a line between the alar cartilage and the nostril itself to separate the nostril wing from the rest of the nose.

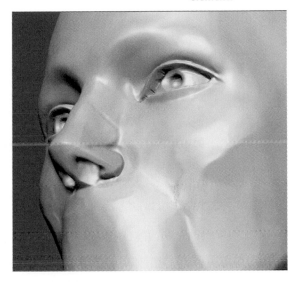

Figure 3.26
Carving in the nose elements

Then cut a line into the side of the nose that describes the outer circumference of the nostril, or *the alar-facial junction*. You want to cut this junction into the model and create the nostril's connection to the front plane of the face. Finish off your carving by using the Standard brush to sculpt in the nostril hole.

Only after you finish carving do you want to start to sculpt the nostril. Remember to avoid adding form. Your only job now should be to round the surface area. Figure 3.26 illustrates our progress here.

3. The alar cartilage is, in simple terms, a plane that folds back underneath itself. It is widest at the point where it turns back upon itself; it is narrowest where it begins and ends. In the nostril hole it forms a C shape that simply disappears along the inside plane of the nostril hole.

In more complex terms, the alar cartilage also contains what plastic surgeons call the tip-defining point and the facet. These two aspects break up the shape of the alar and create the more specific shape of each person's nose. Also note that the alar cartilage connects directly with the columella. You can grab the columella by pinching the center column of skin between your nostrils. Figure 3.27 illustrates our progress so far.

4. Connect the columella of the nose to the upper lip to sculpt the area of the columella-labial junction. We can treat this

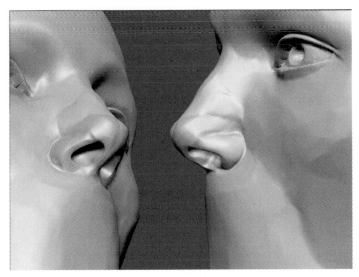

Figure 3.27
Alar cartilage and columella

junction as separate from the surface area of our upper lip. Toward the columella, it creates a wedgelike shape that supports the bulk of the nose. Toward the mouth, it blends into the philtrum. Figure 3.28 illustrates our progress so far.

5. Check over the area of the frontal process of the maxilla and how the nose connects to the nasolabial fold and alar-facial junction. Make sure those planes all work together. Figure 3.29 illustrates our final nose.

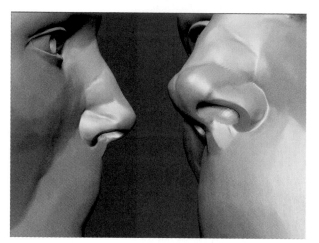

Figure 3.28
Columella-labial junction

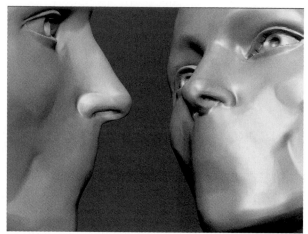

Figure 3.29
Our final nose sculpt

Project: Establishing the Mouth

The mouth is the most mobile part of our face. Small adjustments to the form often have wide-ranging ramifications. We can easily end up sculpting a face that frowns at every moment. But rest assured, I will prepare you for the difficulties of sculpting this part of the face with a few simple concepts and easy-to-follow directions.

Figure 3.30 illustrates each of the bony landmarks that concern us when constructing this part of the face. Keep in mind that some of these landmarks are not visible on the final product and are only part of our construction process.

We will look at the following bones:

- Maxilla
- Zygomatic bone
- Mandible

Among those bones, we will look for the following landmarks:

- Alveolar
- Canine eminence

- Angle of jaw
- Ramus
- Base of mandible

Figure 3.30

Lower face

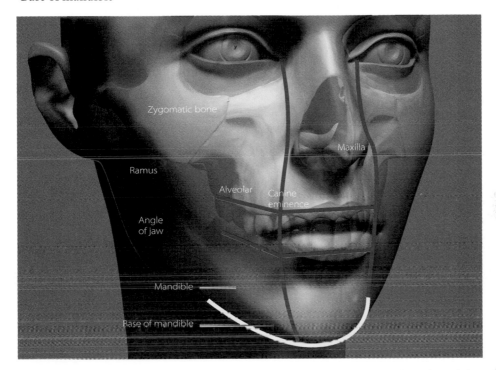

The maxilla defines the front of the face. The *alveolar* defines the horseshoe shape of our teeth. The alveolar is also what our teeth insert into and, with age, fall out of. The *canine eminence* is significant in that it helps define a line from the inside corner of the eye, along the nose and the side of the mouth, and down to the chin. It also defines the transition from the front of the mouth to the side of the mouth as indicated in Figure3.30.

The jaw has three parts to be aware of: the *ramus*, the *angle of the jaw*, and the *base of the mandible*. The base of the mandible deserves an extra mention because artists often miss it, but it can help your model look more authentic. Notice how the base of the mandible creates a round shape that is in contrast the angular shape of the rest of the jaw, and how it echoes the barrel of the mouth and the alveolar.

Follow these steps:

1. Before you begin sculpting the mouth you must establish the barrel of the mouth. What is that? Well, technically it's the alveolar with a lot more thickness. In normal speak, it's your teeth. You can't sculpt lips until you have sculpted the teeth. They define their shape. Have you seen an older person without their teeth? The mouth is a very different shape without them, so we want to make sure we have a nice clean barrel of the mouth, as shown in Figure 3.31, before we move on.

2. The orbicularis oris is more complex than the eye and is not a true sphincter muscle. It is composed of the following elements, as indicated in Figure 3.32:

   - Four independent muscles that connect at nodes and blend into each other at the center line
   - Two distinct areas: inner and outer
   - One node on either side of the face

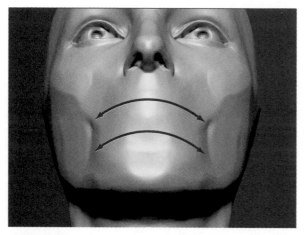

Figure 3.31
Barrel of the mouth

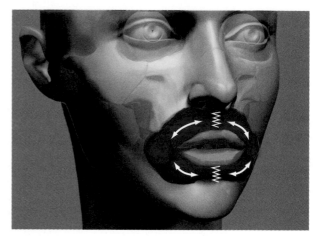

Figure 3.32
Mouth muscle

When you sculpt the mouth area, you will want to dig the corner of the lip in as far as you can stand. Smooth that out just slightly and then build it back up with the Clay brush with Depth set to 3 or 4. Move your brush from the inside outward in a rotating fashion as though you are sculpting the inside of a doughnut, as illustrated in Figure 3.33. Also, to help you get a firm handle on the task, I have included a 15-minute tutorial on sculpting the mouth area on the accompanying DVD, see Chapter3_Mouth.mov.

Figure 3.33
Oh, you have a little doughnut in the corner of your mouth.

3. Before we take a look at any more muscles, make sure you understand what is happening under the surface. Figure 3.34 illustrates the skeletal structure under the cheek area. Pay attention to the frontal process of the maxilla and how it connects to the zygomatic bone. Also, notice how thick the lips are in this cutaway.

Figure 3.34

Skeletal cutaway

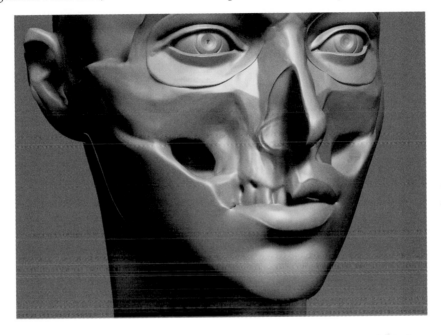

Now, let's look at the zygomatic major and the triangularis. These two muscles help set up very important planes in the face. For example, the zygomatic major helps to define the transition from the front of the face to the side of the face.

The zygomatic major originates on the zygomatic bone and connects to the nodule at the side of the mouth. Figure 3.35 illustrates its position and relationship to surrounding elements.

To understand the triangularis, bring your index finger into the corner of your mouth and then pinch the skin between your index finger and thumb. You should be feeling the nodule at the side of your mouth. Now keep pinching and sliding your hand downward toward your chin. That is your triangularis. This is a very good muscle to spend some time on. Notice how it helps shape the corner of the mouth by providing a ledge, or flat plane, that faces toward the front.

Figure 3.35

Zygomatic major and triangularis

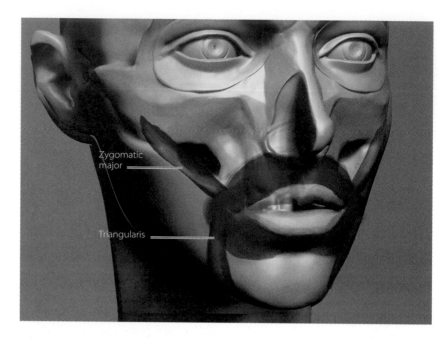

4. The infraorbital triangle is an amazing little shape and very useful as a construction device. Notice how in Figure 3.36 it isn't even really a triangle. The infraorbital triangle is a simple concept that is sometimes a triangle, sometimes a rectangle, and sometimes a landslide (as in the case of an older face).

Figure 3.36

Infraorbital triangle

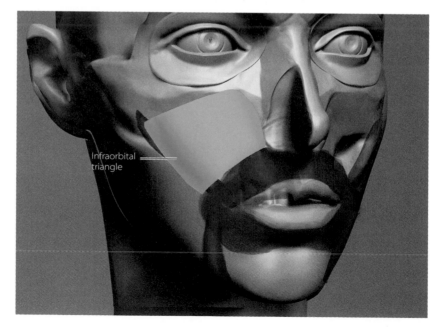

It is bordered by the zygomatic major on the outside, the mouth muscle from below, the infraorbital margin from above, and the nose from the inside. When you look for this device, remember to keep your mind fluid.

This triangle is designed to help us conceptualize the fat of the cheek. In a younger person, it will be smaller and closer to the nose. As we age, it becomes wider and drops downward. When the bloom of youth has gone, you'll also find that this part of the face conforms more and more to the shape of the maxilla underneath it.

Figure 3.37
Final mouth area

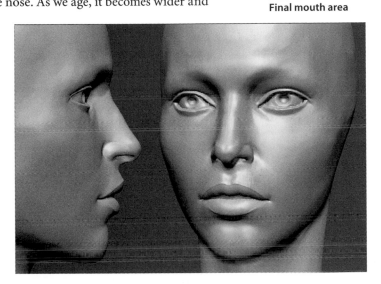

When we are done with the mouth area our model should look like Figure 3.37. There is a lot more to sculpting the face, but so far we have focused on the problem areas: the features. My goal was to break them down into identifiable parts that you can re-create in your sculpts. Our next step is to dive into topology and establish the basic topological layout of our character's head.

Project: Creating New Topology

What is topology? Topology is the polygon layout of the model. It describes where the vertices and edges are placed. It's the map that programs use to render our model to screen or animate its movements. In terms of topology, we have two crucial concerns: edge flow and polygon count.

The dynamic is simple. The more polygons we have, the less we have to think about edge flow. All things being equal, edge flow's inherent value comes in its ability to overcome the weaknesses of most 3D programs: polygon poverty.

I say polygon poverty because in my experience, polygons are like money. You never have enough and you're always trying to find ways to get more. It's a cruel, cruel world, but as ZBrush has shown, the sculptor with the most polygons wins.

In this project, we want to learn the theoretical underpinnings of creating topology. I will be using ZBrush and Maya, but you can use any other app that works for you.

1. You begin with a generic topology map that you paint onto the surface of your model using the Standard brush with RGB on and Zadd off. Figure 3.38 illustrates this topology map. If you are working on a production, you may have to optimize the topology even further than I have here, but this is a good base to start.

There are three important elements to be aware of when you create new topology:

- Stars
- Circles
- Lines

Figure 3.38 illustrates each element. The stars will be weak points in your topology. Wherever there is a star, there will be problems with animation, problems with sculpting, and problems with any dynamic simulations. You want to place these very carefully and selectively.

Figure 3.38

Our topology map

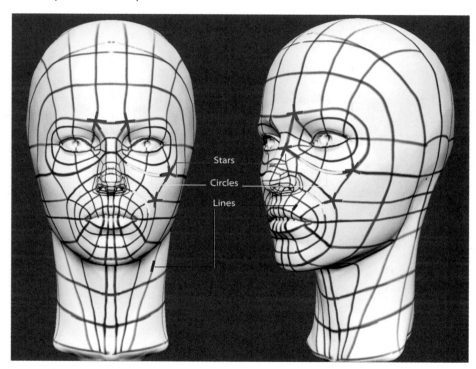

The circles control areas of influence and allow you to selectively add polygons to areas like the eyes and mouth. They also isolate areas of movement to make it easier to animate eye blinks or the mouth opening or closing.

Edges simply describe the direction of the topology. This is important in describing muscle direction and controlling exactly how areas deform.

Figure 3.39

The Rigging subpalette

2. In ZBrush, topology is handled by ZSpheres. Select a ZSphere from the Tool palette. Then, in the Tool → Rigging subpalette, click Select Mesh, as shown in Figure 3.39, and choose your face from the pop-up. Then click Tool → Topology subpalette, click Edit Topology, as shown in Figure 3.40.

3. Before proceeding, make sure you turn Symmetry on. In ZBrush, you create the vertices one at a time. As you create them, ZBrush will connect the dots behind you. I have included a short working example of this on the accompanying DVD, see Chapter3_topology.mov, to help you with the more technical aspects of using ZBrush for topology creation. Figure 3.41 illustrates where we are, mid-project.

Figure 3.40

The Edit Topology button

4. When you get to the eyes and the mouth, it is important that you close them, as shown in Figure 3.42. We will create the eye bags and the mouth bags in Maya. Also, keep the number of edges flowing into these areas equal on all sides or you can run into problems later when making the eye bag and mouth bag.

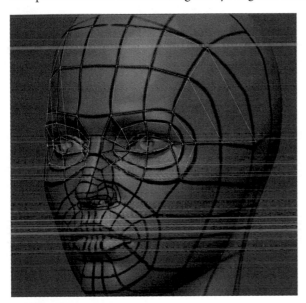

Figure 3.41

Creating new topology

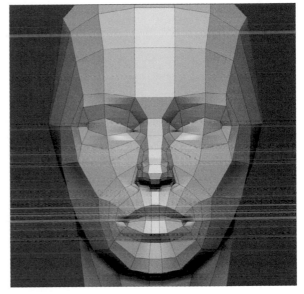

Figure 3.42

The eye and mouth area, with eyes closed

5. When you are done with your topology, you need to convert it to a polygon mesh and export that for use in your other 3D package. To do this, choose Tool → Adaptive Skin and click Make Adaptive Skin, shown in Figure 3.43. Then select the new tool from the Tool palette and export it as an OBJ or a Maya file.

Figure 3.43

The Make Adaptive Skin button

6. In Maya, select all the faces that belong to the inside of the eyes and extrude those inward. Make sure to keep the eye bag as a closed surface. If you delete the face inside, it can cause problems later when you create UVs with UV Master, among other things.

Do the same for the slit in the mouth area. Extrude backward and open it to form the inside of the mouth as you extrude inward. Figure 3.44 illustrates the general shape these should take.

7. Add more polygons around the eyes, mouth, and face area. It would be difficult to add these extra rows inside of ZBrush, but in Maya it's a cinch. Don't worry about repositioning anything just now. All you want to do is to add enough geometry for the face to animate. Figure 3.45 gives you a suggestion of how far to take this. When doing this, I usually set Maya's Insert Edgeloop options to Multiple Edge Loops and then set Number of Edge Loops to 1. This helps preserve symmetry.

8. When I get to the ears, I cheat. Well, some call it cheating. I call it a streamlined workflow. In my book, once you model an ear, there is very little reason to do it again. No one ever says to you, "Wow, your ear has great topology."

   Simply cut the ear out of your other model and then paste it into your new model. To paste it into your new model you must place it exactly where the ear should be. Then delete the ear polygons from your face model. Combine the ear model and the face model by choosing Mesh → Combine. Add new topology as needed to match the ear to the face and you are done (see Figure 3.46).

9. Now add the shoulders. I simply extrude out the bottommost edges of the neck and then extrude the polygon faces along the side. Figure 3.47 shows the final product. Keep in mind, you don't need to sculpt the shoulders at this point. That is what ZBrush is for. When you are done, export the shoulders as an OBJ and make sure to name it _finalTopology.

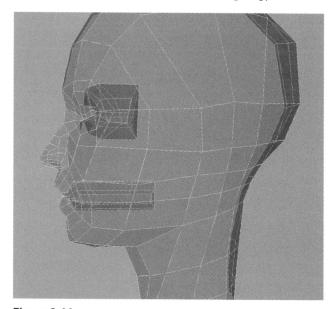

Figure 3.44
Eye and mouth bags

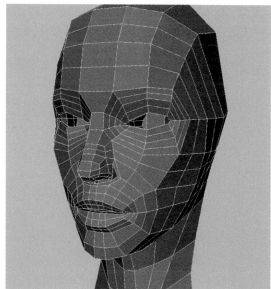

Figure 3.45
Adding Edge Loops

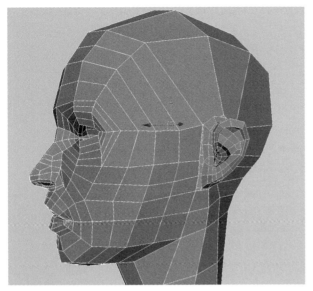

Figure 3.46

Adding the ear

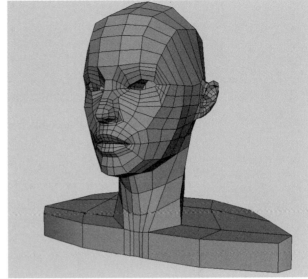

Figure 3.47

Adding shoulders

10. Add eyebrows and eyelashes now to finish the model off. We will append these separately to the model so they will be their own polygon objects. Figure 3.48 shows you an example of how simple the eyebrows, eyelashes, and eyes should be. When you are done creating them, select both eyebrows and export them. Then select both eyelashes and export them separately. Repeat for the eyeballs.

Figure 3.48

Eyebrows and eyelashes and eyeballs

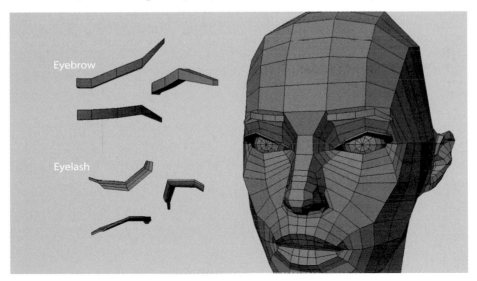

11. Now, back in ZBrush, we will use ZBrush's new projection features on import to transfer the old sculpt to the new topology. Select your sculpt. This is the model that has all of the sculpting that you have done but has the old topology.

Figure 3.49

Reproject higher subdivision levels

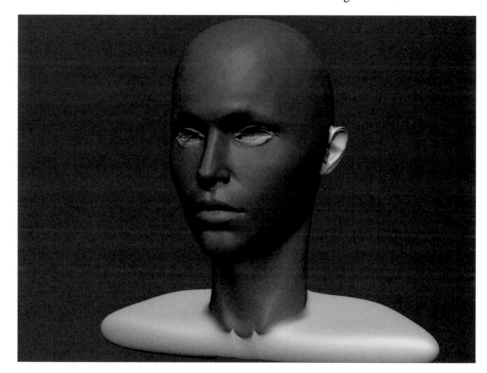

Go to the lowest subdivision level and choose Tool → Import. Navigate to the new topology you exported from Maya. You should get a pop-up that looks like Figure 3.49. Click Yes and ZBrush will attempt to transfer all of the sculpting you did earlier to the new topology you just created. Your model should look like Figure 3.50.

Figure 3.50

Our model after import

12. You will most likely have to clean up the model a bit. The easiest way to do that is to switch the Morph Target by choosing Tool → Morph Target and clicking Switch, as shown in Figure 3.51.

Figure 3.51

The Morph Target subpalette

Then invert the mask and select the Morph brush. Turn Backface Masking on in the Auto Masking subpalette of the Brush palette. Lightly brush over the surface areas of the face. When the polygons go haywire, undo the stroke and avoid that area. That is an area you will have to resculpt. At this point, your model will look something like Figure 3.52.

13. The last thing to do is to sculpt the shoulders and add the eyebrows, eyelashes, and eyes. For the shoulders, remember to indicate the clavicle and to place the acromion process. Try to keep the cylinder of the neck and the top plane of the shoulder distinctly separate. Refer back to Chapter 2 for more information on how to sculpt this area.

To import the eyelashes, select the Polymesh 3D star and then import the OBJ. To import the eyebrows, select the Polymesh 3D star again and import it. Before importing, you must select the Polymesh 3D star. Then simply append each of your OBJs to your face in the SubTool subpalette. Figure 3.53 illustrates our final head sculpt.

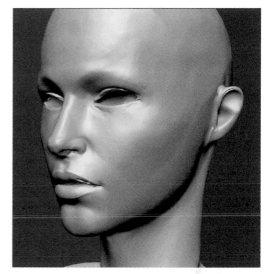

Figure 3.52
After using the Morph brush

Summary

At the end of the day there is a subtle sheen that your model will exude when you have gotten it right. Your job is to be there when it happens and to recognize it, like a painter waiting for daybreak to catch just the right light. You have to be prepared and open to it. Frustration is your enemy and will blind you to the moment. Patience and calm are your allies. The face is one of the hardest things to sculpt, and a female face is likely *the* hardest thing to sculpt. Good luck.

Figure 3.53
Our final head sculpt

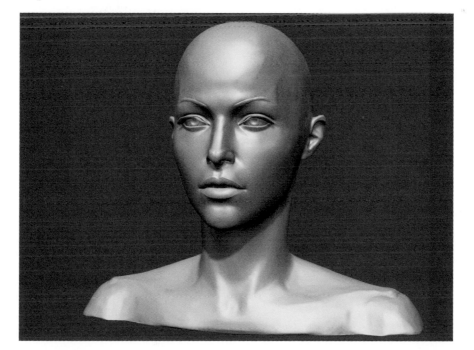

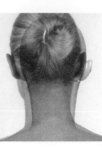

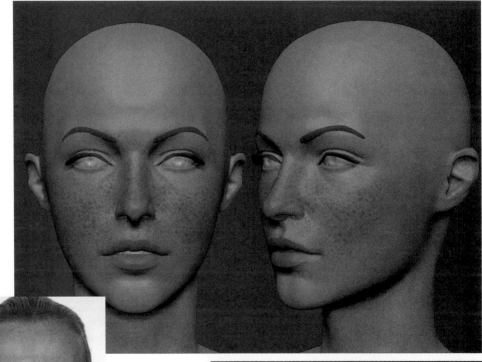

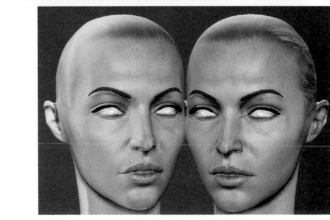

Texturing the Head

Essentially, you have two major ways to texture paint the human head: hand texture using brushes and illustrative techniques and using photographic reference.

That is not to say that you can't blend the two, but each method has its own purpose. You usually determine when to use one or the other by how you plan to create your pore-level details. You can create those manually, or you can use your photographic reference to create them.

In this chapter, we will look at both ways of texture painting in turn, starting with the manual painting approach. The newest approach to texture painting in ZBrush, Spotlight, can be found on the accompanying DVD.

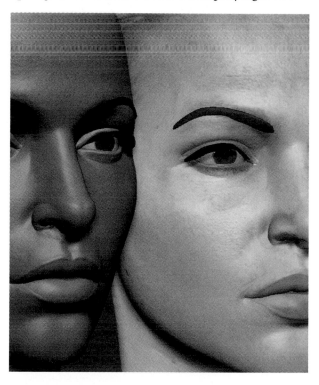

Project: Texture Painting by Hand

Texture painting by hand, as shown in Figure 4.1, gives us a lot of freedom to design the skin of the character, but it does require that we obey a few laws of nature. Among them is the balance between saturated colors and desaturated colors, warm versus cool colors, and the natural distribution of color zones on the face.

We will first look at one of the main reasons we would texture paint by hand: to create our own pore-level detail.

Figure 4.1

Texture painting by hand

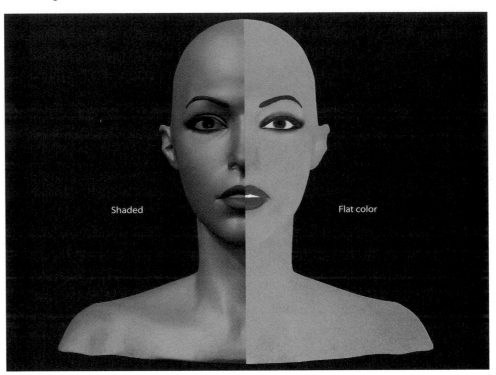

Sculpting Pores by Hand

Pores are the final detail you add to your model. You do not want to make major form adjustments once you have completed them. Our process for pores is to establish a base coat of surface noise, augment that with specific pore types for different areas of the face, and then, finally, bring it all together with some crosshatching.

Several years ago Kris Kosta and Rick Baker both posted several alphas for skin pore texturing on ZBrushCentral. Figure 4.2 shows examples of them. These alphas have been the default alphas that most production artists use to create pore-level detail on their characters.

Figure 4.2

Rick Baker's and Kris Kosta's alphas

bottomlips_wrinkles01.jpg	bottomlips_wrinkles02.jpg	cells.jpg	eyes_bottom.jpg	fine_wrinkles.jpg	lips_contour.jpg	pores.jpg	pores_small.jpg

crosshatch alpha.jpg	long pores alpha.jpg	lots o pores alpha .jpg	neck bumps alpha.jpg	neck stipple 1 alpha.jpg	neck stipple 2.jpg

Follow the steps below to begin sculpting pores.

1. The Kosta and Baker alphas are included in the DVD for your use. Make sure you load them into ZBrush or have them ready before we start texture painting.

2. Create a new layer in which to store your pore-level detail. Figure 4.3 shows what my Layer palette looks like at the end of this process. Notice how each stage is stored in a separate layer to make it easier for me to adjust their intensity and blend them together later.

   When using layers, it's important to exaggerate the effects of the pores. You can always dial the layer down by adjusting the Layer Intensity slider. For now, though, create the *pore-base* layer so that you can use it to store your first pass.

3. We will create our base coat of pores using the powerful Surface Noise feature. Surface Noise can create everything from rocky surfaces to skin pores with just a few setting changes.

   Using it is a two-part process. In the first part, you design how the surface noise will look. In the second part, you apply that noise to your model and bake it into the polygons.

   Turn Noise on and use the settings in Figure 4.4 to get your first pass at pores. Make sure to get the curve as accurate as possible. This is a significant part of the appearance of the noise. When done correctly, your model should look like Figure 4.5.

4. Next you want to make sure your model is at least a million polygons and is at the highest subdivision level. Choose Tool → Surface → Apply To Mesh, shown in Figure 4.6. Click Undo if it doesn't look right, and then adjust your settings and choose Apply To Mesh again. Your model should look the same before and after, but your resolution can affect how much detail you capture. Finally, turn off the layer's recording by pressing REC in the layer subpalette of the Tool palette and adjust the layer's intensity. Figure 4.7 illustrates the base pores with the layer intensity set to .38.

Figure 4.3

The Layer Palette

Figure 4.4

Surface Noise settings

Figure 4.5

Pores created with Surface Noise

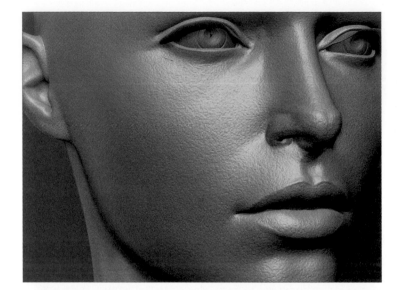

Figure 4.6

The Apply To Mesh button

Figure 4.7

Pore layer with layer intensity set to .38

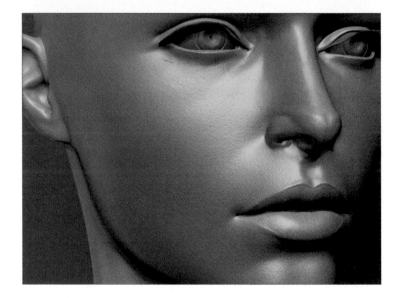

Pore Variations

Different areas of the face have different types of pores as well as different sized pores. Figure 4.8 illustrates the different zones of the face. Of particular note is the area of "long pores." Rick Baker has given us an alpha for this. Also, the areas along the neck are not so much pores as they are skin bumps, so the alpha is used with Zadd on instead of Zsub.

Figure 4.8

Pore zones

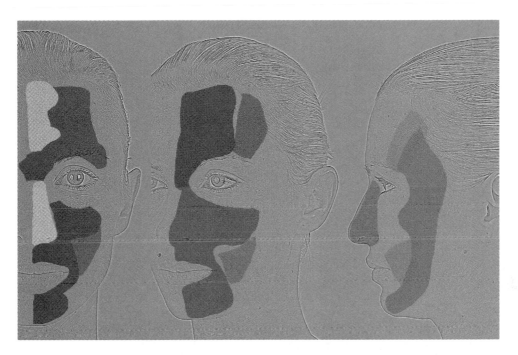

Begin sculpting the pore variations by following the steps below.

1. Let's start out by creating the long pores in the fleshy areas of the cheeks and the bonier side of the forehead. Create another layer and name this layer **poreAccent**. Select the Standard brush with the Drag Rect stroke and the `long pores alpha.jpg`, shown in Figure 4.9. Set ZIntensity to somewhere between 5 and 10.

Figure 4.9

Long pores

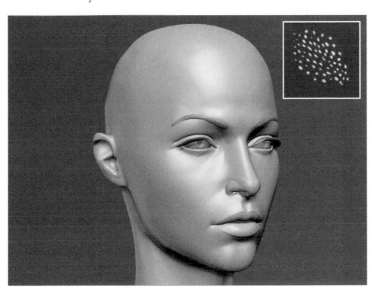

Drag this alpha out continuously in the cheek area. Be careful to make the pore sizes as accurate as possible and keep the pores flowing in the same direction. If the pores are too large, your audience will notice it immediately.

One trick I use is to alternate dragging downward and upward to draw the alpha. Also, don't forget the stretched pores in the temple area. Figure 4.10 illustrates the completed result.

Figure 4.10

Long pores added

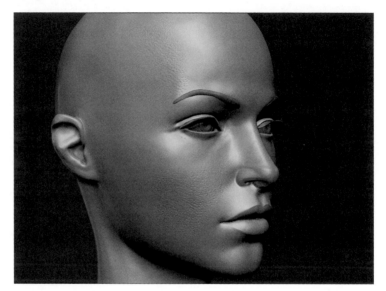

2. Now let's use Kris Kosta's `pores.jpg` file (see Figure 4.11). Use this to drag out the pores in the brow area, chin area, and forehead area. Keep in mind that each of these areas will have different sized pores, so you don't want to rush through this. Take your time. It's better to do it right than to redo it because you rushed yourself.

   Figure 4.12 shows you the final result with long pores and these new pore variations.

Figure 4.11

Kris Kosta's pores alpha

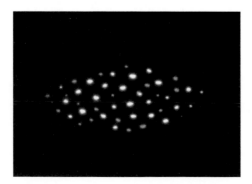

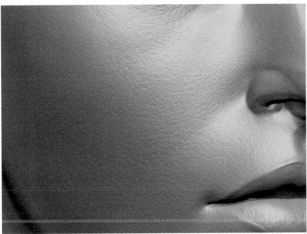
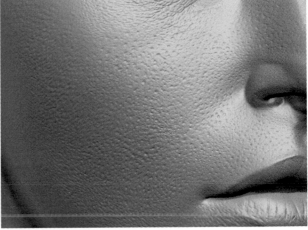

Long Pore Layer's Layer Intensity set to .3   Long Pore Layer's Layer Intensity set to 1

Figure 4.12
Pore variations

3. Now it's time to create the neck bumps. To start, let's create a new layer and call it **neck-FaceHatching**. This layer will contain the remaining details of the skin.

   With the same brush active, select Rick Baker's `neck bumps alpha.jpg` file, shown in Figure 4.13. Click Zadd on the shelf and drag out the bumps along the neck area in a downward circular fashion. You may need to adjust ZIntensity to get the result you need, but remember to exaggerate it slightly, as shown in Figure 4.14.

   When you are done, turn off REC in the layer and double-check the pore sizes and intensity. Adjust Tool → Layers → Layer Intensity to see if you can get a more subtle appearance.

Figure 4.13
Rick Baker's neck bumps alpha

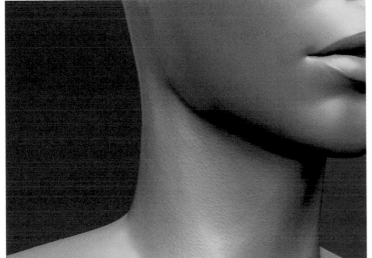

Figure 4.14
Bumps applied to the neck area

Crosshatching

Once the pores are in place, we are 70 percent of the way there, but it may still look like the pores are really just stuck on there and are not really a part of the flesh. This is because they are, in fact, just stuck on there with alphas. Our job now is to tie the textures and sculpture all together and give it some life.

Practical sculptors have a nice little wire tool they use that finds the crevices of the pores and drags out thin lines that connect them all together just like skin. Although we don't have this tool in ZBrush, we can get close with a few adjustments:

1. To create our hatch mark tool, we will use the Standard brush and change the stroke to Dots and the alpha to Alpha 58. We set Brush → Alpha And Texture → AlphaTile to 2. Set ZIntensity to somewhere around 4.

   Cavity masking is essential for us to get an effect similar to the effect that the wire tool mentioned earlier produces. Turn on Brush → Auto Masking → Cavity and leave it as its default.

2. Now let's start sculpting. Using this new brush, draw along the surface of your model trying to connect all the pores. Use small strokes and work along the direction of the skin. Remember to keep the other layers visible but use Figure 4.15 as a guide. Exaggerate the crosshatching a bit; we will soften it later.

Figure 4.15
Making hatch marks in the skin

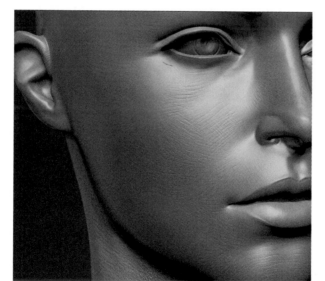

Figure 4.16 illustrates how the hatch marks look when blended with the other layers. You should just barely see the difference. Small as it is, though, it's an incredibly important difference. Using this crosshatching technique adds depth to the pores of your model and can bring more life to them.

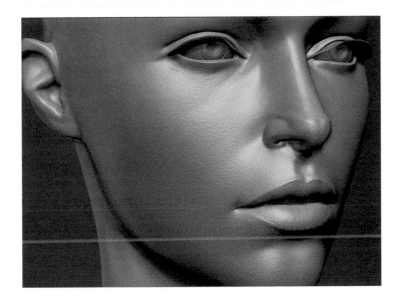

Figure 4.16

Hatch marks blended with other layers

Wrinkles

Once you have the pores established and the crosshatching effectively laid out, you might want to add wrinkles using the other alphas in Kris's and Rick's alpha set. Here's how:

1. Create another layer and name it **Wrinkles**. Then select the Standard brush, set the stroke type to drag rectangle and select an alpha like Kris's eyes_bottom.jpg. Drag out several instances of this alpha along the bottom of the eye as in Figure 4.17. Also try the lips_contour.jpg alpha for the lips.

Figure 4.17

Adding wrinkles to the eyes

2. Once you have laid out a few alphas, it's time to adjust them and give them some realism. You do this with a combination of brushes. I like to use the Inflate brush with a small draw size around the lines created. This creates extra pockets of skin that I can then flatten with the Trim Dynamic brush or H_Polish. Then I melt everything together using the Smooth Subdiv brush and just lightly go over the surface. Figure 4.18 shows you the result.

Figure 4.18
Wrinkles after
sculpting

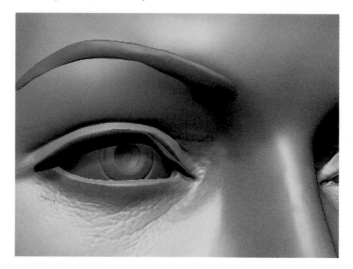

Texture Painting by Hand

When your model's pores are laid out, you are in great shape to start texture painting. This approach relies heavily on the Color Spray stroke and has been around for a long time. It is very flexible, and you can use it to texture paint everything from photo-realistic characters to more illustrative characters. Figure 4.19 shows one example.

Figure 4.19
Example of Color
Spray on a character

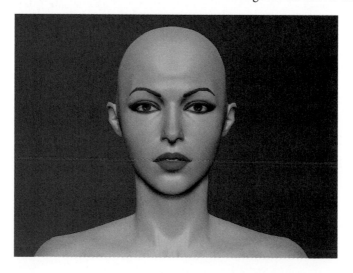

The Color Palette

The color palette will help you get the best color range you can on your model. When we texture paint a model, we are concerned with the following attributes of color:

Color hue

Color saturation/temperature

Value

The color hue spectrum is in the outer circle of the color palette. You establish color saturation and value in the large color box shown in Figure 4.20.

Occasionally, I will suggest cooling a warm color down by desaturating it. You should rarely have to change your hue into the purples or blues to get the color you need. Instead, you can get most of the color you need by balancing between the red and yellow hues and either increasing or decreasing saturation and value. Figure 4.21 illustrates this concept.

Figure 4.20
Setting color saturation and value

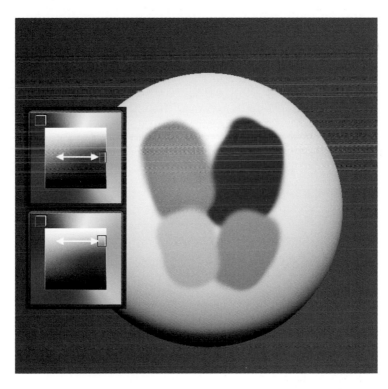

Figure 4.21

Effects of saturation on color

Base Coat

A good place to start with our base coat is to choose one of the RGB values in Figure 4.22 and just test out a few color swatches. You may notice that your material will affect the color value. For example, if you select MatCap_Red Wax as your default material, it will completely overpower your texturing. The SkinShade4 material is used in Figure 4.22.

Figure 4.22

Skin colors in the
SkinShade4
material

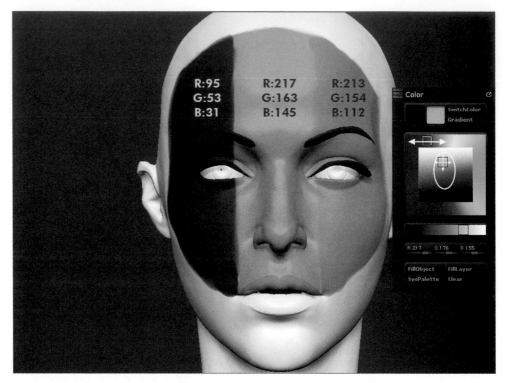

Another option is to use Photoshop's Color Picker to get a good-sized sample and pull from a photographic reference of skin. Make sure to sample from the light area of your reference and not the shadows. Once you have a base color chosen, it's time to start texture painting the model:

1. Make sure RGB is on in the shelf, and create a layer by choosing Tool → Layer → New. Then rename this layer **base coat**.

   Select the Standard brush. Select Alpha 23. Set RGB Intensity between 20 and 50. Select the Color Spray stroke and set the Stroke → Color Variance value to .5. Then set the color swatch to your base color and paint the entire model, as shown in Figure 4.23.

2. If we want to add even more variation to the skin color we can use Surface Noise. This step is optional and could be used in place of using the Color Spray stroke in step 1.

   In the Tool → Surface subpalette, turn on Noise and adjust all the settings to be similar to the image in the section on sculpting pores earlier in this chapter. Set Tool → Surface → ColorBlend to -.22. This should give you a decent amount of surface variation. Feel free to experiment with all these settings.

To bake this noise into our mesh, we have to first store a morph target by choosing Tool → Morph Target → StoreMT. Then choose Tool → Surface → Apply To Mesh. This action will apply the surface noise and the texture noise. Choose Tool → Morph Target → Switch to undo the surface noise and you'll be left with only the texture noise as in Figure 4.24.

Choose the Tool → Layer and click the REC button on your layer to store the texturing down to this point. We'll create another layer for the color zones next so that you'll have more flexibility to experiment.

Figure 4.23

Painting the skin base

Figure 4.24

Skin with texture noise

Zones

The face has several different color temperature zones. The five o'clock shadow of a male character will be cooler (less saturated) than his nose. His nose will be redder and slightly more saturated then the yellow tint of his forehead.

Each area varies slightly in hue, temperature, and value, but as you saw in the section on the color palette, we can use saturation to help us adjust color temperature and even move toward a cooler hue. Figure 4.25 illustrates the different areas and their general color tendency.

Let's start with the nose:

1. Create a new layer and call it **colorZones**. Make sure you have RGB on when you create the layer. Using the Standard brush with Color Spray stroke on, set the hue to a slightly redder value. Set RGB Intensity to somewhere around 10. Lower your draw size so that the brush sprays smaller splotches of color, and then start painting the nose area. Blend the color into the cheek areas and upper lip area as in Figure 4.26.

2. Move the hue toward the yellow spectrum and paint the bony areas such as the forehead and the zygomatic bone. Try to keep the coloring subtle. Refer occasionally to Figure 4.25, which illustrates the different color zones of the face. If you have a significant amount of color variation, make sure Stroke → Color Variance is set to .05.

3. Set your color back to the reddish color from step 1 and desaturate it quite a bit. Use this color to texture the lower part of the face and along the jawline.

4. The eye area of your character will be a cooler, almost purple color. You can get this purplish color by desaturating the red color, but you might find it easier to paint if you drag the color slider ever so slightly into the purple area.

Figure 4.25
Color tendencies of different areas of the face and head

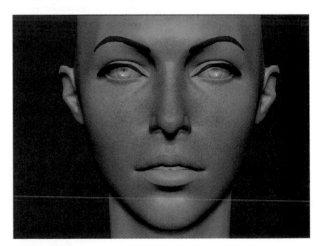

Figure 4.26
Cheeks and nose area

5. Add a few accents of red around the tip of the nose and the frontal process of the maxilla. These color variations will be very subtle in our final female character, so use Figure 4.27 as a guide for general character texturing. In the next step, we'll look at applying some makeup to cover up skin blemishes and unify the color of the general face area as any good butt-kicking superhero chick would.

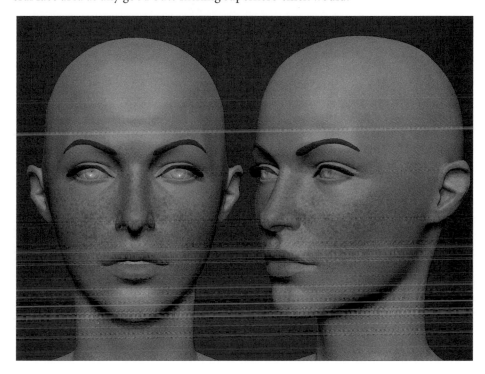

Figure 4.27

Textured skin with color zones

Makeup Time!

Now it's time to add that sexy glamour look to our model with a little makeup. Our goal here is to even out the skin, cover up any blemishes, give the cheeks a bit of life, and apply the lipstick and eye shadow that our character will be using.

If you're like me and not used to applying makeup every day or, uh, any day, then I suggest taking a little trip around the Internet and looking for common techniques and looks. For this example, we'll be using a glamorous shadowy cat-eye look:

1. Our first step is to apply some foundation. Our goal here is to even out the complexion and cover up any blemishes.

   Create a new layer. Then select the Standard brush. RGB Intensity should be low. Make sure the Color Spray Stroke is on and use Alpha 23. Select a color for the foundation from the model by pressing C and hovering over the color you want. Then just paint a light coat over the model to unify the skin tone, as in Figure 4.28.

Figure 4.28

Even skin tone

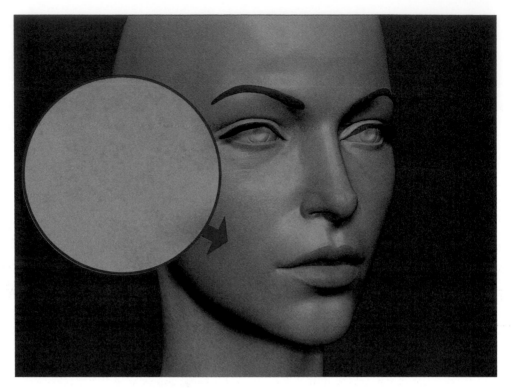

2. Let's also apply a little blush. We just want to add a little color to the cheeks; we do not want to create a clown character. So go easy on how red you make the color and your RGB Intensity setting. Use the Standard brush with the Color Spray stroke but set Stroke → Color Variance to 0.

3. Eye shadow will help us artificially shape the eye. In this case, we're going for a smoky cat-eye look. You need to pair a dark eye shadow with a light eye shadow. You can pick a color close to the color used in step 1 for the light color. Then you can choose a much darker color to apply to the upper eyelid. Note that for our look, the eye shadow does not pass above the eye crease. It is applied only to the eyelid itself, or, if you remember from the last chapter, the palpebral portion of the eye.

4. Eye liner is the next thing to establish. I recommend a dark reddish or bluish color instead of black. Black, as a color, can be very dead. You can add depth to the color by leaving the saturation up pretty high even though the value of it is quite low.

Work your way around the bottom eyelid. Pull the line outward and upward to create the cat-eye effect. Then repeat with the upper eyelid by pulling from the middle of the upper lid and outward.

Figure 4.29 illustrates the applied makeup. Try to keep it subtle, unless your character won't likely be known for her subtle makeup.

Pores

Since we hand-sculpted the pores, we need one extra step to really make the pores sing. The first step is to create a mask for the pores so we can color them separately from the rest of the model. We do this by choosing Tool → Masking → Mask By Cavity.

To use Mask By Cavity, you must first make sure that Cavity Intensity is set to 100, as shown in Figure 4.30. Then click Mask By Cavity. You may have to set the Blur slider to below 10 if you are affecting too much of the skin, but for the first run, use the default settings. Before we start to paint the pores, though, you have to invert the mask and turn off its visibility. Choose Tool → Masking → Inverse. Then choose Tool → Masking → ViewMask.

You can paint the pores with the Standard brush or you can paint them globally using Color → Fill Object. I prefer to use Color → Fill Object. Set the color swatch to a dark, warm color. Set RGB Intensity to about 30, and then click Fill Object. If you find it is coloring the skin of your model too much, then try sharpening the mask by choosing Tool → Masking → Sharpen Mask. Figure 4.31 shows the before-and-after effects of using a mask to enhance the model's pores.

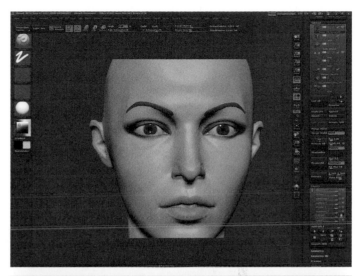

Figure 4.29
Finished makeup

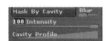

Figure 4.30

Cavity masking
settings

Figure 4.31

Before and after cavity masking

Eyes

You might have noticed that in some of the example images, the eyes are painted in: I find it essential to paint in the character's eyes. Without the eyes painted in, I find it much too difficult to judge the texture job without getting the distinct impression that the character should be staring out from the next *Exorcist* sequel.

Figure 4.32

Alphas used for
painting an eye

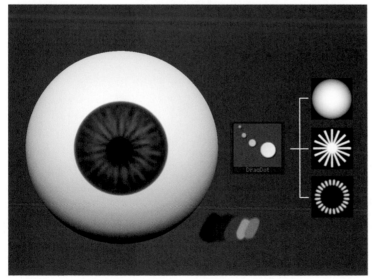

Thankfully, it's fairly easy to paint the eyes, and you don't even need a photo reference, though a photo reference always helps. Figure 4.32 illustrates the alphas used to paint an eye. Notice that the colors vary from dark blue to orange. The orange and yellows were applied with a very low RGB Intensity value. Also, in order to get the hard edges around the outside of the eye, I set my focal shift to -70.

Our model is now textured and detailed with pores and wrinkles and everything was painted by hand. Now let's look at using photographic reference to paint the face.

Project: Texture Painting Approach #2 ZAppLink

When we create models, we always use photo reference in one way or another. For this project, we will use it to directly apply pictures to our model. The primary way to do this is with ZAppLink, but a new tool has come into being with ZBrush 4, Spotlight, which promises to offer even more power. For now, though, we will focus on connecting ZBrush with Photoshop and looking at the production workflow used to create the model in Figure 4.33. Note, we will be starting the texture over from scratch now and looking at a completely different approach towards painting.

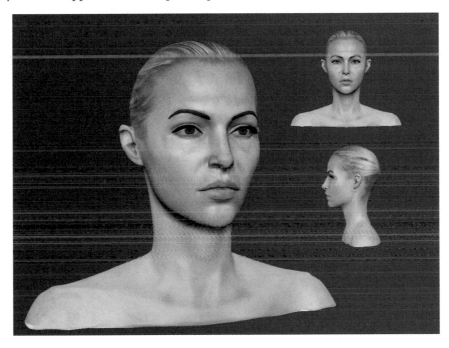

Figure 4.33

Character painted with a photo reference

Texture Painting with Photo Reference

We start this section with a model that does not have any pores or wrinkles. In this workflow, our character will be sculpted to its final shape, but the details like pores and wrinkles will largely come from texture maps.

To start we need to open the ZAppLink Properties subpalette. It is located in the Document palette at the very bottom and looks like Figure 4.34. We will be storing views, saving views, and using views to position our model for texturing in Photoshop.

Let's begin:

1. Begin by loading `femaleHead_chp4_zapp.zpr`. To save views, you simply position the model on the canvas and press one of the views. For example, rotate the model to the front view. Make sure to lock it to the front view by pressing Shift. Then choose Document: ZAppLink Properties → Front.

Figure 4.34

ZAppLink Properties

Figure 4.35

The ZAppLink
button

This will also store the back view. If you don't like the back view it stores, you can delete it by choosing Clear To and then following that with Back in the Document: ZAppLink Properties subpalette.

You'll want to store a side view and a three-quarter view. Once you've done that, I also suggest that you save the views in case something happens or your computer crashes. You can always bring your views back by choosing Load Views.

DOCUMENT SIZE AND ZAPPLINK

Keep in mind that document size is very important to how much texture resolution you can transfer between ZBrush and Photoshop. In the example below, I keep the document size at the default level. If, however, you need more texture resolution, the first step is to double your document size. The only downside to doing this is that it slows ZBrush down as it takes more system resources.

2. Click ZAppLink in the Document palette. Once in Photoshop, all of our views will be stored as both color layers and shading layers. The shading layers will be locked so that we know to avoid them. See Figure 4.35.

    Make sure your photo reference is loaded in Photoshop. We'll start with the front view. Turn all the layers off except the shade layer and the color layer for the front view. Copy your photo reference and paste it into your ZAppLink document directly above the color layer of the front view. If it's too large, use Free Transform to adjust the size. Line up the eye line and the line of the mouth as best you can, as shown in Figure 4.37.

3. Adjust the shape of areas like the eyes, mouth, and nose using Free Transform's Warp tool. The best workflow for doing this is as follows:

    a. Make a selection and press Ctrl/Option+J to copy it into a new layer.

    b. Press Ctrl and click on the layer just created.

    c. Press Ctrl/Option+T to enter Free Transform.

    d. Right-click inside the selection and choose Warp. Adjust points as needed.

    Your goal is to get the shape of these features as close as possible to help minimize any texture fixing at the end. Figure 4.38 illustrates this. Sometimes, though, it is not possible to solve a mismatch of texture and model. This often happens in the corner of the mouth. In those cases, just let it slide. You can adjust it later. Our main goal here is to get the texture about 70 percent done before we start working directly on the texture map.

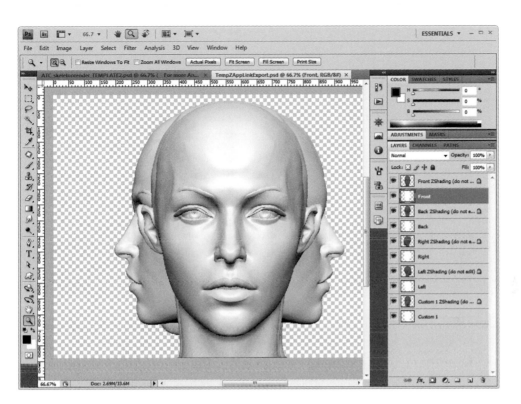

Figure 4.36

The ZAppLink document in Photoshop

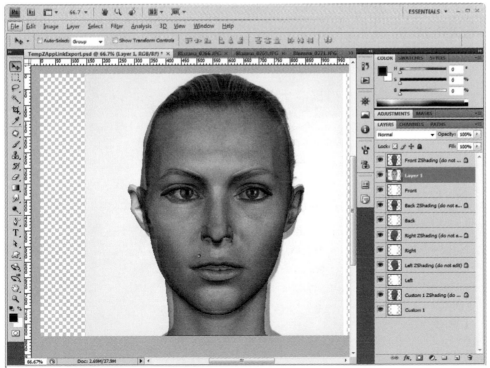

Figure 4.37

The image placed in Photoshop

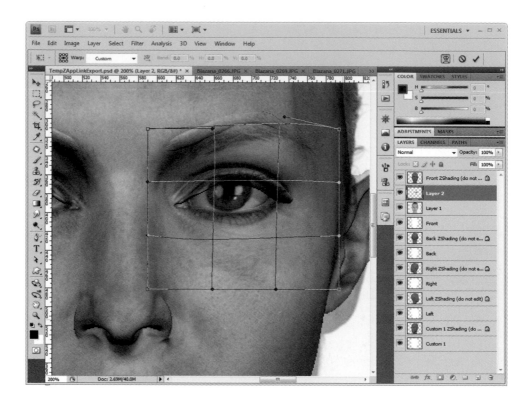

4. Repeat the process in the preceding step for the side view and the three-quarters view as best you can. When you are done, it is wise to duplicate it and save a copy to your hard drive. The file you share between ZBrush and Photoshop is a temporary file. Note that you must duplicate the file before saving it with another name because ZBrush needs the file to be a specific name.

   Once you have duplicated your file, you have to merge down all the layers so that they have the exact same name as when you first brought them into Photoshop and there are no extra layers hanging around. Save the document and return to ZBrush.

5. In ZBrush, accept each layer's projection onto your model, turn off the layer to store the painting, and then save it. As you can see in Figure 4.39, I textured only one side of the model's face, and there is some stretching under the chin and a few other places. This is par for the course; we will fix it when we start working on the texture map itself.

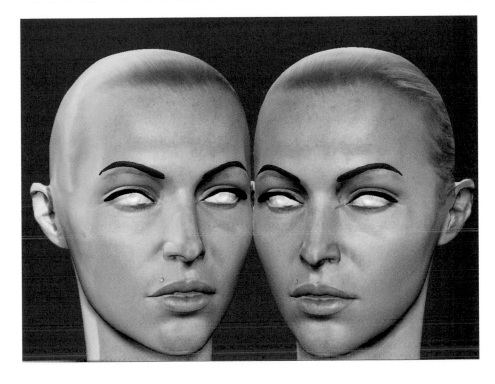

Figure 4.39

Back in ZBrush

Using a UV Map

At this point, our texture job should be about 50 percent done. We are missing texture on one side of the model and there is stretching in other areas that are hard to reach. Instead of fixing those areas in ZAppLink, I have found that the best approach is to switch tactics and start working on the 2D texture map.

To create a 2D texture map, you must create some UVs. UVs are never fun, but they are now incredibly easy to create with UV Master, as shown in Figure 4.40. UV Master ships with ZBrush and is about as push-button easy as it comes.

Follow these steps:

1. Lower your model to its lowest subdivision level and click Work On Clone in the UV Master subpalette. This will create a separate low-resolution file for you to work on and allow you to use the powerful Control Painting feature. Then create Polygroups as seen in Figure 4.41 to specify the UV islands that you want it to use.

2. Use Enable Control Painting to both attract the seam to one side and protect the other side of the model. Just select the Attract button and paint on the model where you want the seam to be. Select Protect and do the same. Figure 4.42 illustrates the final result.

Figure 4.40

The UV Master panel

Figure 4.41
Creating Polygroups

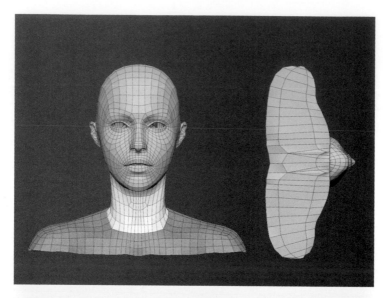

Figure 4.42
Painting the UV
borders

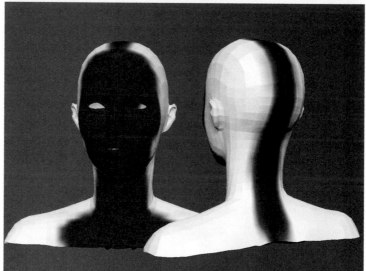

3. Click Polygroups next to the Unwrap button, and finally, click the Unwrap button. To check your new UV layout, turn Polyframe on and then choose Tool → Texture: New from UV Check. When done, your UVs should look like those behind the model in Figure 4.43.

4. By default, UV Master will create all of the UV islands at roughly the same size. Use UV Master's Density controls to specify that the face be four times larger than the rest of the UV shells. To do that, just choose Density and the x4 button. Isolate just the head, Ctrl+click on it, and choose Color → Fill Object. Figure 4.44 shows you the model and the map.

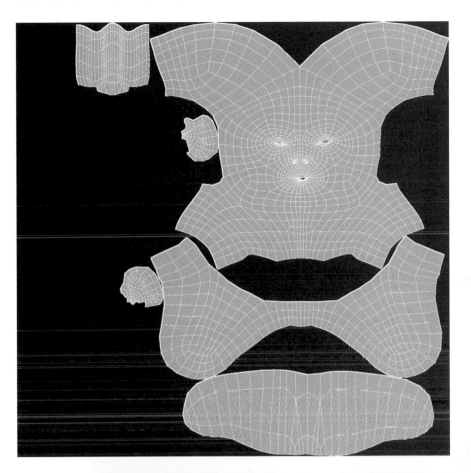

Figure 4.43

UV map from UV
Master before using
Density

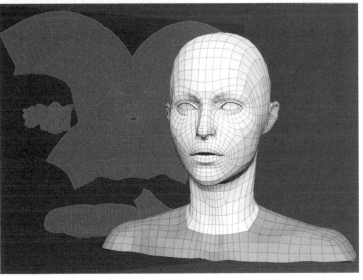

Figure 4.44

UV map and model

Creating a Texture Map

All the texture painting we have done on our character up to this point has been through Polypainting. Polypainting paints directly on your model's polygons. The resolution of your painting depends on how many polygons you have.

For creating a realistic game character, you want to work with a 2 K texture map for each part of the model. A 2 K texture map is 2,048 pixels wide by 2,048 pixels tall. That comes to about 4 million pixels of information.

The standard UV layout is about 80 percent efficient. That means that through UV stretching or empty space, your UV layout is likely to be using only 80 percent of the available 4 million pixels of information. That leaves about 3 million pixels for texturing. It's very easy to get a model up to 3 million polygons in ZBrush, so you usually want to shoot for each part of your model having at least that many polygons.

Before you create your texture map, make sure you have set the map size correctly. You do this by setting Tool → UV Map → UV Map Size. By default, it is set to 2048, so you should be all set to go. Finally, to bake your PolyPainting into a texture map, choose Tool → Texture and click the New From Polypaint button, shown in Figure 4.45.

To export this map painting in Photoshop, you must choose Tool → Texture → Clone Txtr. Then in the texture palette, select the texture and choose Export.

Figure 4.45

Click the New From Polypaint button.

Simple Fixes in Photoshop

As I mentioned earlier, our work with ZAppLink is only intended to get us halfway there. We must rely on Photoshop to get us the rest of the way. At this point, we have a texture map that is 50 percent done and all our efforts will be directed toward making that map better:

1. In ZBrush, you need to export your UV map as an image so you can overlay it on your texture map in Photoshop. To do that, turn on Polyframe and choose Tool → Texture and click New From UV Check. Then clone that texture and export it from the texture palette.

2. In Photoshop, import the UV layout and the texture map. Drag the UV map into the texture map and set its blending mode to Overlay. The first and easiest change you can make is to mirror the side that has texturing to the side that does not. Simply duplicate the layer, flip it horizontally, and position it as best you can. Use the Clone brush to blend the layers together and fix obvious problem areas. When done, your texture should look something like Figure 4.46.

3. To see the effects of these changes on your model, save the texture map with all of its layers intact and import it into ZBrush. In ZBrush, load it on the model in the Tool → Texture subpalette and look around for any problems areas. If you see any, then bake your texture map into Polypainting by choosing Tool → Polypainting and clicking Polypaint From Texture. It's time to start spot fixing.

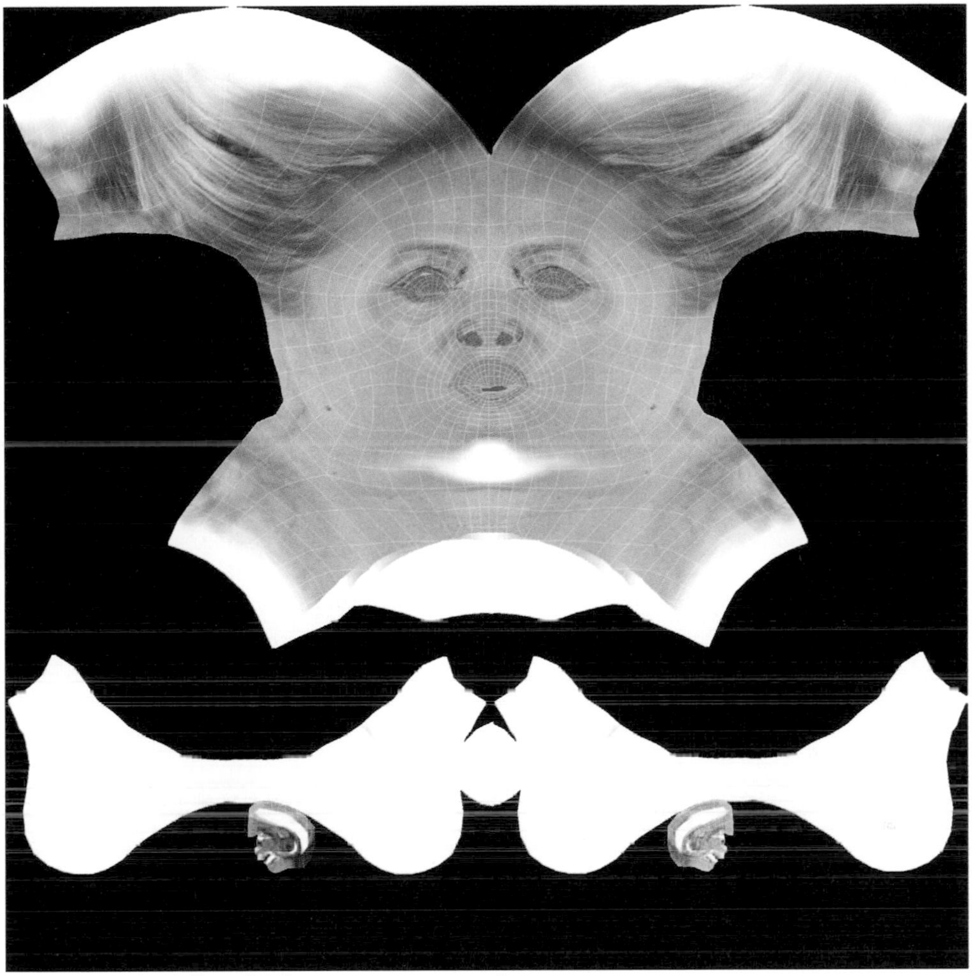

Figure 4.46
The texture map in progress

Spot Fixing

To spot fix an area, we will cycle through a series of steps that dance between Photoshop and ZBrush. At the end, we will get a texture map that has several layers of fixes:

1. First we will use ZAppLink to send over a view of one problem area to Photoshop. We will use this process to texture paint the back, head, chest, and other parts. In ZBrush, set your model up into a three-quarters view. Then turn off Document → ZAppLink Properties → ZAppLink Views, shown in Figure 4.47. By turning this feature off, you disable all the views you created and will send only the current position of the model over to Photoshop. Choose ZAppLink in the document palette and continue to the next step.

Figure 4.47
ZAppLink Views

2. In Photoshop, you will use a photo reference for the back area or whatever area you are working on. Figure 4.48 shows the back area. Make sure to erase parts of the reference that you do not need and merge it down to the color layer. Save the document and return to ZBrush.

Figure 4.48

Fixing the back area

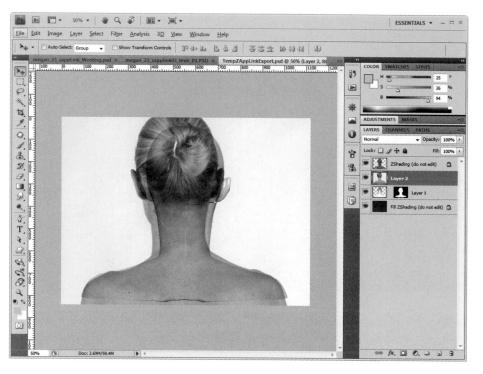

3. In ZBrush, accept the changes. Don't worry about the other views or if the texture has gotten destroyed in other parts of the model. The only area we are concerned about is the cheek area because this is the only area we will be sending to our texture map in Photoshop. That said, let's convert our polypainting to a texture map by choosing Tool → Texture and clicking New From Polypaint. Clone the map and export it from the texture palette with the name **cheekSpotFix.psd**.

4. In Photoshop import cheekSpotFix.psd and overlay the image onto your main texture map. Use Layer Masks to isolate just the cheek area, as shown in Figure 4.49. Save the document and return to ZBrush.

5. In ZBrush, import the texture map again. ZBrush does not auto-update, so you may end up with several texture maps in your texture palette. The last one in the list is the last one you imported. Load that onto your model in the Tool → Texture subpalette and see how it fits, as shown in Figure 4.50. If you see any other areas that need fixing, just repeat steps 1 through 5 for each problem area.

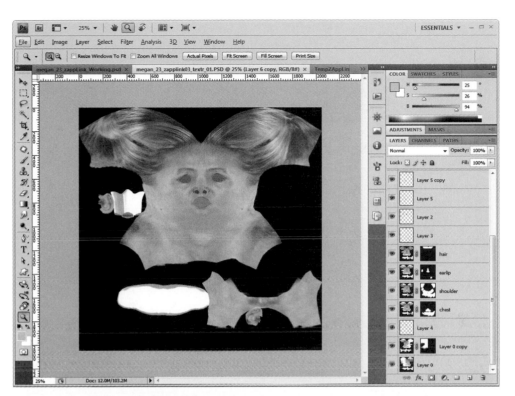

Figure 4.49
Using Layer Masks

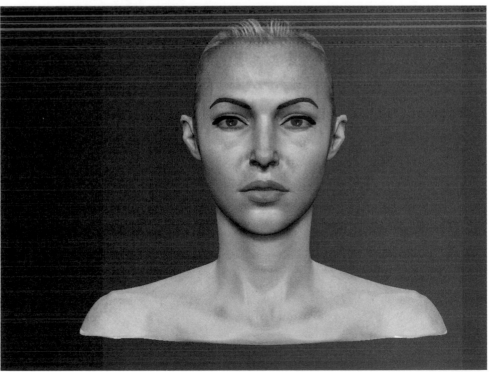

Figure 4.50
Back in ZBrush

Removing Oil and Adding Final Touches

Most photo references will have specular lighting that you will want to remove. Sometimes the lights that these models sit under are incredibly warm and even a few minutes underneath them can cause someone to sweat. Fortunately, removing oil and sweat is a fairly straightforward process:

1. We start by merging all the layers into a new layer. To do this, press and hold Alt while clicking the options arrow for the layer palette and dragging downward to Merge Visible.

    Rename the layer **OilMask**, then desaturate it. Using Levels, adjust the contrast so that the light areas of the face are quite bright, as seen in Figure 4.51.

Figure 4.51

The OilMask layer

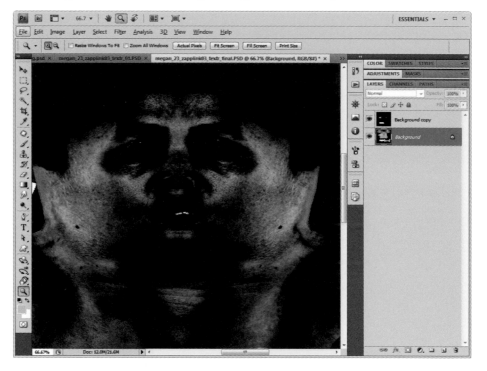

2. Create a Curve Adjustment layer. Then go back to the OilMask layer and copy the contents of the entire layer to the Clipboard. Select the mask of the Curve Adjustment layer by pressing Alt and clicking on it. Then paste the OilMask layer into it.

3. Adjust the curve to remove the highlight, as seen in Figure 4.52. The goal is just to remove the most visible specularity. Be careful not to go too far with this technique.

Figure 4.52

Oil removed

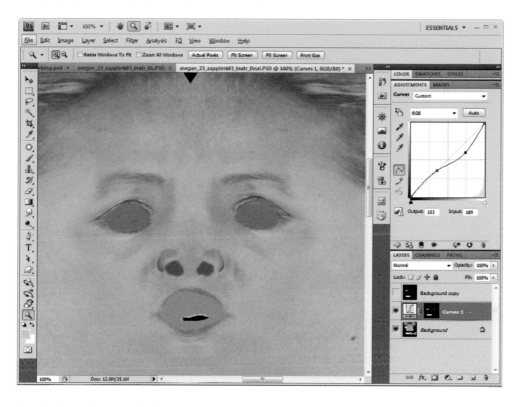

Sculpting Pores via Texture Map

When we use photo references for our texture map, we can also use photo references for sculpting our pores. This way, our texture map and our detail sculpting will match almost 100 percent, and that is a great thing! Follow these steps:

1. To begin, you must load your final texture into ZBrush. Assign it to your model and make sure you are at the highest subdivision level. Create a new layer and name it **Pores**.

2. Then you must convert the texture map to a mask. However, if you just go straight ahead and convert it to a map, you will have resolution problems. ZBrush textures are 8-bit, while its alphas are 16-bit. To get a clean mask, you really should work with 16 bits of information. Otherwise, you'll get stairstepping, as shown in Figure 4.53.

   One option you can use is to blur the mask so that it will blend over the difference. However, if you use the default settings in ZBrush, blurring the mask will largely obliterate its finer details and make getting pore-level detail impossible. Instead, the key is to adjust the amount of blur that happens when you choose Tool → Masking →

Blur. To do that, you must set Preferences → Transpose → Mask Blur Strength down to around 7; maybe even lower (see Figure 4.54). Then choose Tool → Masking → Blur.

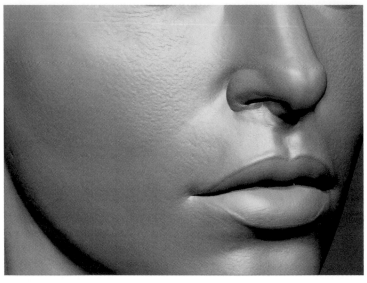

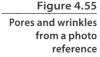

Figure 4.54

Mask Blur Strength

Figure 4.53

Stairstepping

3. Once you have the mask created, turn its visibility off, and in the deformation palette, set Inflate to 5. Set Smooth to 15 and then repeat the inflate. You can do this only a few times before the sculpt starts to get artifacts. Another option is to invert the mask and set Inflate to a negative number. Either way, the goal is the same: Create the pores as in Figure 4.55.

Figure 4.55

Pores and wrinkles from a photo reference

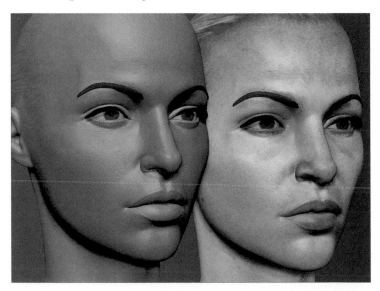

Summary

In this chapter, we have covered much of the texturing process, but there are always new features and workflows popping up. I highly recommend exploring ZBrush's Spin Brush setting with Alpha 58 and the new Spotlight feature and its Spotlight radius. Most important of all, though, is our connection with Photoshop because so much texturing work happens there.

For the latest on using ZBrush 4's new Spotlight feature, check out the accompanying DVD.

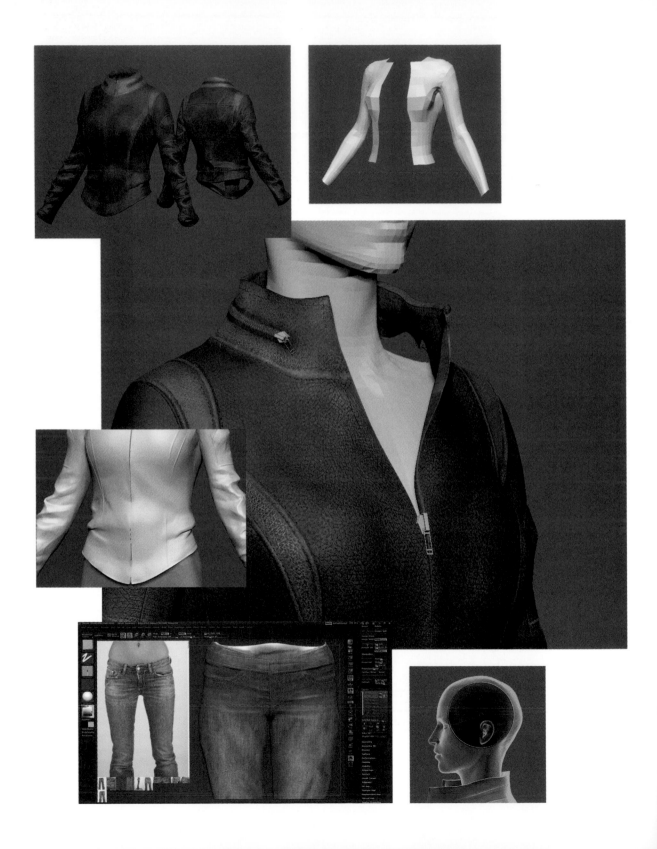

CHAPTER 5

Suiting Up with Clothes

In this chapter we will look at creating our female character's clothing. We will create a jacket, pants, boots, and some beautiful wavy hair befitting any heroine. That's quite a tall order for one chapter, but luckily the workflow for each task is pretty much the same except, of course, the hair. I will, though, introduce small variations on the workflow of each part of the costume to give you a well-rounded sense of all the tools we can use in ZBrush for sculpting the clothing.

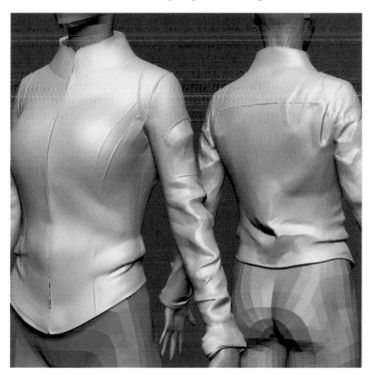

Creating a Jacket

We will start with the jacket. Jackets offer us a lot of possibilities for form. We get to sculpt the different fabric pieces, the seams where they are stitched together, the compression folds that occur around the elbows, and, one of my favorite things to sculpt, the zipper. Figure 5.1 shows our final jacket sculpt.

Figure 5.1
Final jacket sculpt

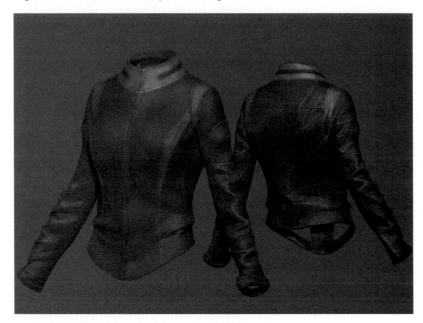

Mesh Extraction

To create the base mesh for the jacket, we will use Mesh Extraction. The controls for it are located in the bottom of the SubTool subpalette of the Tool palette. There are two ways to use it: with masks or with visibility. We will use it with both.

The basic function of Mesh Extraction is to extract either the masked area or the visible polygons of your model into a new SubTool and add a layer of thickness. This allows us to quickly create meshes inside of ZBrush without having to use ZSpheres or another application.

One of the key features of Mesh Extraction is thickness, as shown in Figure 5.2. Thickness will depend on your model's size and will most likely be different for each mesh you use. The other features—S. Smooth and E.Smooth—simply define how ZBrush is to treat the surface and edges of the visible polygons, respectively. In general, I never adjust these numbers and just leave the sculpting to me, myself, and I.

Figure 5.2
The Mesh Extraction palette

Project: Creating the Base Mesh of the Jacket

The base mesh for the jacket should be a simple, easy-to-sculpt form. We do not, at this time, need to create any extensive topology, and because of that, Mesh Extraction is the ideal way to create the jacket. It's simple, fast, and, in a word, cheap. It only costs a little time with masks.

1. To start, load your figure sculpt from Chapter 2 and lower your resolution to a geometry level that is low enough to be easy to work with but can hold the basic shape of the jacket. The model in Figure 5.3 is about 6,000 polygons.

2. Using the Mask Pen brush, mask out the area that represents the jacket. Try to keep the geometry as clean as possible, as in Figure 5.3.

3. When you are done with the mask, choose Tool → Visibility → HidePt to hide everything but the masked area. Make sure the visible selection has clean edges around the cuffs and the bottom.

4. If there are any polygons that you don't want to be included in the jacket, hide them by pressing Ctrl+Shift, clicking and dragging out a selection around the polygon, press Alt, and lift the pen. Repeat as needed until your model looks like Figure 5.4.

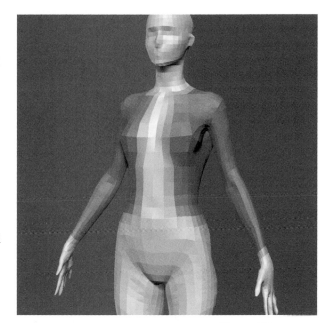

Figure 5.3
Defining the masked area on the sculpt

Figure 5.4
The basic shape of the visible area

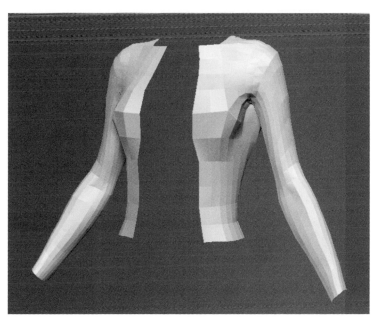

5. When you have the basic shape of the jacket visible, choose Tool → SubTool → Extract. If it is too thick, then select the SubTool and delete it. Select the SubTool that is the body again. Then adjust Tool → SubTool → Thick lower or higher as needed and press Extract again.

6. Select the jacket in the SubTool subpalette. Clear the mask by choosing Tool → Masking → Clear. Use the Move Topological brush to bring both sides of the jacket closer together, as in Figure 5.5. You may want to set Brush → Auto Masking → Range to 1. This will limit the effect of the Move Topological brush to just the area surrounding of the brush. You may also want to turn on Transform → Solo to view just the jacket.

Figure 5.5
Closing the jacket

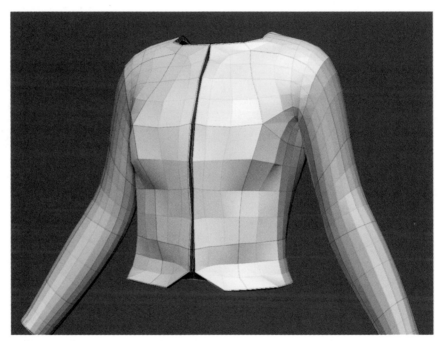

7. Before we begin sculpting the shape of the jacket, it's a good idea to remove unnecessary polygons from inside the jacket. To start, make sure you are at the lowest subdivision level.

   Press Ctrl+Shift and click one of the inside Polygroups. Then press Ctrl+Shift and click and drag outside of the model. Proceed by clicking the other internal Polygroups while keeping Ctrl+Shift pressed.

8. When the last Polygroup is hidden, you'll want to grow the selection slightly by pressing Tool → Visibility → Grow once or twice.

9. Delete the hidden geometry by choosing Tool → Geometry → DelHidden. At this point your model should look like Figure 5.6.

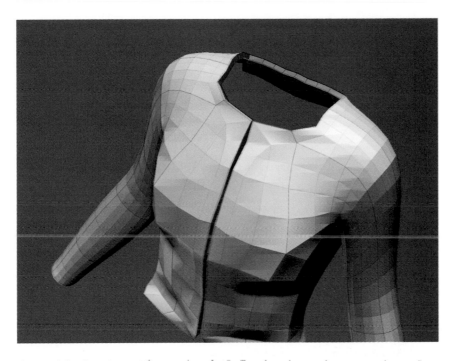

Figure 5.6
Hollowed jacket

10. Divide the model a few times. Then, using the Inflate brush, gently go over the surface of the model to build up the form a little. Use Shift to smooth out cramped areas.

11. Start sculpting by defining the shoulders and getting the correct transition from the top plane of the shoulder area and the side plane of the arms, front, and back. Work all over the model to get its basic shape fairly well blocked in as in Figure 5.7. Remember, your goal at this stage is just to provide the foundation for sculpting later. Don't worry about wrinkles or texture or anything else just yet.

12. Select the Standard brush with Alpha 48 and Stroke → Lazy Radius set to 45. Then outline the different layers of fabric and areas that are stitched together as in Figure 5.8.

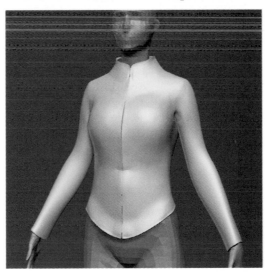

Figure 5.7
The base mesh of the jacket

Figure 5.8

Base mesh with fabric panels

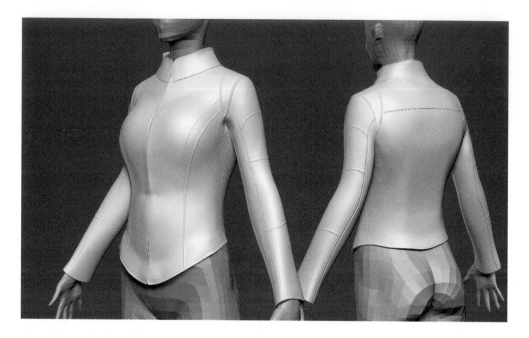

Sculpting Wrinkles for Fabric

Sculpting wrinkles can be very difficult and is one of the harder tests for a digital sculptor to pass. Traditionally speaking, you will encounter the following types of wrinkles, or folds:

- Pipe folds
- Diaper
- Zigzag
- Spiral
- Half-lock
- Drop
- Inert

When sculpting wrinkles, I like to focus on the following items: supporting areas, lines of action, and areas of compression.

Supporting areas are important to define early because they can be seen as the source of wrinkles. All wrinkles will tend to flow from one supporting surface to another. Pipe folds are all anchored along some supporting areas. This also goes for diaper folds and drop folds.

Lines of action will help us sculpt pipe folds, diaper folds, and spiral folds all without having to categorize each specific shape. That will at least get us sculpting wrinkles that are realistic enough while we learn more and get better. Figure 5.9 illustrates how the supporting surface of the shoulders give rise to the lines of action downward along the arm.

Another interesting twist on this is how lines of action can also appear to be spiral wrinkles as the forms underneath the wrinkles are rotated or repositioned like the arm in Figure 5.10.

Areas of compression occur in the knees, elbows, stomach area, and neck. As you saw before, we can map out these areas with the aid of a few shapes: Z, diamonds, and triangles. Figure 5.11 illustrates the compression at the elbow area that results from the line of action above.

Figure 5.9
Supporting areas and lines of action

Figure 5.10
Spiral folds

Figure 5.11
Areas of compression

Converting Polypainting to Masks

We all love to get something for nothing, and that is exactly what painting the wrinkles in does for us. We get more control over the placement and shape of the wrinkles, and then with just a few simple steps, we can convert all of that hard painting work into sculpting.

The key to this process is to covert the Polypainting into a texture map and then from a texture map into an alpha. Before we create the texture map, though, we need to make sure we create UVs, and this is where we learn about UV Master, a Pixologic plug-in for ZBrush.

In our example, you'll learn a fairly advanced workflow for using the alphas as a mask, so make sure to follow each step carefully. Once you have gone through the workflow, I think you'll be quite happy with the results. It's much easier than resculpting the wrinkles.

Working with UV Master

UV Master allows us to create UVs for our model directly inside of ZBrush. While we have always had the ability to create UVs inside of ZBrush, UV Master has one specific goal: to create UV pelts. These are UV maps that you can also paint in Photoshop and that you can easily decipher visually.

Figure 5.12

**The UV Master
palette**

UV Master can be downloaded from the Download Center on Pixologic.com. Simply unzip the file and place its contents in the ZBrush Root/ZStartup/Zplugin folder. Restart ZBrush and UV Master will be located in your ZPlugin palette, as shown in Figure 5.12.

The UV Master behavior is fairly straightforward: choose Unwrap and let ZBrush do its best. I find it very useful to click Polygroups before pressing Unwrap because the meshes we created with Mesh Extraction already have Polygroups created that help us isolate the inside from the outside.

Project: Polypainting and Converting Wrinkles

In this project, we sculpt the compression folds of our jacket using Polypainting and then we convert that Polypainting into a texture map and then an alpha.

This is just one workflow that we can use. One of its biggest advantages is that it is easier to sort through the complexities of compression wrinkles by painting them than it is to sculpt them, make mistakes, smooth the area out, and start over again.

1. Set the Color → RGB sliders to 128 and press Fill Object. Then select the Pen A brush. Set the color swatch to a whiter tone. Then follow your reference and lightly paint in the high points of the wrinkle.

   To paint out an area, you have to sample the original gray from somewhere on the model. To do this, press **C** on the keyboard while hovering over a gray area of the model.

2. Paint in the recessed areas with a darker color. Press Shift to smooth the colors together and remove any sharp transitions. At this point, your model should look like Figure 5.13.

Figure 5.13

Painted wrinkles

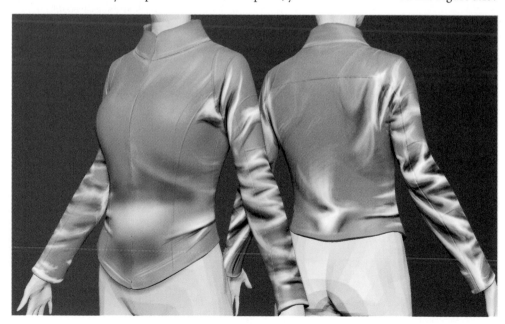

Keep working the wrinkles until you are happy with the results from all views. It's not going to be perfect the first time. It's not even going to be good the 10th time. But the only way you will get better is by moving forward and completing the rest of this chapter. Don't get stuck here.

3. To use our Polypainting to the fullest, we need to create UVs using UV Master. Set your SDiv level to the lowest level. Click ZPlugin → UV Master → Polygroups and then Unwrap.

4. You can check your UV layout by choosing Tool → UV Map → Morph UVs. If everything looks okay, as in Figure 5.14, proceed to the next step.

Figure 5.14

UV layout

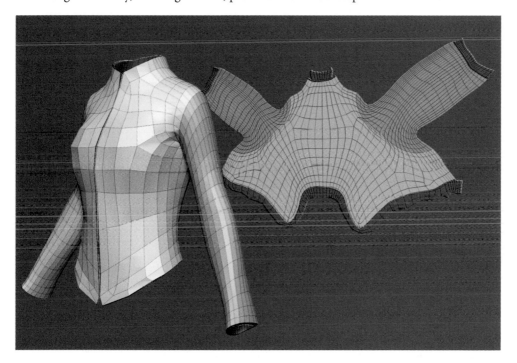

5. As it stands right now, we cannot use our Polypainting as a mask because it will inflate the entire mesh too much since our base color is 50 percent gray. To solve this problem, we need to find a way to separate out the white areas and the black areas of the painting from each other and use them separately as masks.

    First, convert your Polypainting into a texture map by choosing Tool → Texture Map → New from Polypaint, as shown in Figure 5.15.

6. Then choose Tool → Texture Map → Clone to send the map to the Texture palette.

7. Finally, in the Texture palette choose MakeAlpha.

Figure 5.15

Texture Map subpalette

Figure 5.16
AlphaAdjust

8. Once you convert the map into an alpha, you can use the Alpha curve to isolate the white values and the black values. Let's start with the white values.

   Open the AlphaAdjust Curve in the Alpha palette, as shown in Figure 5.16. Click inside of the curve in the exact center to create an edit point. Then drag the edit point outside the curve's rectangular area and immediately back in to convert it to a linear curve. Finally, drag it straight downward. This will completely isolate the white areas of the mask from everything else.

9. To apply the mask, choose Tool → Masking → Mask By Alpha. You may want to turn Polypainting off to see the mask better.

10. Set Tool → Deformation → Inflate Balloon to 5. Repeat as needed to get the high areas of the wrinkle to show up, as in Figure 5.17.

11. Next, let's work on the dark, recessed areas of the wrinkles. In the Alpha palette, drag the rightmost edit point downward and the leftmost edit point upward, as in Figure 5.18. This will isolate the darker areas of the alpha.

12. Choose Tool → Masking → Mask By Alpha to mask everything but the recessed areas.

13. Then set Tool → Deformation → Inflate Balloon to -5 or as needed. Figure 5.19 demonstrates our progress so far.

14. There are two brushes I like to use to sculpt wrinkles. Use Trim Dynamic to flatten wrinkle areas and create hard edges.

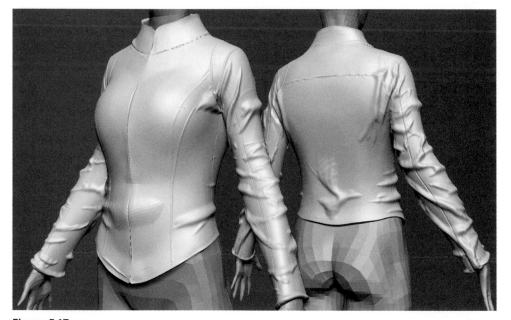

Figure 5.17
Results of Inflate Balloon

Figure 5.18
**Alpha curve for
darker areas**

Also use the Standard brush to smooth often, use the lowest subdivision level possible and build up volume in light, sketchy strokes.

15. It's also useful to set Brush → Depth → Gravity Strength to somewhere around 35 while sculpting wrinkles. This will pull downward on the form as you sculpt and lend some realism to your folds, as demonstrated in Figure 5.20.

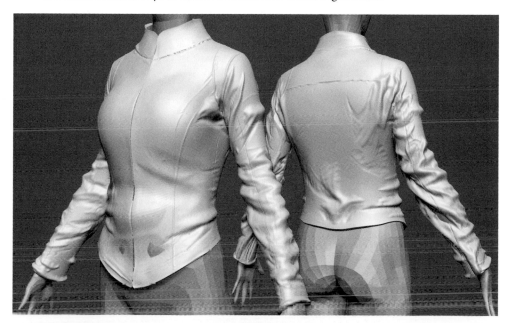

Figure 5.19
Results of Inflate Balloon

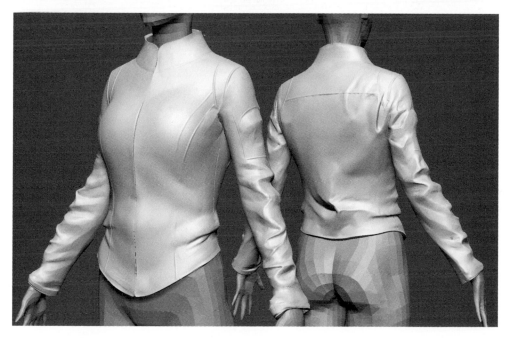

Figure 5.20
Sculpted wrinkles

Figure 5.21

Spin Rate

Project: Sculpting the Texture and Texturing the Sculpt

In this project our goal is to sculpt the leather texture of the jacket. We will use the ZBrush brush system to simulate the surface of real leather.

1. Select the Standard brush, make sure Zadd is on, and in the Brush palette, set Brush → Orientation → SpinRate to 1, as in Figure 5.21.

2. Brush along the surface of the jacket to sculpt the texture until it resembles Figure 5.22. Our goal in this case is just a light texturing.

3. Set your RGB sliders as shown in Figure 5.23 and then choose Color → Fill Object to set the base color of the model as shown in Figure 5.24. Make sure your model is at its highest resolution and that the resolution is at least 1 million polygons.

4. Creating a realistic texture requires us to add some variety to the surface. One way to do this is with cavity masking, where we treat the recessed areas of the model differently than the exposed, higher areas. Set Tool → Masking → Intensity to 100 as shown in Figure 5.25. Then click the Mask By Cavity button. Your model should now look like Figure 5.26.

5. Set the RGB sliders to a lighter, more yellow color. In this example, I used 93, 78, and 68, respectively. Then texture the patches in the shoulder area as well as other areas of the model that would wear over time. This includes along the zipper, in the elbow area, and along the collar, as in Figure 5.27.

Figure 5.22

Sculpted texture

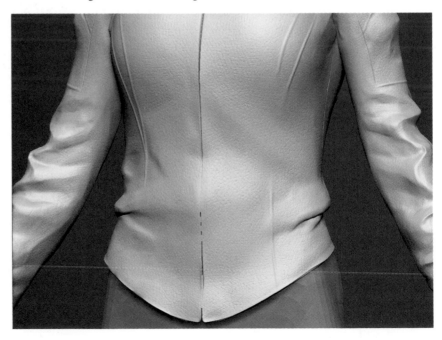

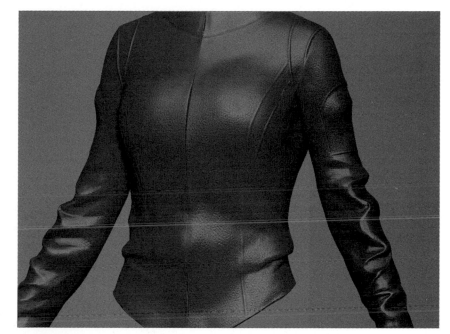

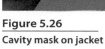

Figure 5.23
Color Interface

Figure 5.24
Color jacket

Figure 5.25
Cavity mask controls

Figure 5.26
Cavity mask on jacket

Figure 5.27
Final leather texture
for jacket

Working with Stitch Brushes

Once you have wrinkles sculpted and a texture painted onto the model, it's time to start adding details like stitching and zipper pockets. This also gives us a chance to create our own custom brushes and learn a few tips and tricks for working with alphas.

Looking at our own jeans or jacket, we can see that most of the stitching is single file, or a *straight* stitch. However, some areas may show a double row of stitches, and some, especially on shoes, may show three rows of stitching for either decoration or extra reinforcement.

The stitch brushes—seam_StitchX1, seam_StitchX2, and seam_StitchX3—located in the resource directory on the DVD, use a combination of ZBrush features to create their effect:

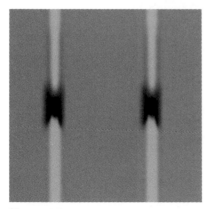

- Stroke → Roll for a tileable stroke
- LazyMouse for a clean stroke
- Alpha → MidValue to enable sculpting in and out simultaneously
- A custom alpha

Figure 5.28 illustrates the alpha of one of these brushes. Notice how the background is 50 percent gray while the stitching is white and the holes for the stitching are black. By setting Alpha → MidValue to 50, we are, in effect, telling ZBrush to sculpt inward and outward at the same time. The value of 50 sets the brush so that anything lighter than 50 percent gray will displace upward while anything darker than 50 percent will displace downward.

Figure 5.28
The alpha of seam_StitchingX2

Stroke → Roll, illustrated in Figure 5.29, is an essential part of getting a tileable stroke to roll across the surface of a model, and the Lazy Mouse settings, also illustrated in Figure 5.29, are key to creating a smooth line of stitching.

Project: Sculpting Stitching

Stitching provides a very important level of reality. Once you finish this brief step, your model will look light years better, but be careful of getting into the seam too early.

To get started follow these steps.

1. Let's open the throat of the jacket first. Set your jacket to the lowest subdivision level.

2. Select the Move Topological brush and set the Range slider in the Auto Masking sub-palette of the Brush palette to 2. This will allow you to pull the left side of the jacket to the left without affecting the right side. Make sure to turn symmetry off when doing this. When you're done, your model should look like Figure 5.30.

   To sculpt stitching for your model, your image needs to be pretty high res. I have found that 6 million is a good number that doesn't tax my computer too much. Try to get your jacket up to at least this many polygons. Avoid using layers when your model is this heavy as they tend to slow your system down even more.

Figure 5.29
Stroke settings

Figure 5.30
The results of opening the jacket throat

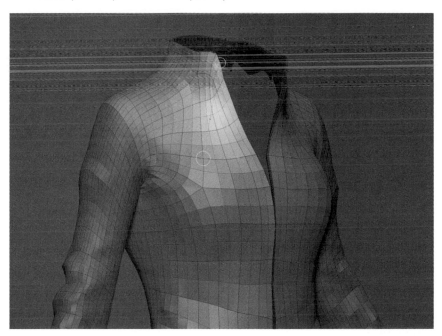

3. Select seam_StitchX1 and make sure that RGB is on as well.

4. Set the color swatch to the color of your seams. This may be dark or it may be light. In our case, the stitching is on the darker side.

5. Adjust Z Intensity to 15.

6. Sculpt along the areas indicated in Figure 5.31.

7. Switch to seams_StitchX2 and use this brush along the areas indicated in Figure 5.31.

8. Use the zipper_pocket brush to create the zippers along the shoulder area.

9. Use the zipper_brush to create the zipper along the back of the neck. Figure 5.31 illustrates both zippers.

Figure 5.31

Seams on the jacket

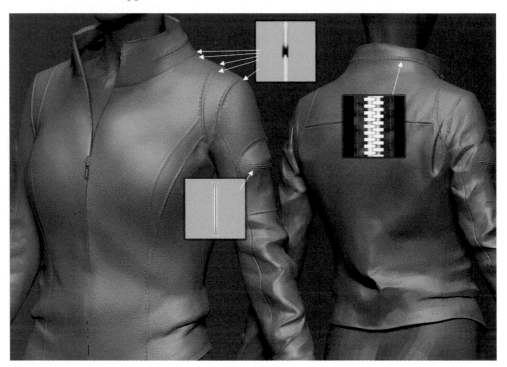

Working with Shadowbox

Shadowbox is a new feature in ZBrush 4. To use it you draw the shape of an object with masks. They call this shape a *shadow*. You can draw the shape from the front view, the side view, and the top view and ZBrush will interpolate between each of the views to create an object.

To enter Shadowbox, you can simply load a Shadowbox from Lightbox or the ZTL folder in the root directory. You can also turn any model you have selected into a Shadowbox model by choosing Tool → SubTool → Shadowbox. Note that this will remove any details you have sculpted and simplify the shape greatly. Do not worry, though; you can always undo.

It's also important to note that Shadowbox has a resolution setting. The more resolution, the more detail you can draw with a mask. To adjust the resolution, you have to adjust Tool →

SubTool → Remesh Resolution. If your Shadowbox is already created, you have to adjust the setting, turn Shadowbox off, and then turn it back on.

Shadowbox also has a smoothness setting that is activated by default. If you do not want it to smooth your models for you, set Tool → SubTool → Polish to 0. You may have to add to your mask to see the change.

Project: Creating the Zipper's Slider Body

In this project, we will create the zipper slider's body using Shadowbox. This is a very fast way to create new meshes in ZBrush, and it is ideally suited to hard surface items like a metal zipper.

1. To create the slider body itself, we turn to Shadowbox. It's a fairly simple procedure, but it does require a few steps.

2. First, load Shadowbox128.ztl from Lightbox, as shown in Figure 5.32.

3. Turn Activate Symmetry on, and then turn Transparency on.

4. Press and hold Ctrl and paint the shape of the main slider body as shown in Figure 5.33. Note that you should be using Mask Pen. If you have a different masking brush selected, simply press Mask Pen in the Brush palette.

5. Switch to the side view and to the Mask Rectangle brush and create the profile of the zipper, as shown in Figure 5.34. Then choose Tool → SubTool → Shadowbox to exit Shadowbox and see the 3D shape.

6. Duplicate the SubTool and then press Shadowbox again. Clear the mask that is automatically created. Turn Transparency on.

7. Use the Mask Rectangle brush to draw the handle's shape from a side view. Then, with the Mask Rectangle brush, press Ctrl+Alt and erase the interior of the handle, as shown in Figure 5.35.

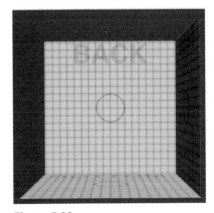

Figure 5.32
Shadowbox tool

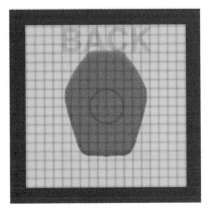

Figure 5.33
The main body's shape

Figure 5.34
Profile of the main body

8. Switch to the front view and make the pull tab's handle is fairly thin, as shown in Figure 5.36. When you're done, exit Shadowbox by pressing the Shadowbox button in the SubTool tab.

9. Duplicate the SubTool again, and again go into Shadowbox. This time set Tool → SubTool → Polish to 0. Clear the mask. Turn Transparency on. Use Mask Rectangle to draw out the shape of the pull tab. Press Ctrl+Alt to remove parts from the interior.

Figure 5.35

Creating the handle for the zipper

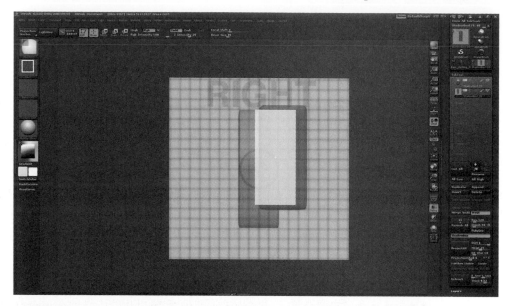

Figure 5.36

The pull tab

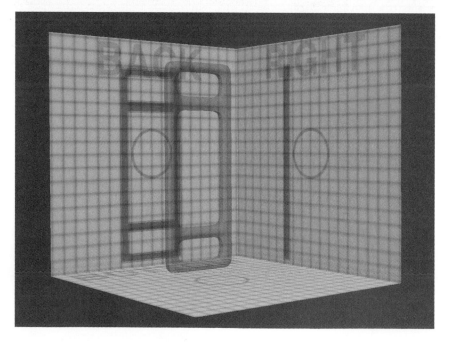

10. When you're done, exit Shadowbox.

11. Finally, combine everything by pressing Tool → SubTool → Merge Visible. Select the new tool whose name begins with the words Merged_PM3D_ and save this for later use. Figure 5.37 illustrates our combined mesh.

12. Select the jacket from the Tool palette. Press Tool → SubTool → Append and choose the zipper you just created.

13. Position the zipper using Transpose or the Offset and Size sliders in the Tool → Deformation tab as illustrated in Figure 5.38.

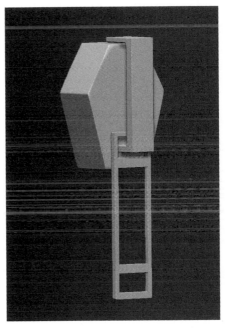

Figure 5.37
Everything combined

Figure 5.38
The zipper positioned

Designing Jeans

Now that we have created the jacket, we can start sculpting the jeans. This will give us the opportunity to study wrinkles in a bit more depth and take a look at a simple workflow for sculpting all the varieties of form that wrinkles present. We will also get to look at a few more custom brushes for creating the seams of a pair of jeans.

Creating the Base Mesh

Create the base mesh for the jeans just as we did for the jacket. Lower your resolution to about 6,000 polygons and use a mask to define the boundaries of the jeans. Then click Hide Pt in the Visibility subpalette to make sure you have the right area selected. Then click Extract in the SubTool subpalette.

Once you create the mesh, you should remove the interior polygons just as we did with the jacket. Then sculpt it using Inflate and some overall smoothing so that it resembles Figure 5.39. Avoid sculpting wrinkles until we have analyzed our reference and have a clear sense of how to progress.

Figure 5.39
The jeans' base mesh

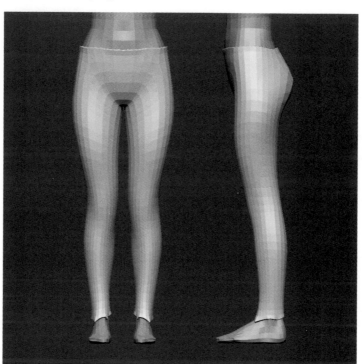

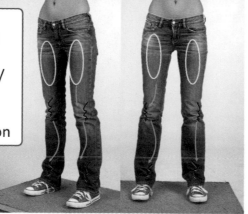

- Yellow = Supporting Surfaces
- Blue = flow/ action line
- Red = Compression

Figure 5.40
Photo reference for creating jeans and their wrinkles

Now let's take a look at our photo reference. In Figure 5.40, you can see how the support surface of the leg is the rectus femoris area of the quadriceps. That means there will be a slight drop fold from here to the compression folds of the knee. Conversely, the knee also serves as the supporting surface for the drop folds of the lower leg, which are then integrated with the compression folds along the ankle.

Project: Wrinkling the Jeans

In the previous example of sculpting wrinkles, we used Polypainting. This is a great way to navigate the complexities of compression folds, but I find it limiting when sculpting drop folds, spiral folds, and the larger compression folds that happen along the length of the lower leg. To sculpt those, we just get in and go to work with the Standard brush or the Clay brush.

1. Start with the drop folds from the rectus femoris area to the knee and then from the knee to the lower leg. Use the Standard brush with a little bit of Gravity Strength to sculpt the spiral wrinkles along the side of the jeans. Figure 5.41 illustrates the basic sculpt we should be creating.

2. The compression folds along the ankle area require us to turn our brain into a trigonometry calculating machine. It is very wise to have a thorough set of references before proceeding.

   Really try to get the large compression fold along the lower leg indicated, as in Figure 5.42. I use a combination of the Clay brush to describe its boundaries and then the Trim Dynamic brush to create the flat planes inside of it.

Figure 5.41

First pass on wrinkles

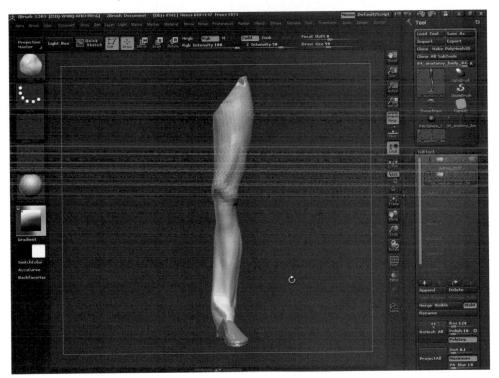

3. For the compression folds in the pelvic area, use the Standard brush with Brush →
Modifiers → Brush Mod set to 25. This will create the hard edge of the folds. Then
go over this stroke with the M_Polish brush and sharpen the falloff of the wrinkle.
Figure 5.43 illustrates our progress so far.

Figure 5.42

**Compression folds
at ankle**

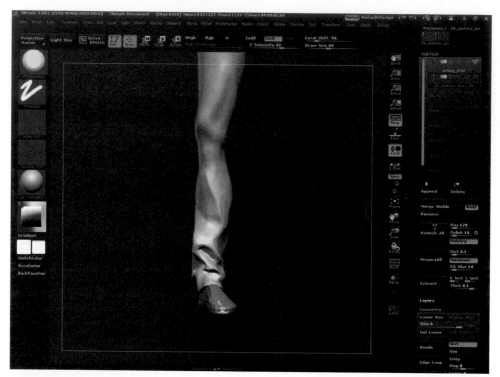

Figure 5.43

Pelvic folds

4. Finally, in the knee area, we use the same process we used in the jacket. Start by set-ting all the Color → RGB sliders to 128 and choosing Fill Object.

5. Select the Pen A brush. Paint the high points of the wrinkles with a whitish color and the dark areas with a darker color as in Figure 5.44.

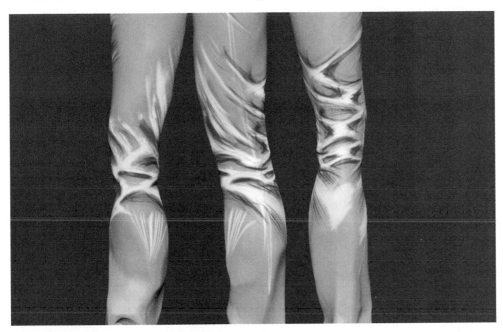

Figure 5.44

Knee folds painted on

6. Create your UVs using UV Master. Make sure to choose Unwrap when your model is at its lowest subdivision level.

7. Convert your Polypainting into a Texture map by pressing Texture Map → New From Polypaint.

8. Press Tool → Texture Map → Clone to send it to the Texture palette.

9. Press Texture → Make Alpha to convert this to an alpha.

10. Open the Alpha Adjust curve in the Alpha palette and adjust the curve as indicated in Figure 5.45.

11. Press Tool → Masking → Mask By Alpha.

12. Set Tool → Deformation → Inflate Balloon to 5 or as needed.

13. Open the Alpha Adjust curve again and adjust the curve to be the same as in Figure 5.46.

14. Press Tool → Masking → Mask By Alpha.

15. Set Tool → Deformation → Inflate Balloon to -5 or as needed. Then clear the mask. At this point your model should look like Figure 5.47.

16. At this stage, we should have a fairly good indicator for our compression wrinkles at the knee. To add a bit more realism to the folds, however, and remove the mechanical quality that we get from the masking and inflating process, we need to adjust the high points slightly and give them some more specific character.

Select the Move brush. Press Alt while clicking on different areas of the wrinkles to push them out along their normal. Then use Trim Dynamic to resculpt the planes and keep the forms clean, as in Figure 5.48.

Figure 5.45

Alpha Adjust curve for the lighter areas

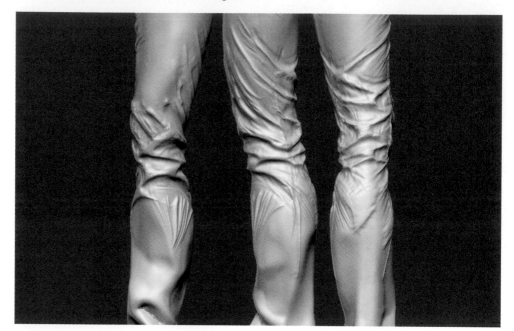

Figure 5.46

Alpha Adjust for darker areas

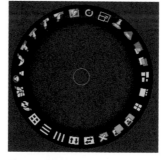

Figure 5.47

Results of Inflate Balloon

Figure 5.48
Wrinkles fine-tuned

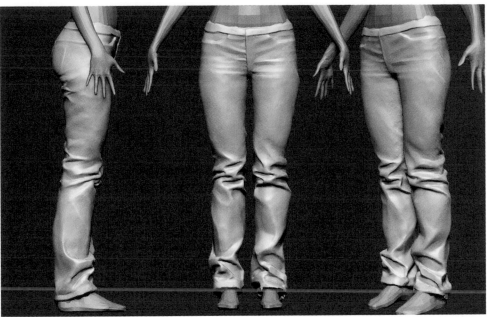

Project: Texturing with Spotlight

Before we sculpt the seams, we will texture-paint the jeans just as we did with the jacket. Jeans, though, are much easier. We can do much of our work by simply pinning a few images in Spotlight and cloning them onto our model.

1. Select the jeans from the SubTool list and divide it until it is at least 3 million polygons, but preferably 6 million.

2. Load the spotlight library Chapter5 Jeans.ZSL from the Texture palette.

3. Press Tile Unified in the Spotlight controller to tile all the images along the left of the canvas as in Figure 5.49.

4. Select one of the images and scale it up to match the size of the model in the viewport as in Figure 5.50.

5. Click the Spotlight Radius button and drag the controller counter clockwise to decrease the Spotlight's brush size.

6. Press **Z** on the keyboard to hide the controller and enter painting mode. Make sure RGB is on in the shelf and Zadd is off. Then simply paint away on the front of the jeans as in Figure 5.51.

7. Press **Z** on the keyboard to bring Spotlight back up. Then select the reference for the back of the jeans, position it, and paint the back. Your model should look like Figure 5.52, where the sides are the main element left.

Figure 5.49

Spotlight Controller

Figure 5.49

Spotlight Controller

Figure 5.50

Positioning the reference

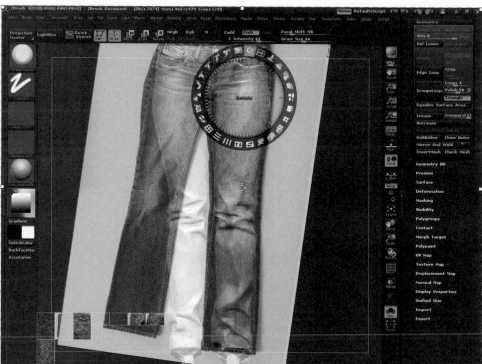

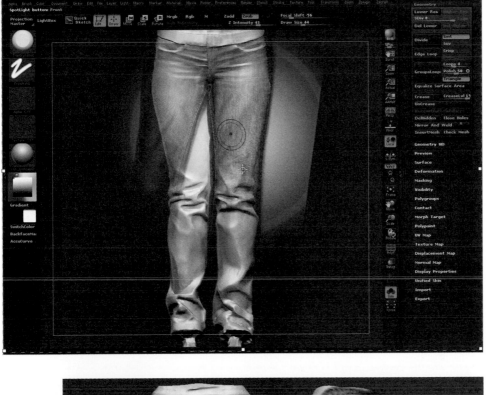

Figure 5.51

Painting with
Spotlight

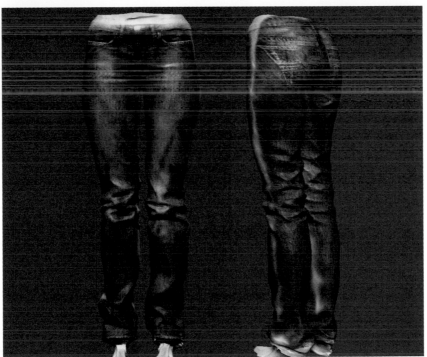

Figure 5.52

Front and back are
painted.

8. Press **Z** again to bring Spotlight back up. Then select the side image and position it and the model as in Figure 5.53. Make sure Symmetry is on so you can paint both sides. Then press **Z** to hide Spotlight and enter painting mode.

9. Press **Z** and this time switch to the image of the model's rear so you can fix any texture stretching that is happening there. Position the reference as in Figure 5.54; then press **Z** to enter painting mode.

10. Finally, select one of the generic denim textures and use it, through Spotlight, to texture over the seams, pockets, or other problems. Your model should look like Figure 5.55.

Figure 5.53

Placement of Texture from Side

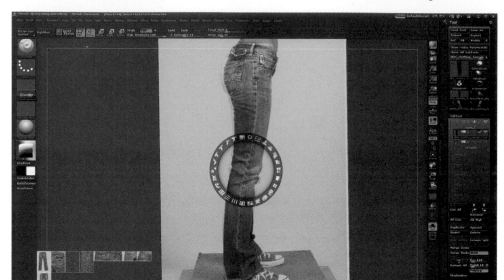

Figure 5.54

Spot-fixed areas

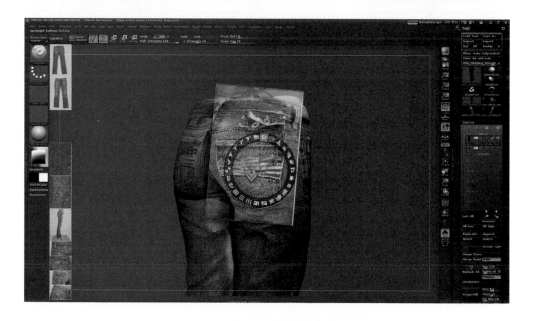

11. Now, it's time to rough up the surface of the jeans all over the place. In this case, we need to *dry brush* the model. To do this, we must first convert our texture into a mask by choosing Tool → Masking → Mask By Intensity (Figure 5.56).

Figure 5.55
Cleaned-up texture

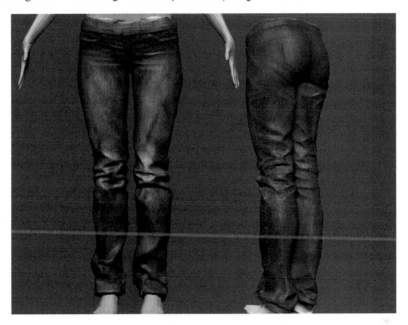

12. Hover your cursor over one of the whiter parts of your texture and press **C** to sample that color.

Figure 5.56
Masking subpalette

13. Select the Standard brush. Select Alpha 58. Set Brush → Orientation → Spin Rate to 1.

14. Our goal now is to replicate the worn look of the jeans near the knee over the rest of the model and especially in those areas that we cleaned up the texture to remove seams. Brush lightly over the model, trying to stroke along the direction you think the wear and tear would occur. Generally, this is along the line of the wrinkles. Work the surface until your model resembles Figure 5.57.

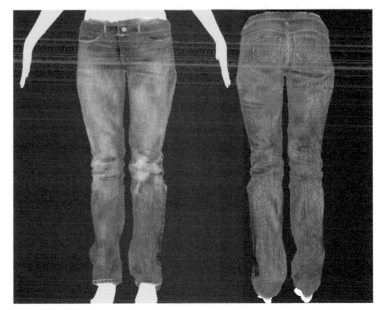

Figure 5.57
Worn areas after dry brushing

Project: Adding Seams and Stitching

Now it's time to add stitching to the jeans. This requires that the jeans have quite a few polygons, but once you put the polygons in, it adds a lot of life to the sculpt.

1. Select the Standard brush and set LazyRadius to 45.

2. Draw along the rim of the front pockets to emphasize them. Also outline the back pockets and smooth only the inside area of the stroke to make it look like the back pockets are raised above the surface or are a separate patch of cloth, as shown in Figure 5.58.

Figure 5.58

Emphasizing the pockets

3. Select the Slash1 brush and set Z Intensity to 30. Quickly draw the seam along the outside and inside of the jeans and anywhere else needed.

4. Select seams_StitchX2 or load it into the Brush palette if it's not there. Set Z Intensity to 20.

5. Set the RGB sliders as follows: 244, 177, 46. Make sure that RGB and Zadd are on in the shelf.

6. Draw along the contour of the inside seam, along the front and back pockets, and in the fly area, as in Figure 5.59. If you are not seeing any sculpt, then make sure your model has enough polygons to actually capture the sculpt. Earlier I mentioned that about 6 million polygons would be necessary to get this level of detail, and there is really no way around that.

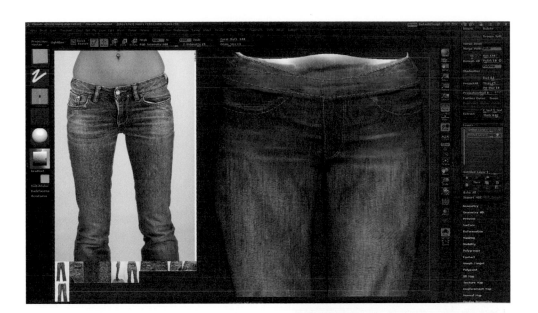

Figure 5.59

The stitching on the pockets and waist of the jeans

Sculpting Boots

Sculpting the boots will give us a chance to walk through the entire process we used earlier one more time and get very clear on the workflow. I'll also introduce one new tool: GoZ. It provides a great way to combine ZBrush with third-party applications like Maya, 3ds Max, and XSI.

Project: Making the Base Mesh for the Boot

In this stage, our goal is to create a simple, basic shape for the boot. Avoid any smaller details like layers of fabric or stitching. We will get to those, but in due time.

1. Extract the boot shape from the model's lower leg and hollow it out so it looks like Figure 5.60.

2. Press GoZ in the Tool palette to send your model over to one of your GoZ-enabled applications. I have enabled Maya as my default GoZ app.

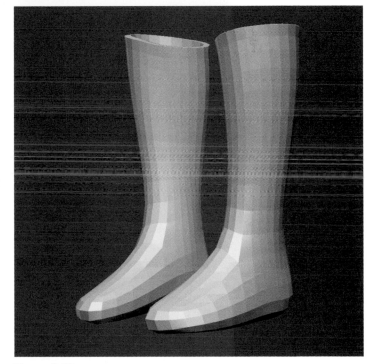

Figure 5.60

Creating the basic shape from extraction

Figure 5.61

GoZ is Located in the Tool palette

3. In Maya, adjust the shape and specifically the bottom of the boot to create a clean surface to extrude the sole and heel downward as in Figure 5.62.

4. Select the faces toward the back of the sole and choose Edit Mesh → Extrude to extrude the heel out as in Figure 5.63.

Figure 5.62

Flattening the sole

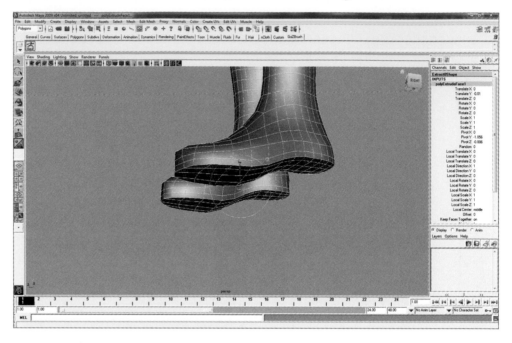

Figure 5.63

Extruding the heel

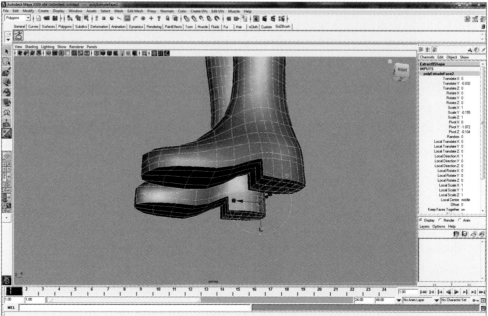

5. Insert edge loops above the sole and along those areas that you want to retain a sharp edge. Adjust the shape of them to resemble Figure 5.64.

6. Press the GoZ button in the GoZ shelf in Maya to send the mesh back to ZBrush (see Figure 5.65).

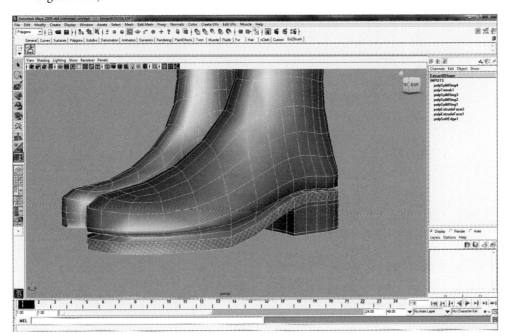

Figure 5.64

Refining the sole's topology

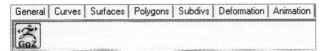

Figure 5.65

GoZ button in Maya's Shelf

7. Back in ZBrush, divide the mesh a few times and adjust the shape, if needed. Your model should resemble Figure 5.66 at this point.

8. Use the Move brush to define the shape of the sole and create the specific kidney bean shape of the foot, as illustrated in Figure 5.67.

9. Use the Clay brush to sketch in the wrinkles and folds of the boot. The leather boots are made of is harder than the leather in a jacket so the boots won't crease or fold back on themselves in the same way jackets do. Instead, they will dent and create distinct facets, as shown in Figure 5.68.

10. Refine the shape of the wrinkles using Trim Dynamic and the M Polish brush, as shown in Figure 5.69. There is an art to knowing which one to use, so experiment with both.

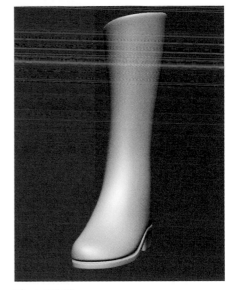

Figure 5.66

The base mesh in ZBrush

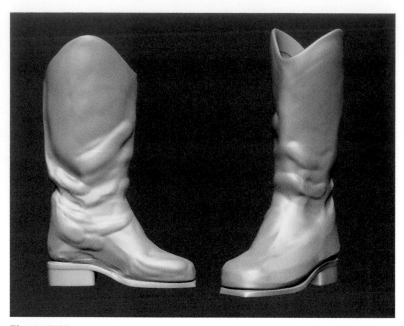

Figure 5.67
The sole defined

Figure 5.68
Wrinkles sketched in

Figure 5.69
Wrinkles defined

Most importantly, though, is to have a pair of boots in front of you while you are sculpting them. Please, pretty please. Don't rely on photo reference. If it took you one day to go out and find a pair of boots to sculpt, you would still sculpt them faster and more realistically than if you struggled through bad photographic references and Google searches.

You don't have enough money, you say? Well, that is no excuse at all. We are artists. We have starved for centuries and still found ways to exist. Head over to your local thrift store and pick up a pair for a few bucks. If that fails, there is always the 30-day return policy at big retail stores.

Project: Sculpting and Texturing the Parts

With the basic shape of the boot sculpted, it's time to start adding more detail to it. We need to add the vamp, or the lower portion of the boot. We also need to sculpt the piping in and define the stitching.

Let's get started.

1. Mask out the area of the vamp using the Mask Pen brush, as shown in Figure 5.70. Don't worry about getting too detailed or precise. Mesh Extraction is not a precise tool, and we'll have to edit our work afterwards.

2. Set the Extract settings as shown in Figure 5.71 and press Extract. If the vamp is too thick, then simply lower your thickness. If it is too general in shape, try setting E.Smoothness to 2.

3. Select the Move brush and click AccuCurve in the Curve subpalette of the Alpha palette. Then pull up any sharp corners that might exist in your vamp. Mine are along the top and in the back. Figure 5.72 illustrates a successful vamp.

Figure 5.70
Vamp masked out

4. Extract the *pulls* from the sides of the boot. These are the leather rings that you use to pull the boot on. I use Move TopoElastic to quickly shape them.

   Then use the Standard brush with default settings to sculpt the piping up the side of the boot and in the vamps. Your boot should look like Figure 5.73.

5. Select the Vamp SubTool and use the same brush we used to sculpt the jacket. Essentially, you select Alpha 58 and turn Spin Rate to 1. Make sure to lower Z Intensity. Then just brush along the surface. Figure 5.74 shows our textured boot.

6. Set the RGB sliders to 67, 63, 55, respectively, and choose Fill Object.

Figure 5.71
Extract setting

Figure 5.72
Extracted vamp

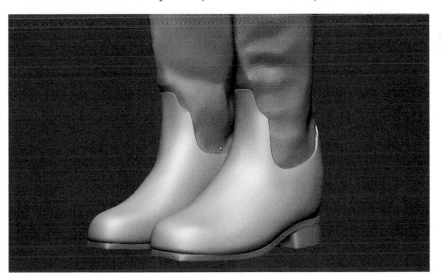

7. Set Tool → Masking → Cavity Masking to 100 and choose Mask By Cavity. You might also want to turn ViewMask off as well.

8. Set the RGB sliders to 38, 32, 26, respectively. Select the Standard brush with RGB on and Zadd off to texture-paint the surface of the boot. Your model should look like Figure 5.75.

Figure 5.73

Extracting more parts

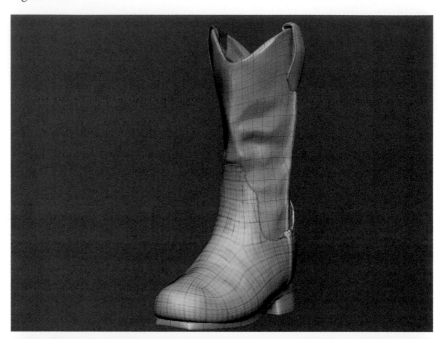

Figure 5.74

Sculpted texture for boot

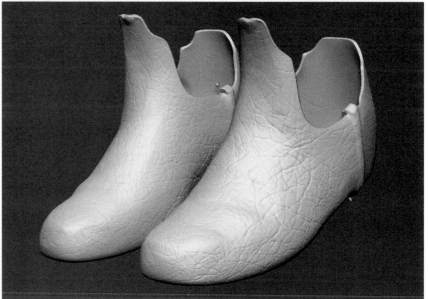

9. Select the Pen A brush and set your RGB sliders to 225, 220, 215. Lower Draw Size to 5 and lightly scratch the surface of your model. Vary this with using the Standard brush with Alpha 25 and the Spray stroke. The goal is to rough up the surface of our model as in Figure 5.76.

10. Select the original boot sculpt from the SubTool subpalette. This will serve as our leather section.

Figure 5.75

Texture-paint result with cavity mask on

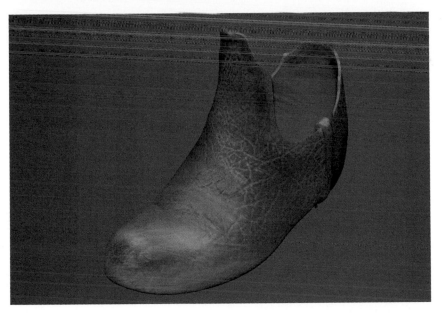

Figure 5.76

Pen A used to paint scratches

11. Set the RGB sliders to 47, 40, 35, and press Fill Object in the Color palette.

12. Select the Standard brush. Select Alpha 28. Select the Color Spray stroke. Set Stroke → Scale to .05 and then set the RGB sliders, in the Color palette, to 77, 64, 55 and paint on the surface of the model. Make sure RGB is on and Zadd is off. At this point, your model should resemble Figure 5.77.

13. With the Leather SubTool selected, choose Tool → Masking → Mask By Cavity. Then lower the color sliders to 21, 18, 14 and paint on the model.

14. Click the Inverse button in the Masking subpalette to invert the mask.

15. Set the RGB sliders higher, to 101, 88, 71, and lightly paint on the surface of the boot so the model looks like Figure 5.78.

16. Set the RGB sliders lower now, to 12, 10, 8, and paint the piping a darker color. Your model should resemble Figure 5.79.

17. The final step to sculpting our boots is to add the seams to the model. Use the seams_Stitch_X1, seams_Stitch_X2, and seams_Stitch_X3 brush from earlier in the chapter. This time, set the RGB values to 120, 100, and 80, respectively. Figure 5.80 illustrates our final boot sculpt.

Figure 5.77
Final texture for vamp with flat render on

Figure 5.78
Cavity mask for boot's leather

Figure 5.79
Leather painted

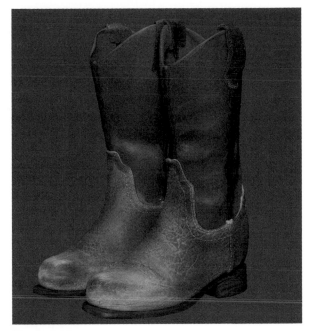

Figure 5.80
Final boots

Combining the Parts

To wrap up this chapter, we can add all of the parts together to create one mesh. In my case, the model is over 20 million polygons. Each of the SubTools is between 4 million and 6 million polygons. This works fine on my system with 8 gigs of RAM, but you do have to be careful depending on your system. If you find yourself waiting for ZBrush to complete simple tasks, then it's time to take the polygon count lower.

Project: Putting It All Together

So, let's combine all of our model's parts and get moving.

1. Before we proceed, make sure to save any ZTLs that you wish to keep and choose Preference → Initialize to start over from scratch. This will clear ZBrush's memory and delete any models, so make sure to save before you do that.

2. Load the following items: the final head from Chapter 4 and the model you have been sculpting in this chapter.

3. Append the head to the body. Most likely your model will look like Figure 5.81 now.

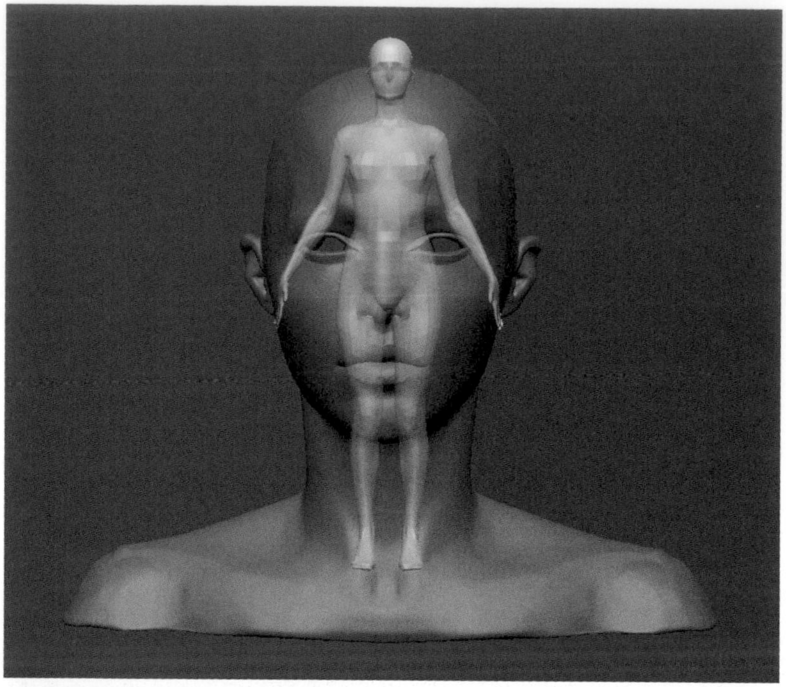

Figure 5.81

Adding the head to body

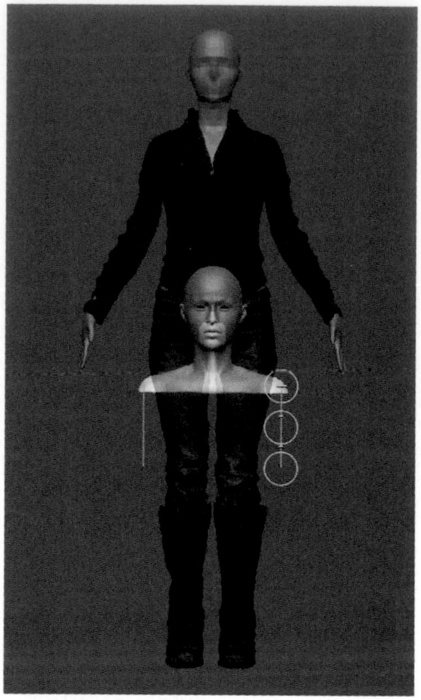

Figure 5.82

Adding the rest of the parts

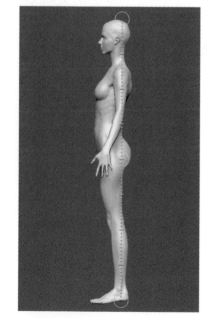

Figure 5.83

Setting the length of the model with a transpose line

4. Scale the model downward by setting Tool → Deformation → Size to -100 twice so your model is roughly the size shown in Figure 5.82.

5. Select Rotate on the shelf. Then draw out an action line from the bottom of the feet to the top of the head as shown in Figure 5.83. Make sure to draw the action line off the model and then bring it back into position. If you do not do this, the action line can be created at an angle and distort the values.

6. Open the Preference palette and set Preference → Calibration Distance to 8, as shown in Figure 5.84. This will establish the model as 8 heads tall and allow us to use the action line's units to make sure the head is the correct size.

7. Select the head from the SubTool subpalette. Click Scale on the shelf, draw out another action line on the head, and scale the head up or down as needed. Draw out as many action lines as you need to check the measurement of the face. You want it to be 1 unit tall. Figure 5.85 illustrates its final positioning.

8. Select the head from Chapter 4 from the Tool palette (not the SubTool subpalette). Then in the SubTool subpalette, select the eyes SubTool. This makes the eyes the active SubTool and will allow us to import them into the model we have been working on in this chapter.

9. Select the model we have been working on from the Tool palette. Then append the eyes from Chapter 4's head. Scale and position the eyes using Transpose and the Deformation palette until they fit, as shown in Figure 5.86.

Figure 5.84

Transpose line adjusted for 8 heads

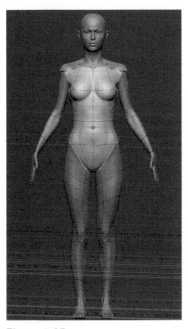

Figure 5.85
Head sized correctly

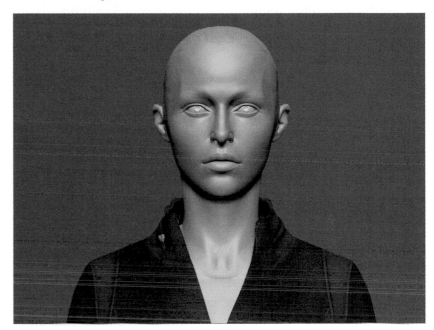

Figure 5.86
Final model with eyes

Project: Sculpting Hair

Before we go any further, we really should give our character some hair, don't you think? She'll look better and just feel better. So, how do you create hair in ZBrush? Well, there are lots of ways, but we're going to use ZSketch.

1. Click Append in the SubTool subpalette and select a ZSphere so your model looks like Figure 5.87. In the SubTool subpalette, select the ZSphere to make it the active SubTool.

2. Press **X** on the keyboard to turn on symmetry.

3. Click Scale on the shelf and scale the main ZSphere down until you think it can fit into the cranium of our model's head. You will probably want to turn Transparency on while doing this.

4. Select Move on the shelf and move the ZSphere upward to fit in the cranial area as shown in Figure 5.88.

5. Click EditSketch in the ZSketch subpalette.

6. Select Sketch2 from the brush pop-up and open the Brush palette's Tablet Pressure subpalette.

Figure 5.87
Appending a ZSphere

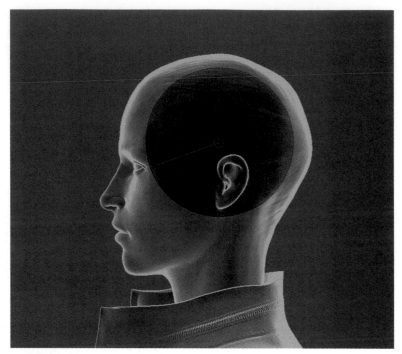

Figure 5.88
Positioning the ZSphere

Figure 5.89
Tablet Pressure subpalette

7. Set the Size curve as shown in Figure 5.89. This is an essential step. Without it the ZSketch lines tend to be too thick and won't really work well for our needs here.

8. Lay down a few strips of hair along the sides of the head and make sure to smooth them out a bit. When you smooth them, you might notice that the tip of the ZSketch stroke will move towards the other ZSketch strokes. You probably don't want that to happen. To solve this, select Smooth3 in the brush pop-up.

9. Lay down a few more strokes to cover the back. The key to getting the right stroke is to vary your pen pressure. Start by pressing hard and then, at the very end of the stroke, use just a little bit of pressure so it trails off. This might take a bit of practice but that's not new to you! Figure 5.90 illustrates our progress.

10. Select Move from the shelf and adjust the shape of your strokes.

11. To adjust individual strokes, you have to first isolate them by pressing Ctrl+Shift and clicking on the stroke you want to adjust. Press Ctrl and click on the canvas to mask the stroke. Then press and hold Ctrl+Shift and click outside of the model. This will show everything. Press Ctrl and click outside of the model to invert the mask so it looks like Figure 5.91. Use Move to adjust the stroke.

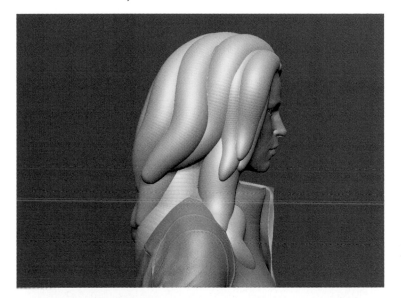

Figure 5.90

Adding ZSketch Strokes

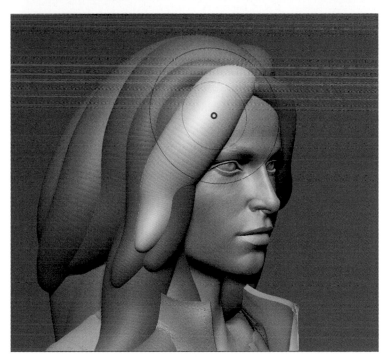

Figure 5.91

Moving a stroke

12. At the end, you should have a full head of hair that you are happy with. Make sure to save the model and then let's create a polygon mesh that retains the overall shape of the hair.

13. Set Resolution to 256 in the Unified Skin subpalette. Press **A** on the keyboard and make sure this is roughly what you want. If it is, then press Make Unified Skin. Figure 5.92 demonstrates our results.

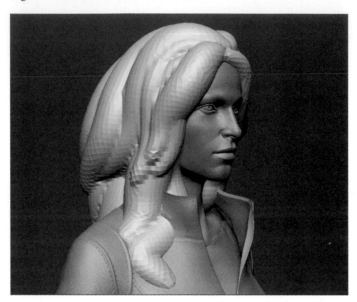

14. Press Append in the SubTool subpalette and select the skinned mesh.

15. Finish up the hair using the sculpting brushes. I like to use Trim Dynamic with Alpha 60. It creates some really nice texture to hair and helps you create clean smooth surfaces. Figure 5.93 illustrates our final result.

16. Make sure to save the model when you are done.

Summary

At this point, we should be done with the body and the face. We should have only the weapon to create, and we should be ready for posing and rendering our model. I say we should be done, but one of the most important things I have learned from sculpting is that I will always find something to fix. If you step away from your model for a few days, you will inevitably see something that you want to fix. As we move on to the next part of our workflow, don't worry if you feel you need to go in and make adjustments to the shape of the model. This is a normal part of our annoying perfectionist nature. Cultivate it.

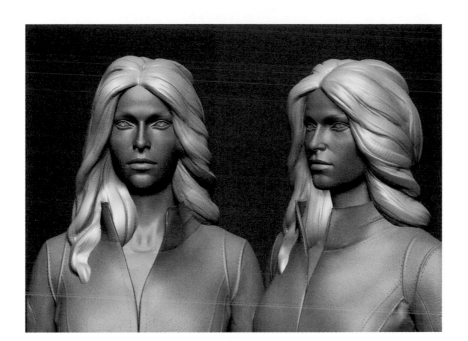

Figure 5.93
Finished sculpt of hair

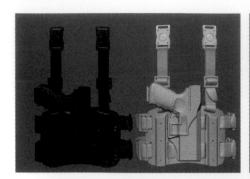

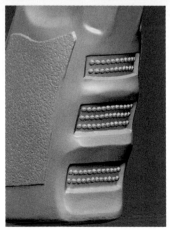

CHAPTER 6

Building Weapons

Weapons give us a chance to talk about hard-surface sculpting and plan our sculpting to make the most of each step. You are probably eager to get into ZBrush and start sculpting—you don't want to think about technicalities or limitations. But if you walked into a carpenter's workshop, you would think twice before turning on the circular saw, wouldn't you? The computer removes this concern, but it can still be useful to force ourselves to think about such things.

As you go through this chapter, you should be planning your own workflow. The workflow I present is not the only one you can use, but it will help your sculpting and will utilize ZBrush to the max.

The Anatomy of the Weapon

When you sculpt something, you understand it in a different way. You can pull it apart, rotate it around in your mind, and look at it from all different perspectives. When I sculpted this weapon, I studied its anatomy. I needed to know the main components, such as the slide and the receiver. I looked for words to describe the weapon's parts, and once I had the words, I got down to the business of understanding those words from a sculptor's perspective.

Project: ShadowBox the Parts

Creating hard-surface models in ZBrush has never been easier, and the ShadowBox tool is the key. In this project we will look at using this tool to quickly create the various parts. Note that we'll use default settings, which create soft forms. The actual hard surface will come in the next project.

1. Load `shadowbox_128` from ZBrush's ZTool directory, as shown in Figure 6.1. Draw the tool onto the canvas and enter Edit mode.

Figure 6.1
shadowbox_128

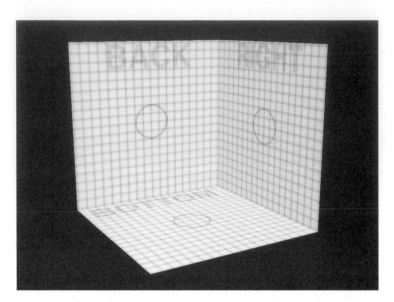

Figure 6.1

shadowbox_128

2. Load the Chapter6Weapon.ZSL Spotlight from the Texture palette.

3. Select the side view of our Gun; position the gun and the ShadowBox object.

4. Press Z to enter Spotlight paint mode. Turn off Zadd on the shelf and paint the side view directly into ShadowBox, as shown in Figure 6.2.

5. Select the MaskRect brush and drag out a mask to create the Gun's slide, as shown in Figure 6.3.

6. Choose Tool → SubTool → Duplicate to duplicate the ShadowBox object.

Figure 6.2

Painting the image into ShadowBox

Figure 6.3

Masking out the slide

7. Choose Tool → SubTool → Shadowbox to exit ShadowBox and complete the slide.

8. Select the duplicated ShadowBox object and clear the mask. Then create another mask, as shown in Figure 6.4. We will create the handle straight up and down and move it back later. This approach helps make our topology easier to work with.

Figure 6.4

The receiver

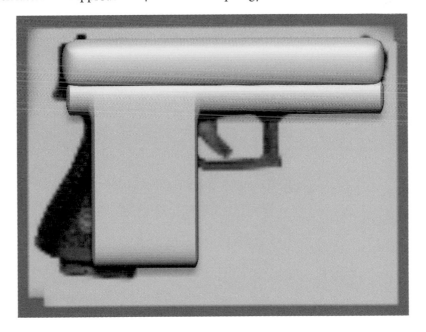

9. When you are done with the mask, choose Duplicate again and exit ShadowBox for the receiver.

10. Select the duplicated ShadowBox object and clear the mask. Then use MaskRect to mask out the trigger guard. To "unpaint" the mask from the interior area, draw out the rectangular mask but press Alt before you lift the pen. This will clear the mask from all the areas within the rectangle.

11. Again, duplicate the ShadowBox object, exit ShadowBox, select the duplicate, and clear the mask.

12. Select MaskCircle and rotate your ShadowBox object to the front view. Draw out the barrel of the gun. Be sure to do this with Symmetry on so you can create a perfect circle—well, as close as possible. You want your circle to be about 75 percent perfect. Don't spend too much time on it.

   Now, draw out another smaller circle using MaskCircle at the center of the barrel, but press Alt before lifting the pen to hollow it out, as shown in Figure 6.5.

13. Select MaskRect and drag out the length of the barrel from the side view to complete it.

14. Continue these steps to create the trigger and the magazine. When you create the magazine, you paint it straight up and down as you did with the handle. Figure 6.6 shows our final result.

Figure 6.5

Using MaskCircle to hollow out the barrel of the gun

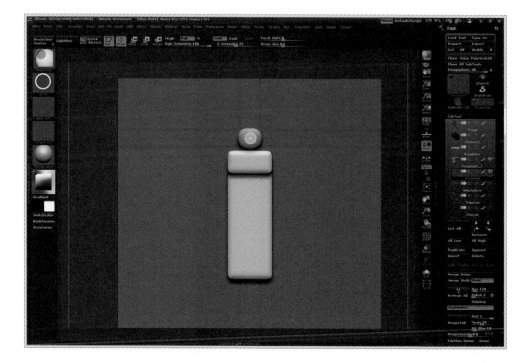

Figure 6.6

Final block-in of form with ShadowBox

Project: Sculpting the Basic Forms

With the clay on the armature, so to speak, it's time to start sculpting the shape. Our goal in this project is to create the basic forms, their specific roundness, and their overall shape characteristics. We will not sculpt line work or details at this stage. It's very important to conceptually separate basic form from details.

1. Select the slide from the SubTool subpalette. Then select the ClipCurve from the Brush palette.

2. Drag out the ClipCurve along the top, bottom, and sides. Then cut a 45-degree angle along the top sides of the slide to create a distinct bevel, as shown in Figure 6.7.

3. Select the H Polish brush and use it to clean up any edges that didn't clip correctly (see Figure 6.8). This step may not even be necessary.

4. Select the receiver and mask the upper portion. Leave the handle unmasked. Blur the mask by pressing Ctrl and clicking on the model or clicking Tool → Masking → Blur. Then select Move from the shelf, drag out an action line, and pull it backward (see Figure 6.9).

5. Select the Trim Dynamic brush and start shaping the curvature of the handle. You can also try the M Polish brush. I will often go back and forth between them (see Figure 6.10).

Figure 6.7

Beveling with
ClipCurve

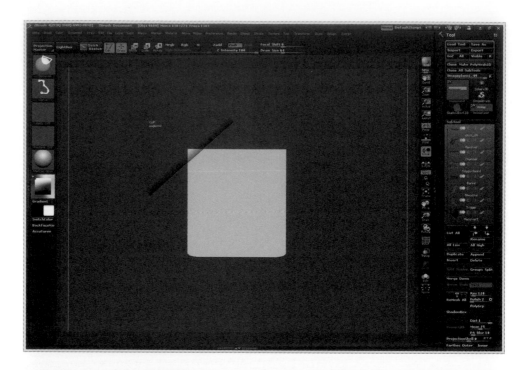

Figure 6.8

Final shape of slide

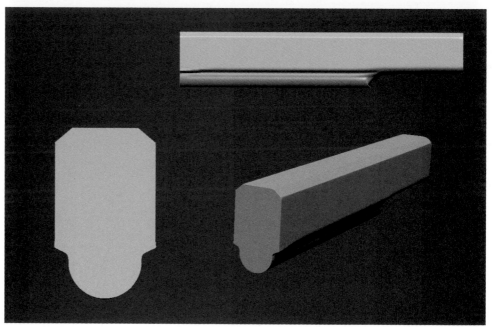

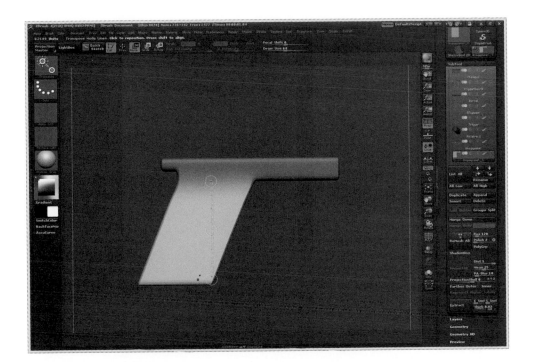

Figure 6.9

Using Transpose to adjust the handle

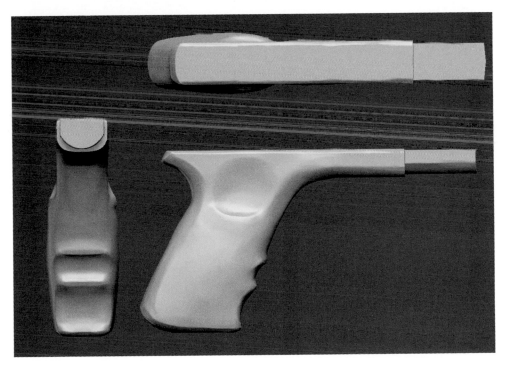

Figure 6.10

Handle's base shape

6. Select the barrel from the SubTool subpalette. Then select ClipCircleCenter from the Brush palette.

7. Looking from the front view and with Perspective off, use ClipCircleCenter to shave off all extra parts of the surface, as shown in Figure 6.11. Remember, you can press the spacebar while still pressing Ctrl+Shift to reposition the selection area.

8. Draw out the ClipCircleCenter brush along the inside of the barrel; press Alt before you lift the pen. This action will shave off all the surfaces within the circle, as you can see in Figure 6.12.

Figure 6.11

Cutting out the center

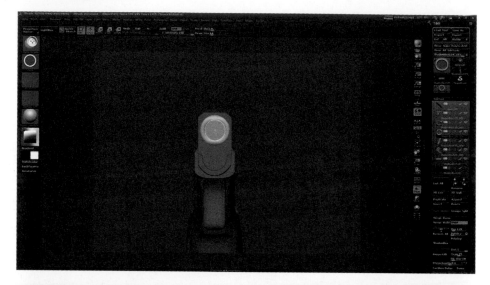

Figure 6.12

Final shape of the barrel of the gun

9. Shape the trigger guard using Move, Trim Dynamic, and H Polish. H Polish is the last brush to use as it will create the hard edges along the sides. Figure 6.13 and Figure 6.14 illustrate the basic shapes of the magazine and trigger, respectively.

Figure 6.13

Shape of the magazine

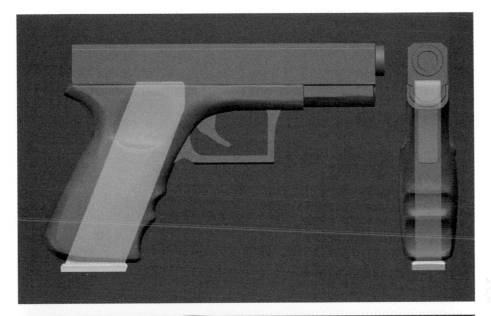

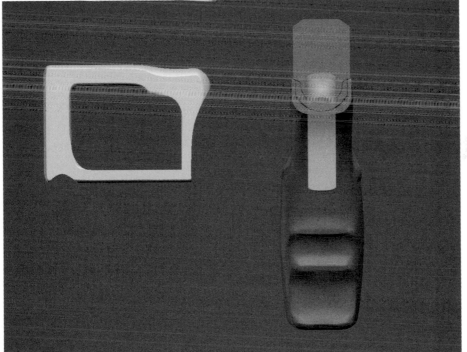

Figure 6.14

Shape of the trigger guard

Working with Stencils

Stencils are like a mask but they work within ZBrush's canvas area. It's just like the stencils you use in craft projects or airbrushing.

Figure 6.15

Stencil palette

The controls for stencils are in their own palette, Stencil, as shown in Figure 6.15. To create a stencil, though, you usually have to start in the Alpha palette. Simply select your preferred alpha and choose Alpha → Make St.

To move a stencil around, press the spacebar to bring up the dime controller.

> The dime controller uses its current location as the pivot point for the action. Make sure to place your cursor where you want the center of the action to occur before you press the spacebar.

Click on the text area to perform one of the actions. For example, to scale the stencil press the spacebar and then click on SCL, to the right.

> When you work with a stencil, select Stencil → Elv to make it easier to see the model through the stencil.

Project: Line Work

Line work and details are always last. Why? Because if you have to redo any of the basic structure you are very likely to destroy your line work and have to redo it—always a bummer.

Our goal in this project is to add just enough detail to sell the weapon. We don't want to go overboard. Too many details can derail us and turn our sculpt into a mess. You want whoever is looking at this sculpt—be it on your demo reel or in a game—to get the sense that this is a made object, that every part of it is designed and has a purpose.

1. Select the slide from the SubTool subpalette. Mask out the bullet chamber and then choose SubTool → Extract (see Figure 6.16). If the chamber is too big or not big enough, delete the extraction it created, lower the thickness, and try it again.

2. Hide the chamber that is created, press Move on the shelf, and drag out an action line from the side view. It should be pointing straight up and anchored right at the bottom of the chamber. Click the top red dot and drag it all the way down to the bottom of the action line. This will flatten out the chamber area, as shown in Figure 6.17.

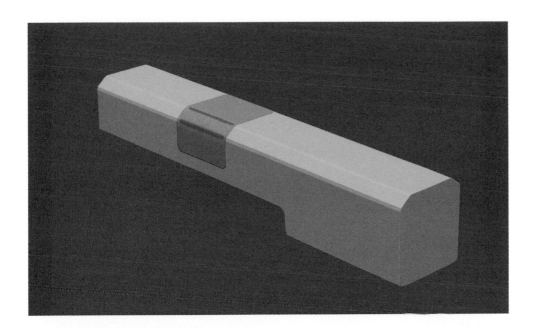

Figure 6.16

Extracted chamber area

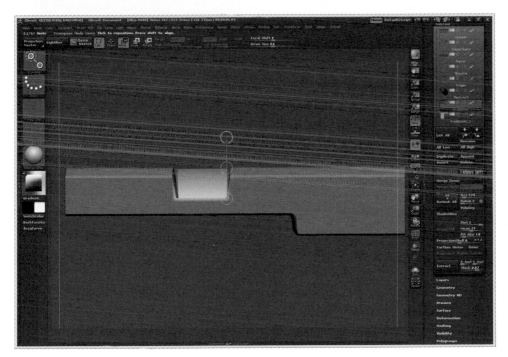

Figure 6.17

Using Transpose to create the chamber

3. Now, let's create the lettering. Position the slide along its side. Then zoom into it on the canvas. You want to get very close but have enough room to write the text along the side of the gun.

4. Click ZAppLink in the Document palette (see Figure 6.18) and then click OK in the pop-up menu. This will open Photoshop or your preferred photo editing application.

5. In Photoshop, select the topmost layer. Then select the Type tool and write your text along the side of the barrel (see Figure 6.19).

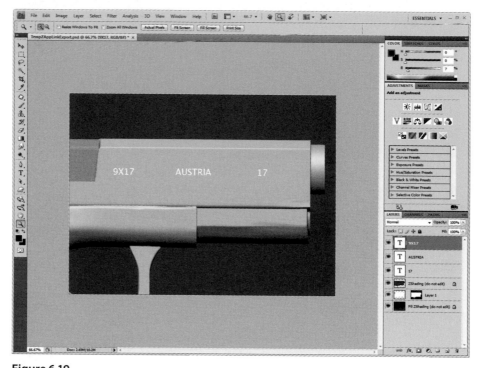

Figure 6.19

In Photoshop, write your text along the barrel's side.

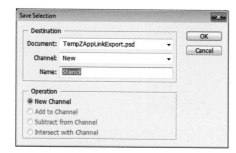

6. Press Ctrl and click on the text layer. Then choose Select → Save Selection. Name the selection **Stencil**, as shown in Figure 6.20.

7. Now you can safely delete the text layer and save the Photoshop file.

8. Switch back to ZBrush and click OK (Unchanged).

9. ZBrush will then tell you the document has a stencil and will automatically load that for you (see Figure 6.21).

Figure 6.20

The Save Selection dialog box

10. Turn off Stencil → Show so that the stencil doesn't get in your way.

11. Select the Move brush, then press and hold Alt while clicking on the surface of the model to bring out the relief of the text, as shown in Figure 6.22.

12. When done, you turn off the stencil by choosing Stencil → Stencil.

13. Select the receiver from the SubTool subpalette and make sure Perspective is off.

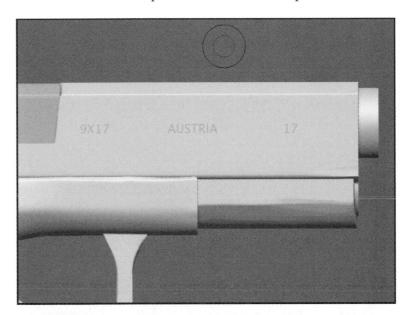

Figure 6.21
Stencil active in the interface

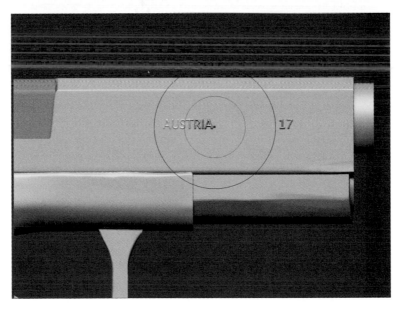

Figure 6.22
Using Move to pull out the text

14. Mask out a selection along the sides of the handle, as shown in Figure 6.23.

Figure 6.23

Mask along the sides of the handle.

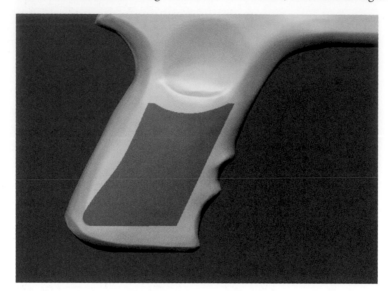

Figure 6.24

Surface Noise settings

15. Once you have the side patch masked out, invert the mask by pressing Ctrl and clicking on the canvas or click Tool → Masking → Inverse.

16. Set Deformation → Inflate to 2 to push this patch outward.

17. Now, let's use Surface Noise to create the texture along the grip. Choose Tool → Surface → Noise and set Scale to **2.7** and Strength to **.13**. Adjust the curve as shown in Figure 6.24. Then choose Apply To Mesh. Figure 6.25 illustrates the result.

Figure 6.25

Final grip

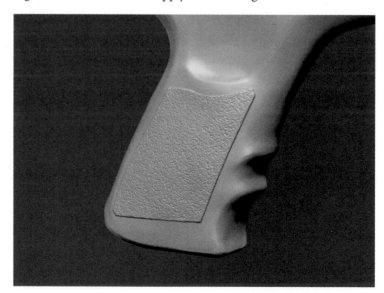

18. We are not done with the grip yet, though. Mask out the section between grips, as shown in Figure 6.26.

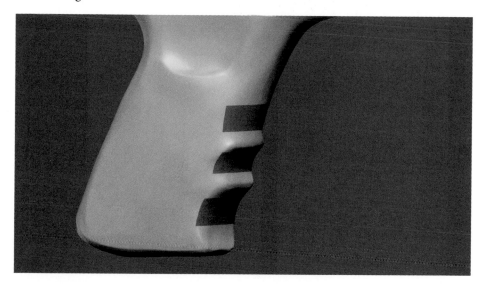

Figure 6.26
Masked-out grip
sections

19. Invert the mask and use Transpose to move them inward, as shown in Figure 6.27.

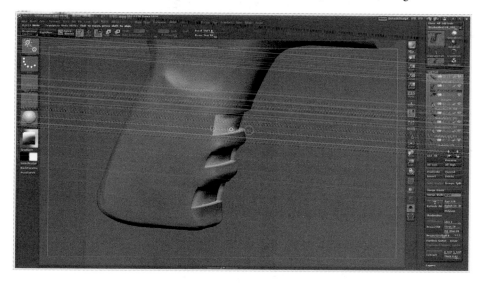

Figure 6.27
Using Transpose to
push grip areas in

20. Store a morph target so you can clean up any loose sculpting later.

21. Load the 2x6Dots brush from the resource folder on the accompanying DVD. Take a moment to look at the settings for this brush. It has some important changes in the Tablet Pressure subpalette of the Brush palette as well as some changes in the Stroke palette.

22. Sculpt as straight a line as you can inside the recessed areas. Use the Morph brush to clean up any areas that are a bit sloppy. This is just a precautionary step and is not absolutely essential. When you are finished, your receiver handle should look like Figure 6.28.

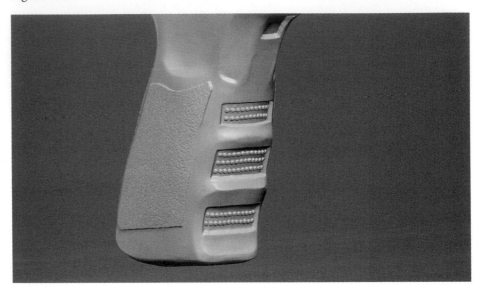

23. The back of the grip also needs some sculpting, as shown in Figure 6.29. Now, put your thinking cap on and ask yourself, "How would I do that?" Let's look at a few options:

Masks Masks could work, but it would be difficult to create them and then painful to get the nice, clean repetitive pattern. I wouldn't use masks here.

Alphas Using an alpha with the DragRect stroke might work, but how would you know how big to make the alpha and what if it was scaled too wide? An alpha would be good but might need too much work to make it functional.

Line in the Backtrack Subpalette This option is a really good idea. Combine it with the Layer brush and its Constant Depth feature and you will be on to something. The only problem would be keeping the precise distances.

Stencils This is the approach I used. Stencils via ZAppLink allow you to use Photoshop's grid for the precision and its brush and selection tools to help you create a clean pattern. Once the stencil is placed in ZBrush, it's really easy to just push the forms out or in by using the Move brush while pressing Alt.

Although there are lots of options for creating forms in ZBrush, my goal is to make you aware of your options and of their limitations and their advantages.

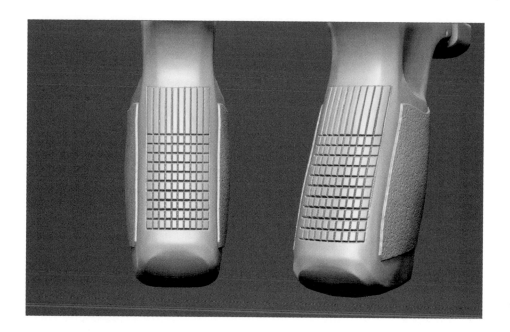

Figure 6.29

The back of the handle's grip

Project: Small Parts and Details

It's time to create the smaller pieces of the gun, like the magazine catch and the slide lock. Our goal is not to get caught up in creating the perfect magazine catch because no one will ever see it. Our goal is to put in enough detail to make it look realistic.

1. Select the receiver from the SubTool palette. Use the Clay brush and Trim Dynamic to notch out the slide lock and slide stop lever areas, as shown in Figure 6.30.

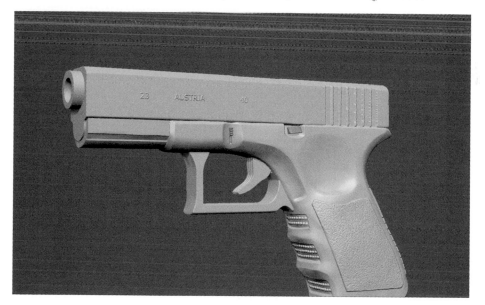

Figure 6.30

Slide lock and slide stop lever areas

2. Load PolyCube from ZBrush's `ZTool\Image Plane` directory.

3. Select our gun and append the PolyCube. Rename it **slideLock**. Once it's appended to your model, it should look like Figure 6.31.

Figure 6.31

PolyCube appended to the pistol

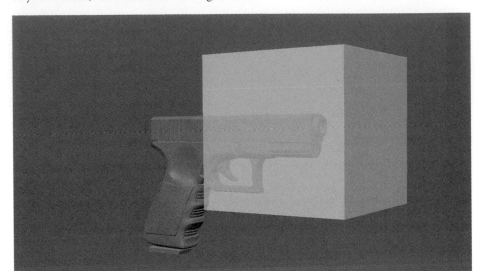

4. Decrease the size by dragging the Deformation → Size slider to the left a few times. Then use Transpose to scale it further and place it along the side of the gun. The Deformation palette is shown in Figure 6.32. When your model is positioned, it should look like Figure 6.33.

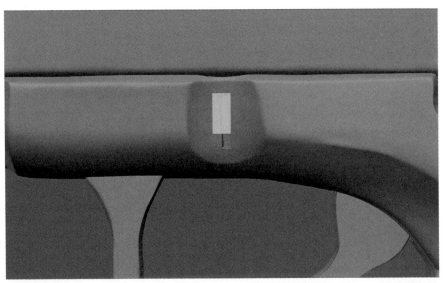

Figure 6.32

The Deformation palette

Figure 6.33

The slide lock scaled and placed

5. Repeat steps 3 and 4 for the slide stop lever. When these are sculpted and placed, your model should look like Figure 6.34.

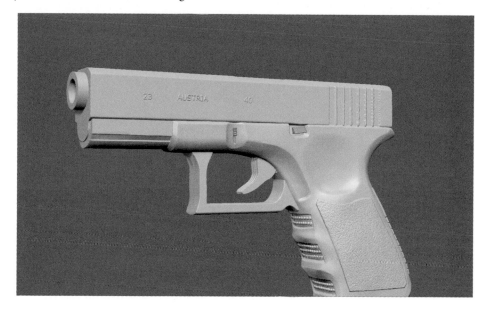

Figure 6.34

The right side of the pistol

6. Now, rotate the model to the other side. On this side we created the magazine catch and some pins to add detail. Figure 6.35 illustrates the final result.

7. Let's talk about creating the pins. Select MaskCircle and mask out small pin areas, as shown in Figure 6.36.

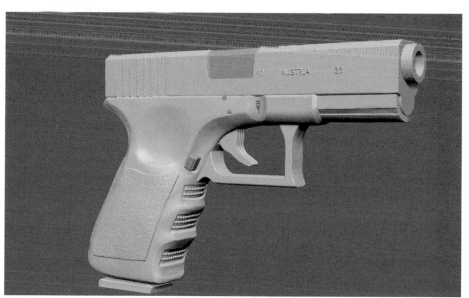

Figure 6.35

The left side of the pistol

Figure 6.36

Masking out pin areas with MaskCircle

8. Extract these areas using SubTool → Extract. Adjust the thickness as needed.

9. Hide the extracted parts, invert the mask, and use the Move brush while pressing Alt to quickly push the pin areas in. This is a simple trick but adds a nice layer of detail. Figure 6.37 shows the results of this process. Figure 6.38 illustrates our final gun sculpt.

Figure 6.37

Extracted pins

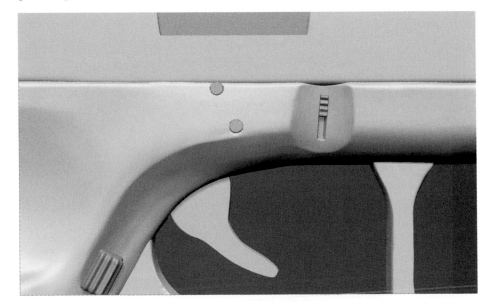

Figure 6.38
Final pistol

Anatomy of the Holster

Our next series of projects will focus on the holster and thigh rig. We are using a Level 3 Tactical Serpa Holster from Blackhawk as our source of reference. There are three parts to the tactical holster: the holster itself, the platform and the rigging or straps.

Project: Creating the Platform

The platform is strapped to the thigh and serves as the base for the holster. You'll first create a template of the platform on a simple flat plane. Once you have created the template, you will add depth to it and work with it as a 3D object.

1. Select Plane3D from the Tool palette. Then choose Tool → Make Polymesh. This will convert the model into a sculptable 3D plane.

2. Divide this plane twice to add enough polygons to create a detailed mask.

3. Sculpt its shape to resemble our platform, as shown in Figure 6.39.

4. Mask out the shape of the platform complete with holes (see Figure 6.40). I used a combination of MaskRect and MaskCircle to create the shape.

5. Select Tool → SubTool and set Thickness to 0 and E.Smt to 0. Then choose Extract. This converts your mask into a flat 3D plane that you can refine before converting it again into a 3D shape with depth (see Figure 6.41).

6. Use the Clay brush, Trim D, and H Polish to sculpt the raised surfaces along the outside of the platform (see Figure 6.42). These are the areas where you would place extra magazines or light holders. Make sure that the form is solid and the lines are clean before proceeding.

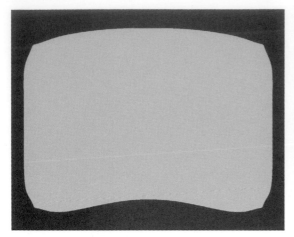

Figure 6.39
Basic shape of the platform

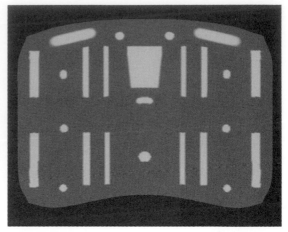

Figure 6.40
Masked areas

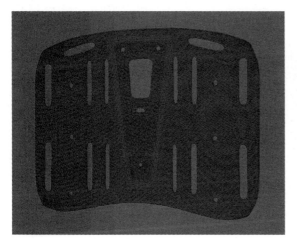

Figure 6.41
Extracted platform mesh

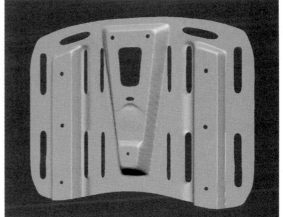

Figure 6.42
Sculpted platform

7. Store the morph target by choosing Tool → Morph Target → Store.

8. Position the platform so you are looking at it from a side view and press Shift+S to snapshot it to the canvas.

9. Click Move on the shelf and draw out an action line. Then move the platform backward just enough to cover the thickness of the platform, as shown in Figure 6.43.

10. Choose Tool → Morph Target and click CreateDiff Mesh, as shown in Figure 6.44. CreateDiff is an old feature of ZBrush that is still incredibly powerful. It will create a new mesh that is the difference between your stored morph target and your model's shape now. Since all we did was move it backward, this step creates a new mesh with the required depth. To select the new mesh, look for a new tool that starts with MorphDiff in the Tool palette (see Figure 6.45).

11. You will probably have to flip the normal. To do this, choose Tool → Display Properties and click Flip, as shown in Figure 6.46. Be sure to do this before you subdivide the model.

12. Finally, to get rid of the hard machined shape that you get from CreateDiff, drag the Deformation → Relax slider to 30 (see Figure 6.47 and Figure 6.48).

Project: Creating the Holster

Now it's time to create the holster. You will do this in multiple stages. The first stage is similar to our previous workflow. You create a mask of the holster's 2D shape, then extract that shape, sculpt it, and add depth to it with CreateDiff. The difference with our approach here is that you have to create two sides. To do that, you will duplicate one side and Merge Down.

1. Select your gun model. Append a 3DPlane from the Tool palette, rename it **holsterDrawing**, and divide it twice.

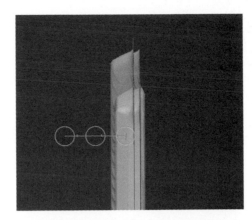

Figure 6.43

Using Transpose to move the platform back

Figure 6.44

Morph Target subpalette

Figure 6.45

Final result

Figure 6.46

Display Properties subpalette

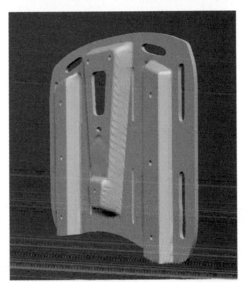

Figure 6.47

Deformation subpalette

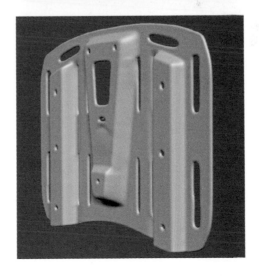

Figure 6.48

Final result of the platform

2. Rotate it using Transpose so you are looking at the side of the gun.

3. Mask out the shape of the holster (see Figure 6.49). Keep it general but make sure your edges are clean lines. You can avoid trouble later by keeping the lines very smooth.

4. Set Tool → SubTool and set Thickness to 0 and E.Smt to 0. Then choose Extract (see Figure 6.50).

5. Select the extracted mesh and rename it **holsterTemplate**.

6. Select the ZProject brush from the Brush palette. Click Zadd on the shelf and brush along the gun to project the gun's shape into the holster template (see Figure 6.51).

7. Selcct the TrimFront brush, press Alt, and use this brush to create flat plateaus in the area of the trigger and the ends of the barrel of the gun. Work all over the model to create the overall shape of the holster (see Figure 6.52).

8. To add some details, mask out the trigger lock, as shown in Figure 6.53. Then extract it and adjust the thickness as needed.

9. Invert the mask, hide the trigger lock, and push the unmasked area inward with Transpose, as shown in Figure 6.54.

Figure 6.49

Masked-out holster shape

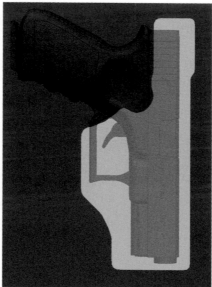

Figure 6.50

Extracted holster shape

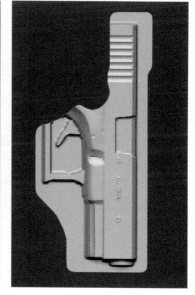

Figure 6.51

Gun projected into the holster with the ZProject brush

Figure 6.52
Sculpted holster

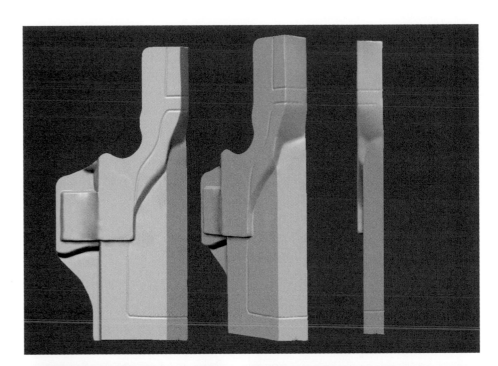

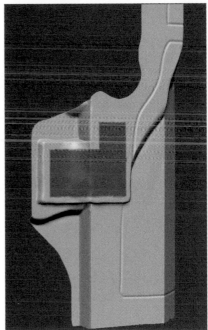

Figure 6.53
Mask for trigger lock

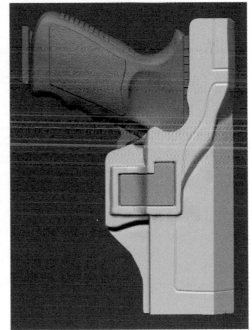

Figure 6.54
Holster with trigger lock

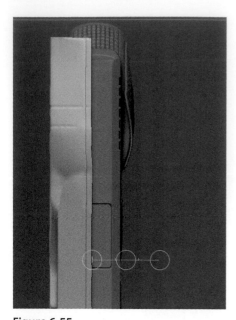

Figure 6.55

Creating depth for CreateDiff

10. When you have the shape sculpted, it's time to create the thickness. Store a morph target by choosing Tool → Morph Target and click StoreMT.

11. Position the holster so you are looking at its side, as shown in Figure 6.55. Snapshot it to the canvas by pressing Shift+S.

12. Click Move on the shelf and drag out an action line. Move the line just enough to cover the thickness of the holster.

13. Choose Tool → Morph Target and click CreateDiff.

14. Select the new mesh that starts with MorphDiff in the Tool palette (see Figure 6.56).

15. Choose SubTool → Duplicate.

16. Click the small Y in the Mirror button in the Deformation subpalette. Click the small X to turn off mirroring in the X direction.

17. Choose Deformation → Mirror (see Figure 6.57).

18. If necessary, reposition each side slightly.

19. Select the topmost holster side and choose SubTool → Merge Down to combine them into one shape (see Figure 6.58).

Figure 6.56

One half of the holster with depth

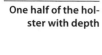

Figure 6.57

Mirror button in the Deformation subpalette

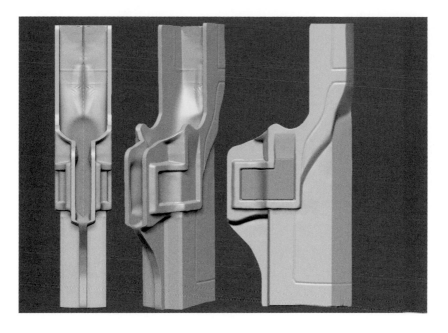

Figure 6.58

Merged sides of the holster before the final sculpt changes

20. At this point, you may have to alter the shape slightly. For example, I have to drag out an area that closes the holster in the trigger area. I also have to select the faces along the top of the holster to create a top plane that locks the gun into place. Figure 6.59 shows the results.

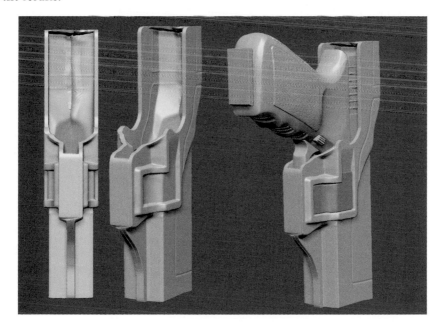

Figure 6.59

Holster after the final sculpt changes

Project: Adding the Plastic Buckle and Tri-Glides

In this project, we will create the plastic buckles. The process is fairly straightforward and, once again, ShadowBox is key. You'll have to adjust the size and scale of the buckles for other projects, so don't sweat how big or small they are. Just create them within `shadowbox_128`'s default size.

Figure 6.60

Female component of the buckle

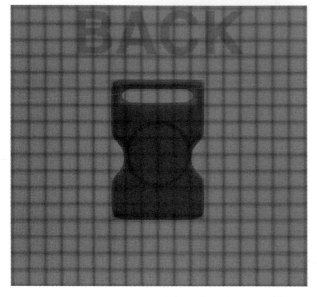

1. Load `shadowbox_128` from ZBrush's ZTool directory.

2. From a front view, mask out the female component of the buckle. I used MaskRect and adjusted its shape with MaskPen (see Figure 6.60).

3. From a side view, draw out a thin rectangle with MaskRect and create its depth (see Figure 6.61).

4. Choose SubTool → Duplicate and then exit ShadowBox by choosing SubTool → ShadowBox.

5. Select the duplicated subtool and clear the mask.

6. Create the mask for the male component of the buckle using MaskRect and MaskPen, as shown in Figure 6.62.

7. Choose SubTool → ShadowBox to exit ShadowBox.

8. Select the topmost subtool and choose Merge Down. Then save the ZTL file for later reference.

9. Repeat the previous steps to create the Tri-Glide fasteners, as shown in Figure 6.63.

Figure 6.61

Side view of the female component of the buckle

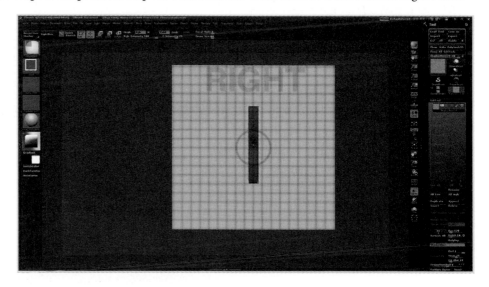

Figure 6.62

Male component of the buckle

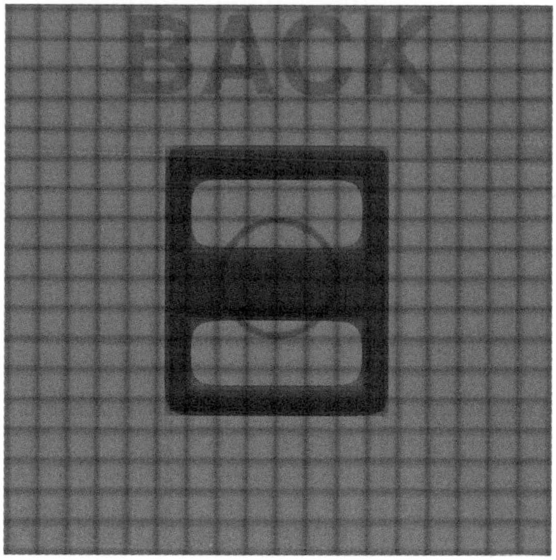

Figure 6.63

Tri-Glide fasteners

Project: Creating Straps

Straps are fun to create but they can be problematic to handle in ZBrush, especially the thigh strap, which turns in on itself and doubles up. No problem, though—you just won't use ZBrush to make straps. Instead, you will use GoZ, which makes short work of connecting ZBrush and, in this case, Maya.

1. Select the gun from the Tool palette. Append a Cylinder3d and position it to stand in for the thigh of the model (see Figure 6.64).

2. Press Ctrl+Shift and select a cross section of the cylinder that could serve as a stand-in for a thigh strap.

3. Choose Tool → SubTool and click Extract. Adjust the thickness as needed (see Figure 6.65).

4. Rename the SubTool that is created by Extract to strapTemplate.

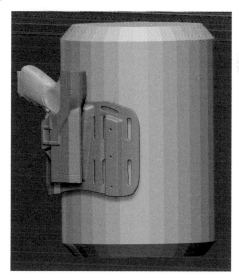

Figure 6.64

Temporary leg shape

Figure 6.65

Extracted strap

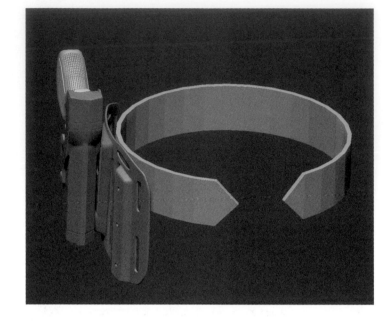

Figure 6.66

GoZ interface

5. Click GoZ in the Tool palette (see Figure 6.66).

6. Duplicate the strap and scale it outward, as shown in Figure 6.67.

7. Delete the polygon faces at the tail of the duplicate strap (see Figure 6.68).

Figure 6.67

Scaling the other strap

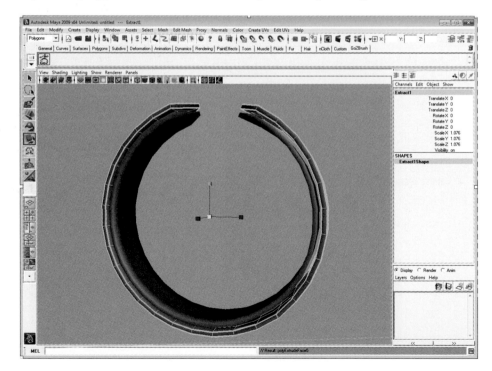

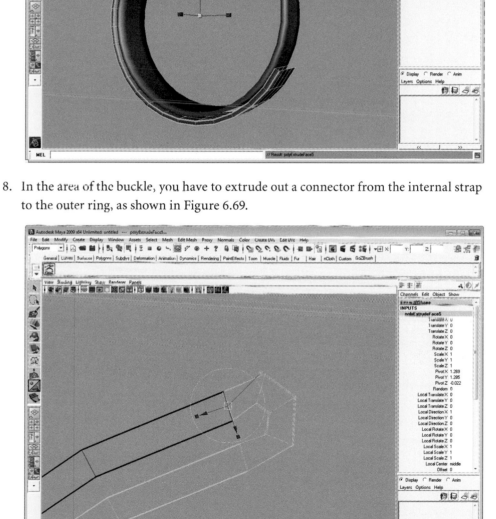

Figure 6.68
Removing unnecessary polygons

8. In the area of the buckle, you have to extrude out a connector from the internal strap to the outer ring, as shown in Figure 6.69.

Figure 6.69
Connection extruded

9. Also, extrude out a portion of the strap that folds back on itself where it locks the male component of the buckle in place (see Figure 6.70).

Figure 6.70

Strap extruded back upon itself

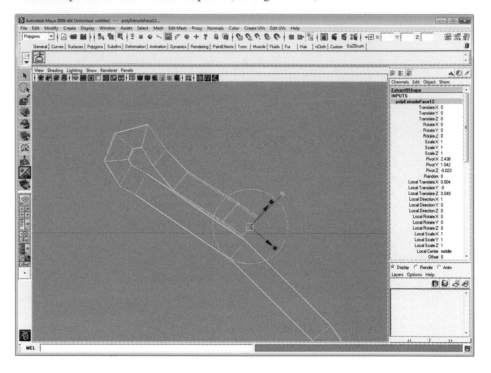

10. Select both straps and choose Mesh ➔ Combine.

11. Select the Merge Vertex tool from the Edit Mesh menu and use it to merge each vertex one at a time (see Figure 6.71).

12. Select the Insert Edge Loop tool from the Edit Mesh menu and add edge loops around the edges both on the top and the bottom (see Figure 6.72).

13. Select the resulting mesh and click the GoZ button in the GoZ shelf to send it back to ZBrush.

14. You may need to append the mesh back to your gun. Once it's placed, use MaskRect to mask out sections and use the Move Elastic brush to weave the strap through the platform (see Figure 6.73). You may need to divide the mesh to get a smooth weaving of the strap.

15. Duplicate the strap and move it upward to become the upper strap. Then click Merge Down to combine the straps into one subtool. (This step may not be necessary.)

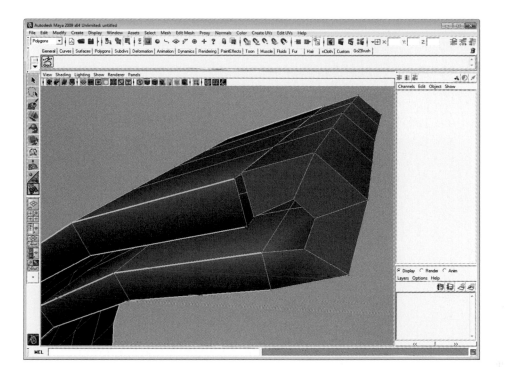

Figure 6.71

Using the Merge Vertex tool

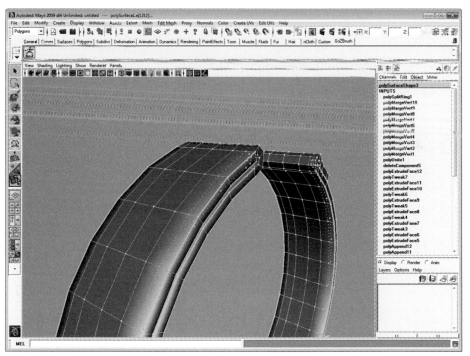

Figure 6.72

Edge loops at edges

16. Append the buckles you created in the previous project and position them as shown in Figure 6.74.

17. To create the strap to the hip, you need a guide to give you a sense of scale and placement in Maya. Select the platform template, then click GoZ in the Tool palette. The polygon count of the strap should be low enough that you can send the strap right into Maya (see Figure 6.75).

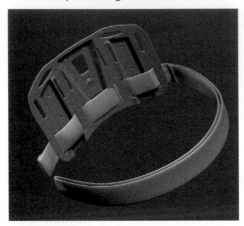

Figure 6.73

Straps woven through the platform

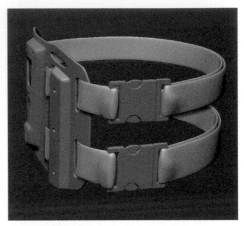

Figure 6.74

Buckles positioned

Figure 6.75

Importing the platform into Maya

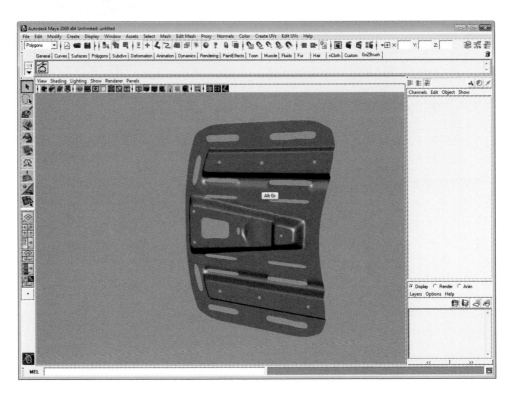

18. In Maya, extrude the strap for the hip, as shown in Figure 6.76. You may want to bring in some buckles to help you place it.

Figure 6.76

Hip strap

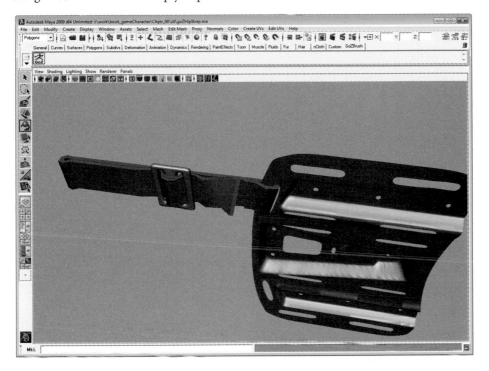

19. When done, select the strap and click GoZ to send it back to ZBrush.

20. Choose Duplicate in the SubTool subpalette.

21. Choose Deformation → Mirror to create the left strap. Your model should look like Figure 6.77.

The buckles are placed on our final straps. Also, notice we used a different buckle for the top. You can create this buckle using the same steps that you followed for the generic buckle design. We also added another belt loop on top to connect the straps to the character's belt. Figure 6.78 shows our results.

Figure 6.77

The platform with hip straps

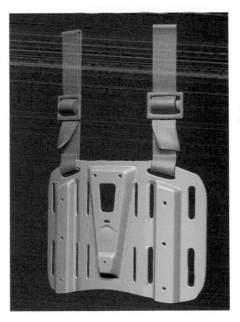

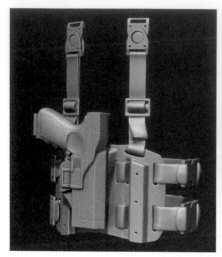
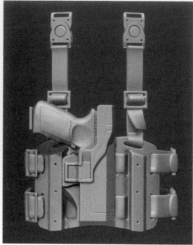
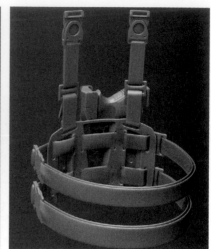

Figure 6.78

Our pistol and holster

Texturing

Texturing weapons is a subtle art but it is very important. In this project we will look at a few simple tools to help you while texturing your gun and holster.

Although we do much of the texturing for props in Photoshop, 3D texture painting offers some compelling features, such as Ambient Occlusion and Cavity Masking.

Project: Texturing

This project will focus on a few simple but powerful features in ZBrush's texturing toolset. These features make short work of texturing props like our Gun handgun and holster.

Figure 6.79

Specularity curve

1. Select the receiver from the SubTool palette and select SkinShade4 from the Material palette. Use SkinShade4 because it gives you a good clean view your texture. I find the other materials can darken the color too much.

2. To adjust the material properties, open the Material palette and then the Modifiers subpalette.

3. Set Specularity to 55.

4. Open the Specular Curve and adjust it so that it is a very, very sharp corner. Let Figure 6.79 guide you.

5. Set the RGB sliders to 29, 30, 33 and then click Fill Object (see Figure 6.80).

6. Select Masking and set Intensity to 100; then choose Masking → Mask By Cavity. You may also want to turn off View Mask.

7. Set the RGB sliders to 61, 63, 75 and set RGB Intensity to 15.

8. Select the Standard brush. Set the stroke to Color Spray. Select Alpha 23. Paint lightly along the barrel of the slide and in areas of wear.

9. To start painting the wear along the edges of the gun, set the RGB sliders to 87, 88, 97 (see Figure 6.81).

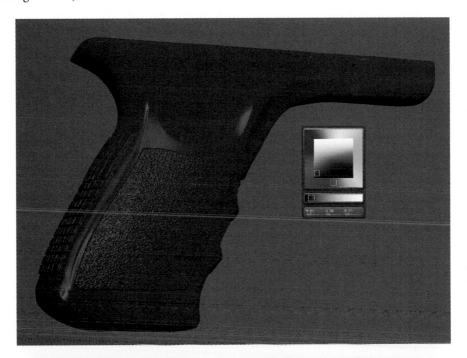

Figure 6.80

Base color

Figure 6.81

Painting some wear and tear

Figure 6.82

Ambient Occlusion settings

10. Ambient Occlusion, on the Masking subpalette, is one of those cool things you can only do in 3D. Before you use it, set Occlusion Intensity to 10 and then lower the AO ScanDist to .05 in the Masking subpalette. Then click Mask Ambient Occlusion (see Figure 6.82).

11. Invert the mask so you can paint into the crevices.

12. Set the RGB sliders to 25, 25, 29.

13. Set RGB Intensity to 30 and click Fill Object to darken those areas (see Figure 6.83).

14. Repeat this for each part of the gun and holster. You want to do each part quickly. Figure 6.84 illustrates our final texture painting. However, you can consider this more of a first pass on the texture. Once you redo the topology and create UVs, then you can get more detailed with it.

Figure 6.83

After further painting

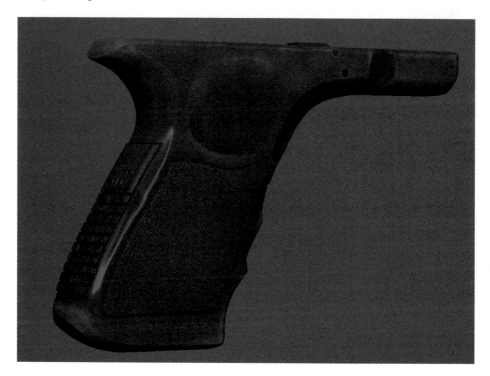

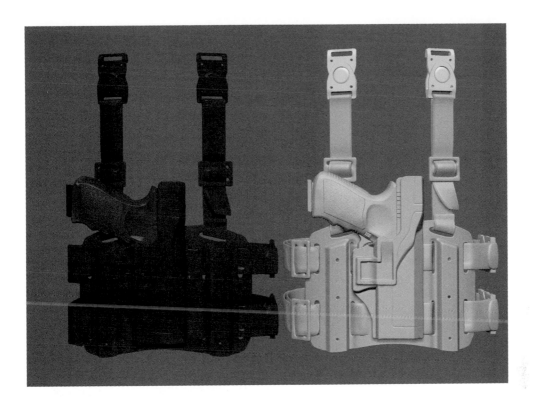

Figure 6.84

**Final texture for gun
and holster**

Summary

So, our gun and holster are all finished. You should feel more comfortable with ShadowBox and the Clip brushes and have a warm, fuzzy feeling for GoZ. The next step is to piece all this together, but we have deliberately left that process for another chapter.

Take another look at your model and congratulate yourself on a job well done. So far, you have sculpted a character, a face, clothing, folds, stitching, and now a hand gun using ZBrush 4 and a few accomplices. Take a breather. Relax. We still have a bit of a road ahead of us.

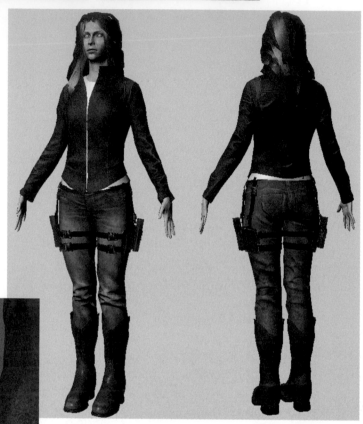

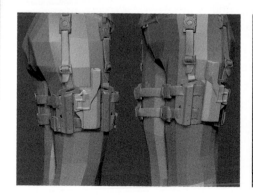

CHAPTER 7

Getting It Into the Game

Putting our model into the game requires a couple of steps. The first step is to begin refining the topology for the in-game mesh. Second, we need to generate the normal maps, texture maps, and any other maps that we might need.

There is a lot of debate on the topic of topology. What constitutes correct topology can be debated in all directions. However, there are a few concrete, essential concepts that you should understand. We'll explore those in the next section, Topology Spectrum.

The Topology Spectrum

When we create the low resolution model we have two major concerns. We need to optimize our topology to show as much form with as few polygons as possible and we need to optimize the topology to be as animation friendly as possible.

There are a few important variables: the kind of rigging system used in the game and our expected level of realism. If there is any sort of dynamic rig on the model such as jiggle deformers than you need to heavily weight your topology to be all quads and as evenly distributed as possible.

If you want to emphasize lower resolutions, with more focus on the form of the model than how it moves in the game then you need to create more elaborate topology to describe the form of the model's wrinkles. You can see an example of that in the Project: Topology and Clothing Folds section of this chapter.

So to restate the solution, your topology should allow you to accurately describe the form of your model up to the level that your rigging and animation setup can process.

The more specific your topology is, the harder it is for a more dynamic rig to create folds and wrinkles. In film work triangles and n-gons are avoided at all cost whenever a dynamic skin solve is used because triangles and n-gons do not behave as well as quads do. That said, games happen in real-time and cannot rely on a building full of computers to render one frame. In games, you have to make hard choices between how specific your topology is and how dynamic your rigging system is.

Project: Topology - Removing Interior Polygons

In this project we will adjust the topology of the jeans and the jacket to get them ready for viewing in Maya. Our goal at this point is not to create specific topology, but to get the model into Maya so we can begin to make realistic decisions about how to re-organize our topology.

1. Load your original model that you worked on in chapter 5. This model should have the hair sculpted with it. Immediately save this model as our `in-game_SourceMesh`.

2. Select the Jacket SubTool and go to the lowest subdivision level.

If you created the jacket like we did earlier in the book you will have a separate group for the outside of the jacket; the thickness of it and some of the inside is shown in Figure 7.1.

3. Press Ctrl+Shift and click on the outside of the jacket. Make sure to select all of the polygroups that belong to the outside of the mesh like Figure 7.2.

4. Go to the highest subdivision level for the jacket and click Tool → Masking → Mask All.

Figure 7.1

Jacket with Polygroups

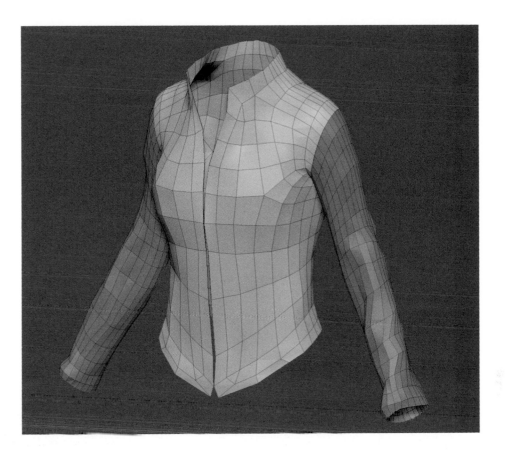

Figure 7.2

Jacket after removing inside polygroups

5. Go to the lowest subdivision level and press Tool → Geometry → Delete Hidden, as shown in Figure 7.3.

6. Select the Jeans from the SubTool subpalette.

7. Press Ctrl+Shift and drag out a selection around the bottom of the jeans. Press Alt before releasing Ctrl+Shift to hide the area inside of the rectangle. Hide any other parts that you think should be deleted to create a base for our low resolution mesh. My example is shown in Figure 7.4.

8. Go to the highest subdivision level, mask all, then return to the lowest subdivision level and click Delete Hidden in the Geometry subpalette.

9. Repeat steps 6 through 8 for the belt and any other SubTools that need it.

10. As a final step make sure your SubTool has polygroups as indicated in Figure 7.5. We will use them later when we create UVs.

At this stage your jeans and jacket should be one-dimensional with no thickness. However, they should still have their entire subdivision history and polypainting.

Figure 7.3

DelHidden button

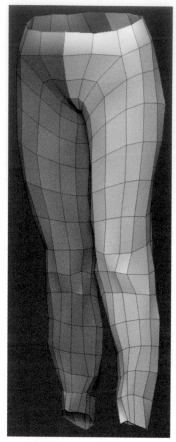

Figure 7.4

Removing the bottom of the jeans

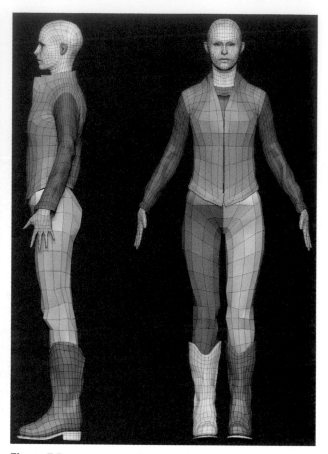

Figure 7.5

Your final Polygroups should look like this

Project: Topology - Combining Parts

The boots give us a chance to explore another way to work with the topology of our models. In this case, we will use the ZProject brush to project the vamp, the lower part of the boot, into the body of the boot.

1. Select the boot SubTool.

2. Click Rotate on the shelf and zoom in on the area around the lip of the boot. Press Ctrl and drag out a mask as shown in Figure 7.6.

3. Invert the mask by pressing Ctrl and clicking outside of the model.

4. Click Visibility→ Hide Pt, as shown in Figure 7.7, to hide the masked areas. Make sure this corresponds to the lip of the boot. Adjust your selection as necessary.

5. Go to the highest subdivision level and click Mask All in the Masking subpalette. Then click Delete Hidden in the Geometry subpalette.

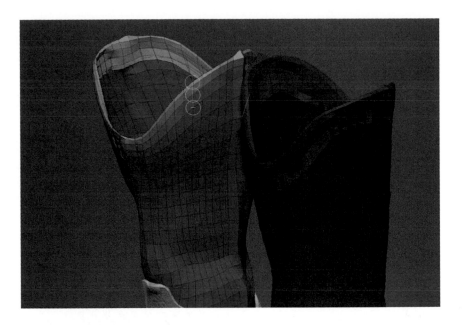

Figure 7.6

Using Topological Masking on the boot

6. Make sure that the boot and the vamp are both visible in the SubTool palette and then select the ZProject brush.

7. Click RGB and Zadd on the shelf. Make sure that symmetry is off. ZProject doesn't work well with symmetry. Then brush along the surface of the model as shown in Figure 7.8. Only brush the areas that are facing you. Avoid brush along the sides as this will create artifacts and damage your topology.

Figure 7.7

Hide Pt button

Figure 7.8

Projecting the vamp into the boot

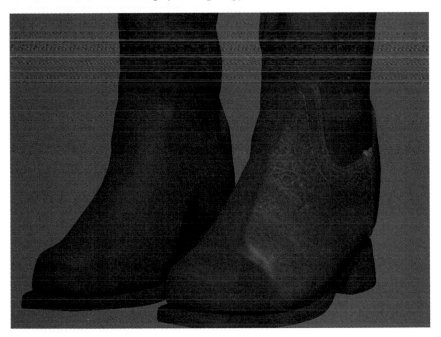

8. To access the inside of the boots you'll have to hide the left and the right side respectively. Use Ctrl+Shift and drag out a selection for each SubTool. Then use ZProject to project the details as illustrated in Figure 7.9.

Figure 7.9

Projecting the inside of the vamp into the boot

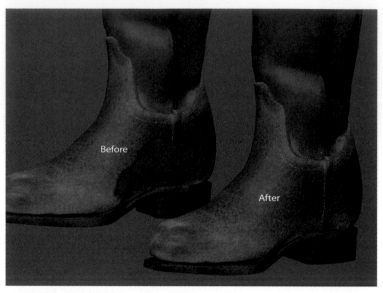

9. Once the vamp is projected into the boot you can delete the SubTool by clicking Delete in the SubTool subpalette.

10. If you have not saved your model by now you are living dangerously. This is just a friendly reminder. Save now, save often, and save again in 5 minutes.

11. As a final step make sure your SubTool has polygroups as indicated in Figure 7.10. We will use them later when we create UVs.

Figure 7.10

Final boot

Project: Adding the Holster

Let's add the holster we created in Chapter 6. This will require a few steps and we want to make sure that we get everything appended to our in-game-SourceMesh as cleanly as possible. In the very next project we'll adjust the topology to be useable in the game engine.

Follow the steps below to begin.

1. Load the pistol we created in Chapter 6 (shown in Figure 7.11).

2. Select the pistol and select the Strap_top subtool from it.

3. Select the in-game_SourceMesh and append the Strap_Top.

4. Repeat steps 3 and 4 until you have appended the strap_bottom, hip straps, buckles, holster, platform, and holster release. Don't worry about the pistol itself. We can import it later as its own model. Figure 7.12 illustrates our progress.

5. Once the parts are appended, it's time to position them. Use Transpose Master to rotate, scale and move them into place. When done, your model should look like Figure 7.13.

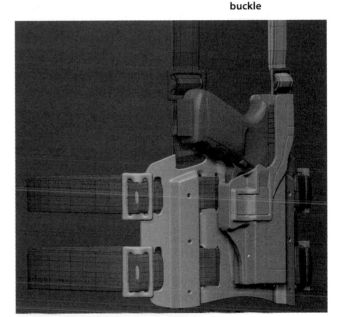

Figure 7.11

Our holster with platform, straps and buckle

Figure 7.12

Holster parts appended to in-games_SourceMesh

Figure 7.13

Holster after being positioned

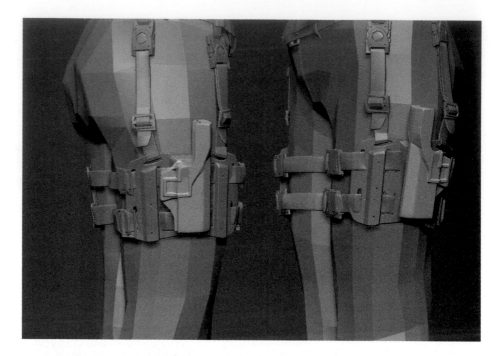

6. Use the Move Up and Move Down arrows in the SubTool list to position Strap_Top, Strap_Bottom and Hip_Strap on top of each other.

7. Select Straps_Top. Open the Geometry sub-palette and check how many subdivision levels it has. If it has three levels, set it all the way to subdivision level 3.

8. Select Straps_Bottom and open the Geometry sub-palette. If it has more than 3 subdivision levels, then set it to SDiv 3 and click Del Higher in the Geometry sub-palette. It if has less than, divide it till it has at least three levels. The goal here is to make sure that all of the straps have the same number of subdivision levels and that they are at the exact same subdivision level.

9. Select Straps_Top and click Merge Down in the SubTool sub-palette. This is not an undoable operation so you want to make sure that each strap is at the same subdivision level and that they have the same number of levels. You might consider saving your model before doing this step in case something happens.

Figure 7.14

Our SubTool list

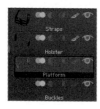

10. Use the Move Up and Move Down arrows in the SubTool list to position all of the buckles on top of each other. Then click Merge Down to combine them, as well.

11. At this point you should have 4 SubTools, shown in Figure 7.14, that belong to the holster: straps, buckles, platform and holster. Double check this and make sure before beginning.

Project: Topology - Decimation Master & Polypainting

When we created the platform and the holster we used Mesh Extraction from a fairly high polygon mesh. This means that these SubTools have way too many polygons to be used in the game.

In our specific case, we are not going to retopologize these SubTools. Instead, we are going to use Decimation Master. Now, depending on your game pipeline, you may have to retopologize it. My interest, though, is to show you another way that you can keep your polygon count low and still retain all of its form.

There is one big roadblock standing in our way though: our Polypainting. How do we transfer the Polypainting from our design sculpt to our decimated topology? Well, I'm glad you asked.

Figure 7.15
The Holster

The short answer is that we will use the ZProject brush but follow the steps below to see how it ends.

1. Select the Holster, seen in Figure 7.15 from the SubTool list.

2. Click Duplicate in the SubTool sub-palette.

3. Click Pre-Process Current in the Decimation subpalette of the ZPlugins palette, as shown in Figure 7.16. Note, you only need to process the current selection for now.

4. Set % of Decimation to .1% click Decimate Current. Hover over the Tool palette thumbnail and check how many polygons it is. You may need to set Decimation % as low as .05%. If you need to set it lower, simply change the number in the Decimation % and click Decimate Current again.

5. Click Divide, in the Geometry sub-palette, several times. We want our decimated model and our original holster to be roughly the same number of polygons.

6. Select the ZProject brush and make sure that RGB is on and Zadd is off on the shelf. You may also want to hide all the other SubTools. Then just brush along the surface to transfer the details the painting.

Now, you might be wondering how you will be able to UV the holster with this type of topology. Well, for the holster there is no problem. We'll be able to create UVs using UV Master and get a decent amount of control over it. The Platform SubTool, however, is another story. It has too many openings for UV Master to function correctly so we'll look at how we retopologize it and create the UVs for it in the Project: UVs, Topology and the Platform section.

Figure 7.16
Decimation Master

Project: In-Game Hair

You're going to hate me. I almost hate myself doing this step but it has to happen. We have to convert our beautiful sculpted hair into hair that can sit in our game engine. That said, though, this is a great opportunity to relook at the planes of hair and get a fresh perspective on how to create curls.

To begin follow the steps below.

1. Load `hairNet.obj` from Chapter 8's resource folder in the resource DVD. This strip will be roughly positioned for an 8 head character so you might have to adjust its placement. Figures 7.17 and 7.18 illustrate our placement.

Figure 7.17

Polygon hair groups

2. Click Autogroups in the Polygroups subpalette.

3. Use Move Elastic and Transpose's Move and Rotate to position the hair. Create a wavy quality that matches your design sculpt of the hair. Figure 7.19 shows our progress.

4. Try not to get too specific as that will slow you down and make this even more painful. You can adjust further once you have the general shape of the model's hair. When you're done your hair should resemble Figure 7.20. Notice how the groups of hair interpenetrate each other. Let's fix that.

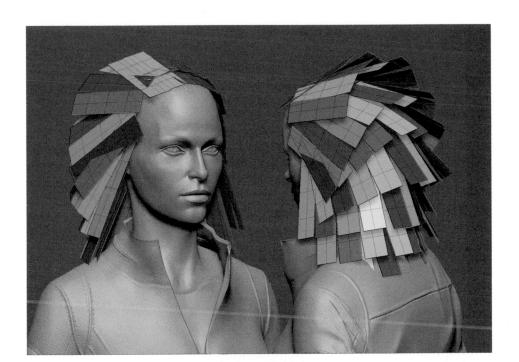

Figure 7.18
More polygon hair
groups

Figure 7.19
Progress with hair

Figure 7.20
First pass on hair

5. Let's make sure that each layer lays on top of the layer below it. To do that we need to make sure that each layer has its own polygroup or SubTool. I like to use SubTools because it isolates the different layers of hair. Press Ctrl+Shift and click on one of the strands along the bottom. Then press Ctrl+Shift and click and drag outside of the model to invert that. Then press Ctrl+Shift and click the remaining groups of hair along the bottom row.

6. Click Split Hidden, as shown in Figure 7.21, in the SubTool subpalette to separate the hidden parts of the model into their own SubTool.

7. Repeat steps 9 and 10 for each layer of hair groups.

8. Using Move Elastic tuck the tops of the hair underneath the layer above them and the bottom of the groups above them. Figure 7.22 demonstrates our finished hair.

9. Select the highest hair grouping in the SubTool list and then merge it all back together using Merge Down.

Figure 7.21
Split Hidden

Figure 7.22
Final hair

Project: Create UVs using UV Master

Once you have the Polygroups created we are ready to create the UVs. The groups are an essential part of UV creation because they create the different islands.

Make sure that you have UVMaster installed and follow the steps below to continue.

1. In the UVMaster subpalette, shown in Figure 7.23, of the ZPlugins palette click Polygroups.

2. Select the jacket in the SubTool subpalette and set it to the lowest subdivision.

3. Click Work on Clone in the subpalette so we can start to get more detailed with our model.

4. Click Polygroups directly under the Unwrap All button as shown in Figure 7.24.

5. Click Unwrap, in the UV Master subpalette, to see what UVMaster will create by itself.

6. Click Flatten in the UV Master sub-palette to see the UV layout. Most likely you will have to adjust these but it's worth a try to see if UV Master got it right from the start.

7. Click Enable Control Painting and then click Attract. Paint the model where you would like the seam for the UVs to show up. The blue lines in Figure 7.25 show where the seams will be.

8. Click Protect, under the Enable Control Painting button, and paint the model red, as shown in Figure 7.25, wherever you do not want a seam to appear.

9. Click Unwrap to create the UVs for your model again. Then click Flatten, towards the bottom of the subpalette, to see how your UVs look. Figure 7.26 demonstrates our final UV Layout. If they look fine, then it's time to transfer them back to the mesh. If they do not look good, then make sure that you have the area correctly painted and repaint if necessary.

10. Click CopyUVs.

11. Select the original jacket from the SubTool sub-palette of our sculpted model and click PasteUVs in the UV Master sub-palette.

12. That completes our UV creation for the jacket. Repeat this for each of the SubTools that require UVs. Don't worry about the Platform, though, we'll look at how to work with it in the next section.

Figure 7.23
UV Master plugin

Figure 7.24
Polygroups button

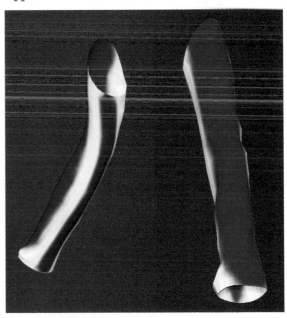

Figure 7.25
Control painting for jacket

Figure 7.26

Final Uvs

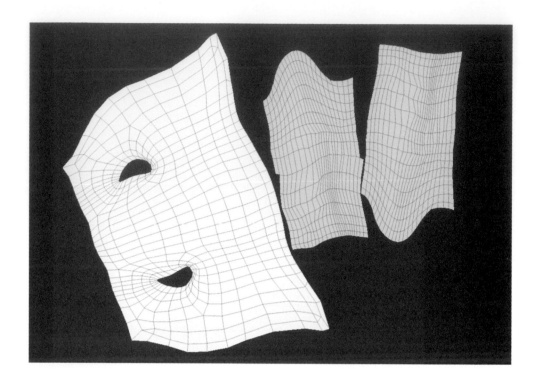

Project: UVs, Topology, and the Platform

The platform we created in Chapter 6 has issues with UV Master. These issues give us a chance to showcase a really cool feature of UV Master: Keep UVs. The problem with the platform is that there are too many holes in it. UV Master doesn't really know what to do with them. To fix the problem we have to use our PolyGroups from the original sculpt to help us create the UVs.

Figure 7.27

the Platform

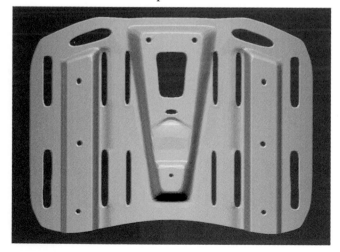

Follow the steps below to continue.

1. Select the Platform, seen in Figure 7.27 from the SubTool list.

2. Turn on PolyFrame and make sure you still have the groups from the front and back of the platform. In this case we are going to keep the back of the platform. It's entirely reasonable for you to delete the back for your in-game mesh.

3. Click Polygroups in the UV Master sub-palette and then click Unwrap.

Figure 7.28

Our UV Layout

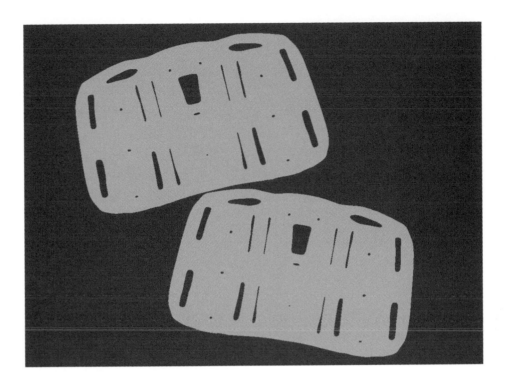

4. Click Morph UV in the UV Map sub-palette of the Tool palette and make sure that your UVs look like Figure 7.28.

5. Set SDiv, in the Geometry sub-palette, to the highest subdivision level.

6. Click New from Polypaint in the Texture sub-palette to create a texture map with all your Polypainting on it.

7. Click Keep UVs (Figure 7.29) in the Decimation Master sub-palette and then click Pre-process Current.

8. Set % of Decimation very low. Remarkable, a number as low as .1 still provides decent results and keeps your UVs.

9. Click Decimate Current.

10. When your model is at the resolution level you like click Export from the Tool palette and navigate to where you would like to save the low-resolution in-game mesh.

11. In the Texture sub-palette click Clone to send the texture to the Texture palette.

12. From the Texture palette click Export to save it alongside your low-resolution OBJ file.

Figure 7.29

Decimation Master interface

Figure 7.30

Decimated Platform

Figure 7.31

Multi Map Exporter palette

Figure 7.32

Displacement Map settings

Figure 7.33

Normal Map settings

Figure 7.34

Mesh Export settings

Project: Creating Maps

With our new topology and new UVs we are ready to generate our texture maps, normal maps, cavity maps, and bump maps.

1. Make sure you have MME loaded. If not, visit Pixologic's Download Center and install it before continuing.

2. Open the Multi Map Exporter subpalette in the Zplugins palette, shown in Figure 7.31. Click all of the maps so that we get everything all at once.

3. Click SubTools in the MME subpalette. It is located directly below the Create All Maps button.

4. Click Export Options to open its controls.

5. Click Displacement Maps and then click Adaptive, 3 Channel, and 16 bit Scale. Then click Get Scale and make a note of the number in the Scale slider. Figure 7.32 illustrates our settings.

6. Click the Normal Map button to open its controls. Then click Tangent and Adaptive. For your game engine you may need to also click SwitchRB or FlipG. For now, leave them at defaults. We'll switch or flip only if necessary. Figure 7.33 illustrates our settings.

7. We'll leave Ambient Occlusion and Cavity at their default settings for now.

8. Click Mesh Export to open its controls. Then click MRG to make sure that your model's vertices stay merged. Figure 7.34 illustrates our settings.

9. Finally, when all done with the settings click Create All Maps towards the top of the subpalette. Set a folder to store them in and click OK.

Creating the Specular Map

The last map we need to create, we can't create in ZBrush: it's the Specularity map. This is a very important map that really helps us create the illusion of reality.

Follow the steps below to create your specular map. Note, you'll likely have to tweak this after previewing the map in the next project, Viewing the Game Model.

1. In Photoshop, copy the Texture map into a new document. Then desaturate it entirely by pressing Ctrl+Shift+U.

2. Copy the cavity map into the new document and set its blending mode to Multiply.

3. Create a Levels or Curves adjustment layer and adjust its settings to clamp the light and dark values down and increase the contrast.

4. Save the document as both a .PSD file and a .TGA file. You want to make sure to save a .PSD file so you can alter the document later after previewing it in the game engine.

Figure 7.35 demonstrates our final spec map for the face along with the layer settings. Repeat this as necessary for the rest of the maps.

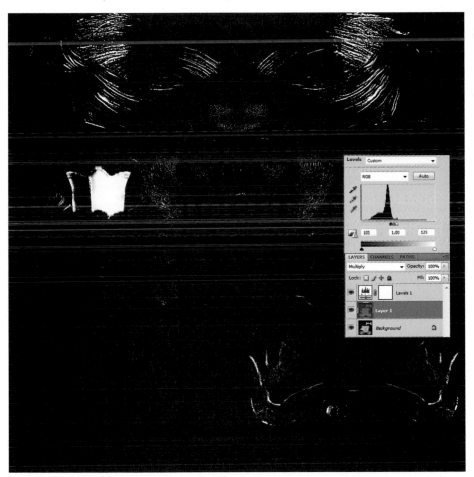

Figure 7.35

Specular map with layers and adjustments

Project: Setting Up Model in Maya

Figure 7.36

**Low Resolution
objects in Maya**

To see how our model is doing and where we'll need to redo the topology we want to preview the model with its normal map in a 3D application like Maya.

Figure 7.36

**Low Resolution
objects in Maya**

1. In Maya, click Import in the File menu and import each of the low resolution meshes, demonstrated in Figure 7.36, that ZBrush's MME exported.

2. Open Hypershade and create a new Blinn. In the Hypershade window create a Blinn and drag it to the jacket in the viewport.

3. Open the attribute editor by double-clicking the Blinn or press Ctrl+A.

4. Click the Bump Mapping node. Set the Use As text box to Tangent Space Normals as shown in Figure 7.37.

5. Choose File from the pop-up and then click the arrow next to Bump Value to go to the file node. Click the folder next to Image Name and navigate to the normal map for the jacket.

6. Click the checker next to the Color node. Choose File from the pop-up. Click the checker next to the Image Name folder and navigate to the color map.

7. Repeat step 6 for the specular map as well.

8. Press **6** on your keyboard and then click High Quality Rendering in the Renderer menu of the viewport. You should now see the normal map and texture map on the jacket.

9. Repeat steps 2 through 7 for the remaining parts of the model. Figure 7.38 demonstrates the model with all of the maps set up.

Figure 7.37

Bump Map node

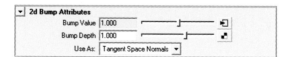

Figure 7.38
Model in Maya with all her maps

Assessing Your Topology

When you have the entire mesh in Maya with the normal maps you can plainly see the limitations of them; they only work within the interior of the model. They cannot create outside contours. Now we need to decide if we will "hard-code" the clothing folds into our mesh or not.

If we only need to reflow the topology a bit we can refer back to the Project: Topology section in chapter 3. Towards the end of that chapter there are about three or four steps where we import different topology into the lowest resolution and use the Morph brush to fix up areas.

If, though, we plan to hard code the topology then we need to talk for a moment about how to do that and how our topology might look. We'll look into that in the next section, Project: Topology and Clothing Folds.

Project: Topology-Optimized for Form

Topology that describes folds invariably has triangles and n-gons in it. Use it only when you need the absolute highest amount of optimization in your model as it causes problems both when you sculpt and when you use more advanced rigs.

Follow the steps below to re-topologize the jacket.

1. Select the jacket from the SubTool list and click Clone in the Tool palette.

2. Select the cloned jacket. Then set the color swatch to white and click Color→ Fill Object.

3. Select the Standard brush and set the color to black. Then start by defining the halfway points along the front and side of the arm as seen in Figure 7.39.

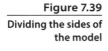

Figure 7.39

Dividing the sides of the model

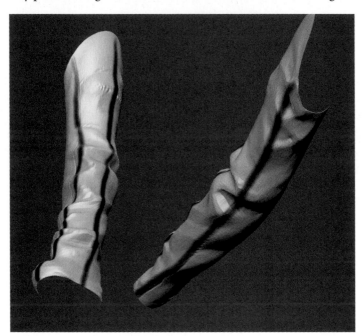

4. Next start to define the high points and the low points of the major wrinkles. You'll want to make sure that you define both the high points and the low points at the same time. Look for the blue lines in Figure 7.40 to see the main flow lines.

5. Use triangle-shaped quads to create the corner of the folds. Figure 7.40 illustrates these polygon faces in red.

6. In the back of the arm you can see where you can use triangles to describe the diamond shape of compression folds as shown in Figure 7.40 and highlighted in green.

7. When you have the major folds outline, it's time to integrate it with the upper part of the arm and to final topology. This step will take time and it does take patience to become profient with it.

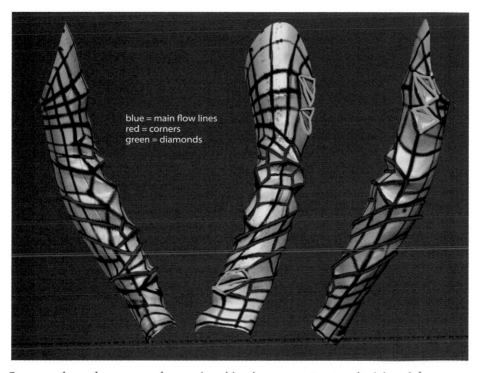

Figure 7.40

Topology Lines

blue = main flow lines
red = corners
green = diamonds

8. Once you have the arm topology painted its time to start re-topologizing. Select a ZSphere from the Tool palette.

9. In the rigging tab click Select Mesh and select the jacket with the topology lines painted on it.

10. Click Edit Topology in the Topology subpalette.

11. Make sure that Symmetry is on and start to create the topology for the arm jacket as shown in Figure 7.41. Use the PolyPainting as your guide.

12. When done, set Density to 1 in the Adaptive Skin subpalette and click Make Adaptive Mesh.

13. We've only created the arms, but that is all we really wanted to re-topologize. Export the arm jackets as OBJs. Make sure the MRG is on in the Export sub-palette.

14. In Maya or another 3D application import the re-topologized arm. Also, import the low resolution jacket that MME exported.

15. Select the jacket, right-click on it and choose faces. Delete the faces that correspond to the arms that we have retopologized.

16. Select both objects, the arms, and the jacket, and click Combine in the Mesh menu.

17. Click the Select Edge Loops tool from the Select menu. Press Shift to select multiple edge loops and select all the edge loops that are not needed for the arm or do not have corresponding edge loops in the arm of the jacket as demonstrated in Figure 7.42.

18. Click Delete Edge/Vertice in the Edit Mesh menu to remove them.

19. Select the Merge Vertice Tool in the Edit Mesh menu and go one-by-one around the arm to merge the vertices of the arm to the jacket, as shown in Figure 7.43.

20. Check the mesh to make sure that both arms attached correctly. You might need to conform the normal or delete extraneous edge loops. Sometimes, I have to delete some polygon faces and recreate them using Maya's Append to Polygon tool.

21. Select the jacket and click Export Selected in the File menu.

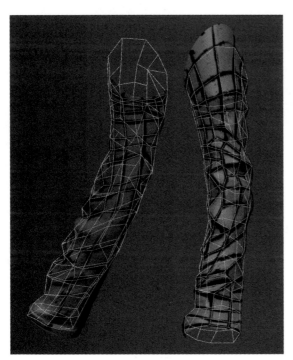

Figure 7.41
Final topology using ZSphere's Topology feature

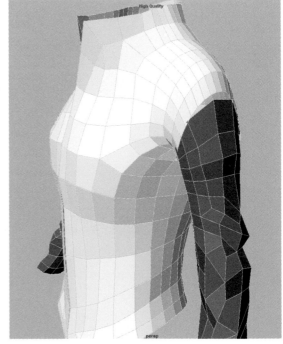

Figure 7.42
Deleting extra edge loops

Figure 7.43
Merging Vertices

Project: Importing Jacket's Reflowed Topology

I want to take a moment to look at a few tricks and tips for importing the jackets new topology into its original sculpt. Follow the steps below to get started.

1. In ZBrush, select a PolyMesh3D star and import your jacket's reflowed topology. It's important that you select the PolyMesh3Dtool, shown in Figure 7.44, to do this.

2. Click Divide once in the geometry sub-palette.

3. Go to the lowest resolution and click Export. Let's call this jacketReflowedSmoothed. OBJ.

4. Select the jacket SubTool in our in-game_SourceMesh and go to the lowest subdivision level.

5. Click Import and navigate to the jacketReflowedSmoothed.OBJ.

6. At the prompt, click Yes to reproject all of the higher frequency details.

7. Click Switch in the Morph Target sub-palette to return the mesh to its preprojected state.

8. Select the Morph brush and brush the projection back in. Watch for areas where the polygons go astray. Those are areas you'll have to resculpt. Figure 7.45 illustrates the results of our re-projection.

9. One downside to this is that it destroys your UVs. However, UV Master makes it very easy to create them. I recommend that you

Figure 7.44
Polymesh3D

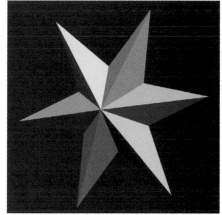

recreate the Polygroups along the arms of the jacket and then click Unwrap in the UV Master sub-palette. You can, however, just click Unwrap and let UV Master sort it all out for you.

10. Once your UVs are created then hide all of the other SubTools in the list. You can do this by clicking the eye icon of the jacket. If you already have objects hidden then you'll have to click it twice.

11. Make sure SubTools, the Multi Map Exporter, is orange. Then click Create All Maps to recreate the maps.

Figure 7.45

Final topology for jacket

Project: Getting Model into Marmoset

Once you have your model all set up in Maya it's time to export directly into a game engine. There are a lot of game engines out there but most of them take more time than we have in this section to get into.

Marmoset, however, is a game engine for us sculptors. It is designed for game artists who want to quickly see what their model will look like in a game engine.

I would like to thank Mark Dedecker, freelance character artists, for vetting this section and providing its framework. Note, you'll want to do this step only after getting the model into Maya as it does require the use of a Maya plugin.

So, to get into Marmoset follow the steps below.

1. First we have to install Marmoset. There is a 30 day trial on the DVD that comes with this book or you can download from http://www.8monkeylabs.com/. Double click the installer executable and follow the prompts.

2. We're not done with just that though. Next you have to install the Maya plugin. Make sure to read Marmoset's documentation to see the how and the where.

3. After you've restarted Maya, open the Maya scene file that you had when you finished from the Project: Setting Up Model In Maya section. However, if you don't have that scene file you can import all the OBJ files into a new scene file. Make sure, though, that you smooth the normals of all the objects before you continue. To smooth the normals, click Normals: Soften Edge. Your model should look like Figure 7.46, at this stage.

4. The final step before exporting is to rename the separate parts of your model so that they are easily identifiable in marmoset. Note, Marmoset calls these separate parts "chunks."

5. In the Plug-in Manager, shown in Figure 7.47, under Window: Settings/Preference, load stoogeExport and click Auto-load so it starts with Maya. If you do not have the plugin listed here, it has not been installed. Check the Marmoset documentation and reinstall the export plugin.

6. Select all of the parts that you want to export and then type "stooge" in the Mel script line shown in Figure 7.48. This will bring up Marmosets export window.

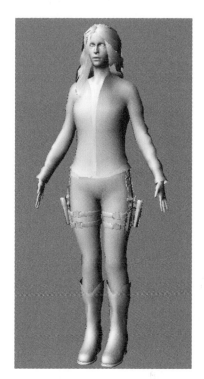

Figure 7.46
Smoothed Normals in Maya

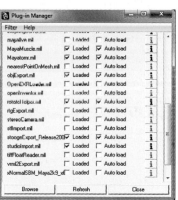

Figure 7.47
Plugin Manager

Figure 7.48
Maya's Mel window

7. Leave everything at its default unless you already know what you want and click Export. Choose a location to save the new .mesh file. It can take a bit of time to export so be patient and wait for it to finish.

8. Open Marmoset and click Open Mesh in the File menu. Navigate to the .mesh file you saved in step 7. In Marmoset your model should look like Figure 7.49.

Figure 7.49

Our model in marmoset

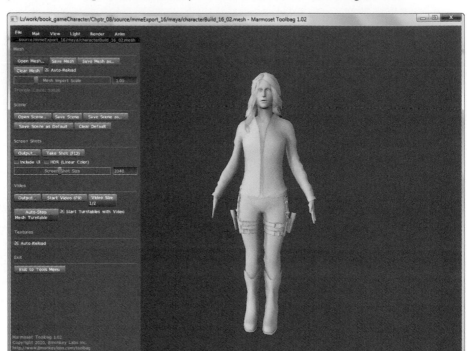

9. Navigation in Marmoset mirrors Maya. Rotate the model around and check for any flipped or reversed normals. If you see any, you'll have to go back to Maya and fix them.

Figure 7.50

Material List

10. Open Mat menu. On the right hand side there is a material list as shown in Figure 7.50. Only a default mat is created at this point.

Click New Mat, in the bottom right of the interface, to create a new material and choose the directory you want to save it in and save it as FaceMat.

11. Select the face chunk from the Chunks list, shown in Figure 7.51. Select the FaceMat material in the Material list. Then, click Apply Selected Material to assign it the new face material to the face.

12. Repeat steps 10 and 11 for each chunk until you have a separate material for each part, as shown in Figure 7.52. When you're done, click Save Mesh & Materials in the bottom right hand corner of the interface.

Figure 7.51

Chunks List

13. Select the FaceMat material from the Material list. On the left click Diffuse, seen in Figure 7.53, and navigate to where ZBrush exported your texture map. Keep in mind it will have a suffix of "-TM".

14. Click Normal /Height and navigate to the normal map for the face. Click Spec/Gloss and find the face's specular map we made ealier. You can experiment with the other maps but this covers our immediate needs.

15. To turn on specularity you need to click Use Specularity, shown in Figure 7.54, for each material that you want to have it. If you don't have a specular map you can fake it by assigning the color map into the Specular/ Gloss channel. Adjust Specular Intensity as I find its default settings a bit high sometimes.

16. Check your specularity by holding down the shift key and LMB and slide the mouse around to move the light.

17. Repeat steps 13 through 15 for each material in the Material list. Once your done make sure to click Save Mesh & Material. Figure 7.55 shows what our first pass on the materials should look like.

Figure 7.52

Material List with All Materials

Figure 7.53

Diffuse Settings

Figure 7.54

Specularity settings

Figure 7.55

Our model with materials setup

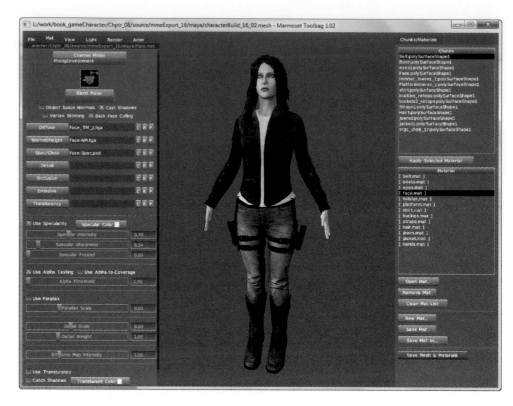

Figure 7.56

Channel Mode

18. Now, we want to change the type of material for the face and any other skin. In our case, we change the material for the hands and head. Select the FaceMat material again and click Channel Mode in the Mat menu. Select Skin Environment from the list as seen in Figure 7.56.

19. Increase Scattering to get more of the Subdermis Color to show through. Adjust Subdermis Depth to limit some of the effects of Scattering. Scatter Smoothing can be used to soften the lighting and shadows just as real world SSS does.

    My settings are as follows:

    Scattering = .7

    Subdermis Depth = .6

    Scatter Smoothing = .8

20. Select the Light menu. Click Sky Lighting Presets and select Sunlight (Figure 7.57). Adjust Sky Brightness to increase or decrease the light intensity.

Figure 7.57

Sky settings

Figure 7.58

Adding a rim light

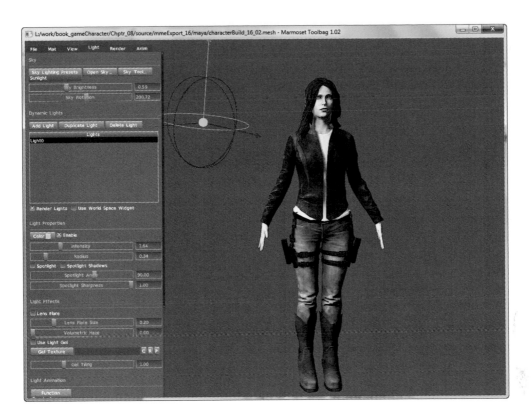

21. To add a rim light, click Add Light. Use the manipulator to position the light behind the model as shown in Figure 7.58.

22. Click the Color swatch to change the color from purple to white or whichever color you choose.

23. In the File menu click Save Scene. Then open the Mat menu and save the Materials. This is just a safety check. I'm sure you've been saving all along.

24. Now we are ready to render a turn table. Position your model in the view finder just as you want it for your turntable.

25. Open the View menu, shown in Figure 7.59. Set Mesh Turntable to 45.

Figure 7.59

Turntable settings

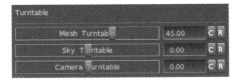

26. With the model still rotating, open the Render menu and click Ambient Occlusion (Figure 7.60).

Figure 7.60

Ambient Occlusion settings

27. In the File menu, while the model is still rotating, click the Output (Figure 7.61) and navigate to where you want this to be exported to.

Figure 7.61

Output settings

28. Click Video Size and choose whether you want your turntable's resolution to be half of the screen, a quarter of the screen, or full screen.

29. Click Auto-Stop and select Mesh Turntable from the list.

30. Press the SPACEBAR to clear the UI from the screen and press F9 on the keyboard to begin recording. A small, red video icon will flash on the bottom right of the screen as seen in Figure 7.62. It will continue to flash until it has completed one revolution. Once it's done, you can press "t" on the keyboard to pause the turntable.

Figure 7.62

Recording Icon

31. Navigate to where your file was saved and double click it to open it. Make sure you have all of the model rendered and it is positioned as you want it. There is more you can do but at this point you've rendered it out.

Summary

At this stage our model is in the game and we have a turntable. We are almost completely done with the model and you deserve a round of applause for your efforts so far. Keep your spirits up. In the next section we will look at creating a dynamic pose for our model. We'll also learn how to use ZBrush's new rendering and animation system.

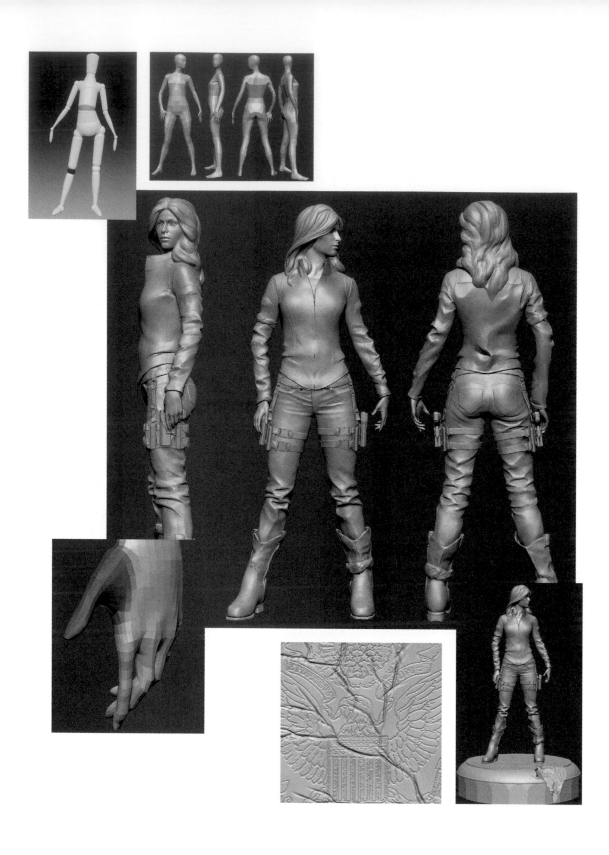

CHAPTER 8

Posing and Rendering in ZBrush

In this chapter you'll find a pose that works and explore ZBrush's new Best Preview Render. As always, you'll do each step with a sense of craftsmanship. You may find that this is one of the hardest stages to complete. You are, in effect, finishing your model and creating its presentation. Along the way you'll see things you missed. You'll notice things you don't like, and you'll feel a lot of pressure to make everything perfect. Don't let that stop you, though. There is always the next model.

Project: Finding the Pose with Mannequins

Simply put, it's just not easy to find a pose. I find it easier to iterate through and create a bunch of poses without judging them too much in the beginning. Then I look over the results to find that spark that I can build a dramatic pose around.

To do this, I use Mannequins. Mannequins are not entirely new to ZBrush. They use a feature that has been around for a long time, Mesh Insert. This time, though, Pixologic created some default mannequins to give you an extra push into creating exciting poses for your models.

Your first task is to iterate through a bunch of poses to try to find one that works. You'll use mannequins to help you figure out the pose.

1. Load 8HeadFemale_Ryan_Kingslien.zpr from the Mannequin folder. Your screen should resemble Figure 8.1.

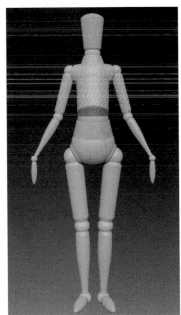

Figure 8.1
Load the mannequin.

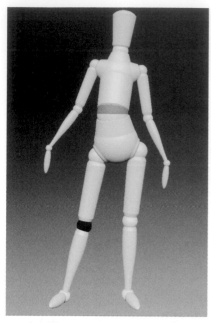

Figure 8.2

Mannequin with the
hip posed

2. Click Rotate on the shelf. Then click on the linking spheres between the hip and the root ZSphere. Let's start with just a bit of attitude. Drag the sphere to the right for a little contrapposto.

3. Do the same for the rib cage. Drag just slightly to the right.

4. Rotate the hip itself by clicking directly on the hip ZSphere and dragging left. Since the left leg will be weight-bearing, you want it to tip forward slightly while the other leg falls slightly behind it, as shown in Figure 8.2.

5. Rotate the chest by clicking directly on the chest ZSphere and dragging to the left. Since the chest is on the other side of the root ZSphere, it will move in the opposite direction.

6. Now rotate the legs to get the model standing on her own two feet. To rotate her leg, just click above the knee and drag left or right. In this case you are dragging her left leg toward the left. Do the same with her right leg.

7. Rotate the arms and head until your model resembles Figure 8.3.

8. When you're done, click Clone at the top of the Tool palette and alter the position of the new cloned mannequin as well. Repeat this step until you have at least 10 different poses.

9. When you are done will all the different poses, save the project by pressing Ctrl+S. Be sure to rename it.

Figure 8.3

Mannequin posed

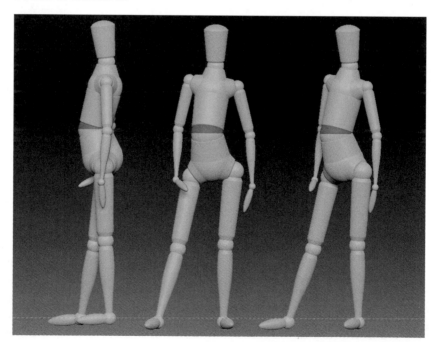

10. To choose a pose, you need to create a character sheet of all your poses. Simply zoom out on the model so it's small enough to fit all of your poses into it. Then position the first pose in the upper-left corner and press Shift+S on the keyboard to snapshot that pose to the canvas. Move the model slightly to the right and rotate it for a three-quarter view. Press Shift+S to snapshot this view as well.

11. Repeat step 10 for each pose that you have. Figure 8.4 demonstrates our results. Export your canvas by clicking Document: Export.

12. In an image editor like Photoshop, load your exported file. Review all the images and cross out the images that you do not like. Leave yourself with four images.

13. Copy each of the remaining four images into their own file and see if one really sings for you (Figure 8.5). If not, go back to the drawing board and make more poses. Then when you find a favorite, move on to the next step and start to rough out the pose. Please note, though, that this stage can and should take time. It's only a few lines of text but could easily consume half the day. Once you get the right pose, the hard work will all be worth it.

Figure 8.4
A canvas of poses

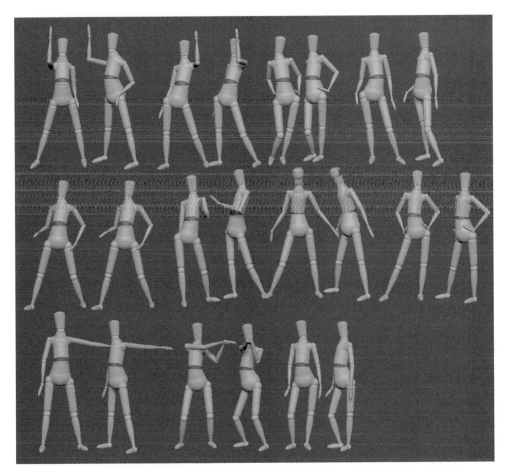

Figure 8.5

Short listed poses

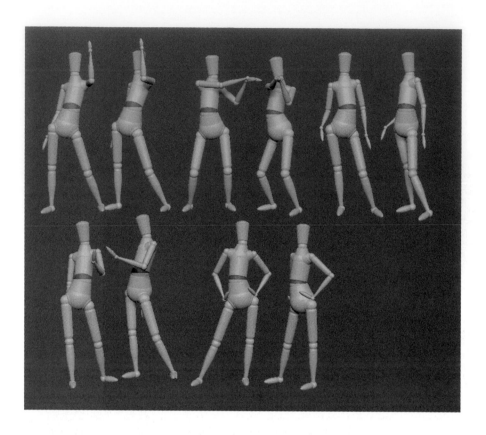

Project: Establishing the Pose for the Body

Once you have a pose that you are happy with, you need to re-create it using just the body. It's too early to get involved with all the other subtools, and there are some subtle issues that we want to be clear up, such as the tilt of the head.

1. Click Initialize in the `Preference` folder to clear all the tools and start over from scratch.

2. Load the ZTL file you created in Chapter 5, "Suiting up with Clothes."

3. Select the body subtool. If the head is hidden, then press and hold Ctrl+Shift and click on the canvas to show everything, as in Figure 8.6.

4. Click Clone in the top of the Tool palette and select the cloned mesh.

5. Lower your resolution level. You need just enough resolution to be able to retain the shape of the hips. I kept mine at SDiv Level 2, as shown in Figure 8.7.

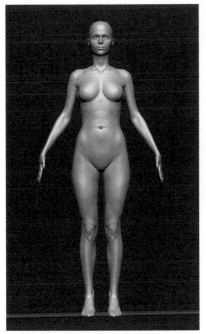

Figure 8.6
Our body sculpt

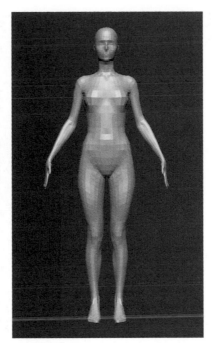

Figure 8.7
SDiv Level 2 of our body

6. Draw the action line outward from the pivot of the rotation, as shown in Figure 8.8. Then rotate the whole body while keeping an eye on the hip. Your goal here is to establish the overall orientation of the hip. You are rotating the whole body, though, because it helps you re-create the complex motion of the spine better, in this case.

7. Draw out a topological mask from the hip to the chest, as shown in Figure 8.9.

8. Draw out an action line from where you think the tenth rib would connect with the spine. The tenth rib is the fulcrum for the rotation of the rib cage. Then rotate the chest slightly to the right.

9. Mask out the character's left leg and draw out an action line from the great trochanter outward. Use this to rotate the leg outward (see Figure 8.10).

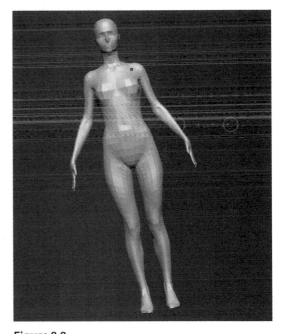

Figure 8.8
Rotating the hips

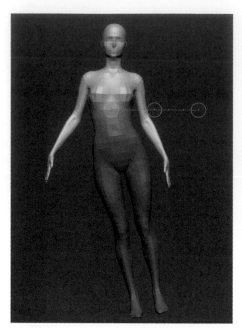

Figure 8.9
Rotating the chest

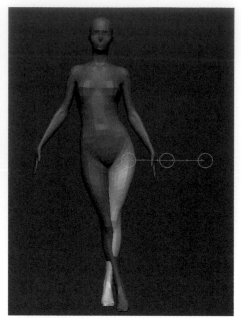

Figure 8.10
Rotating the leg

10. Repeat step 9 for the other leg. Rotate this outward as well, as shown in Figure 8.11.

11. Continue adjusting the rib, head, and upper arm of the model to get close to the final pose. Don't worry about the lower arm. We will look at that in the next step.

12. To rotate the lower arm, you will need to mask out half of it. To mask out the top half of the lower arm, press and hold Ctrl, then click a little bit below the elbow and drag downward to the wrist. Doing so usually creates the perfect mask. Then, draw an action line along the ulna, as shown in Figure 8.12.

    Once you have an action line drawn, you rotate the forearm by clicking and dragging on the center red dot in the action line. You may need to move the action line slightly inside of the body, but it will work fairly well regardless.

13. You can also use the procedure in step 12 to rotate the lower leg and the rib cage of the model. When you are done, your model should look like Figure 8.13.

14. Export an OBJ file and call it `poseRough.obj`. Then save your model as a ZTL for later use. I always save a ZTL file—it's just habit but a good one.

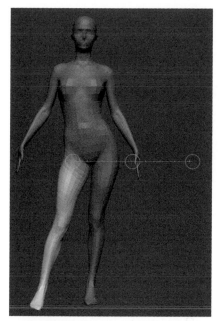

Figure 8.11
Rotating the other leg

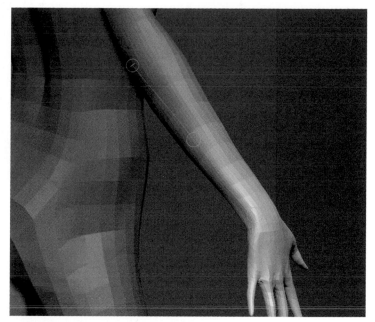

Figure 8.12
Rotating the arm

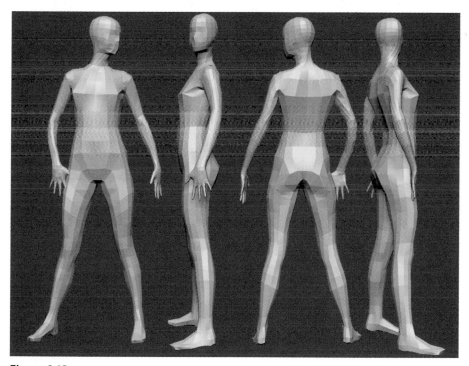

Figure 8.13
The final pose

Project: Posing Multiple Objects

Once you have the pose, it's time to re-create it again with the goal of posing all the other subtools. We will have to use Transpose Master, so make sure you have downloaded and installed it. You can find more information about it at Pixologic's Download Center.

Transpose Master creates a combined mesh that is composed of the lowest resolution of each of the subtools. Since all of the subtools are combined, we can move and adjust them in concert with each other.

Follow the steps below to begin.

1. If you have restarted ZBrush since the last project, select PolyMesh3D and import poseRough.OBJ.

2. Click Load Tool and load the final in-game_SourceMesh from Chapter 7, "Getting Into the Game." Note, because I am rendering in ZBrush, I am using the hair we sculpted in Chapter 5 instead of the in-game hair from Chapter 7. You could use either one.

3. Click Append and select the poseRough model. This will give you a reference to work from.

Figure 8.14
Transpose Master results

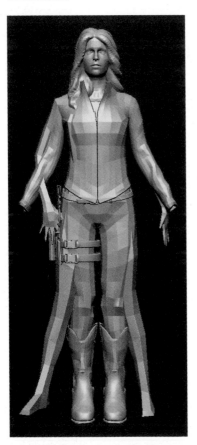

4. In the Transpose Master subpalette, click TPoseMesh. Doing so will create a new mesh that consists of the lowest resolution of each subtool, as shown in Figure 8.14.

5. The key to using Transpose Master is to use the Lasso Mask brush, as shown in Figure 8.15, not topological masking. You lasso an area that you want to pose, and then you invert the selection by pressing Ctrl and clicking in the canvas area. Finally, you press Ctrl and click on the mesh to smooth the mask.

6. Don't worry about fingers at this stage. You want to get as close as you can to the pose that you created earlier in the chapter. You'll have time to fine-tune it later.

7. Once the pose is completed, as shown in Figure 8.16, it's time to send it back to the original mesh. To do so, choose TPose → SubT.

8. Save the model. In the next section you will spend a bit of time finessing the model and pose.

Figure 8.15

Using a lasso to mask an area

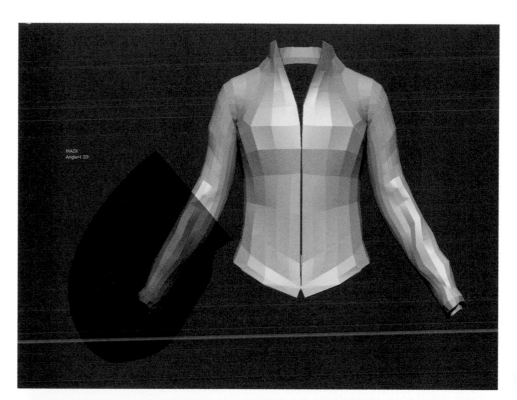

Figure 8.16

Posed TPose mesh

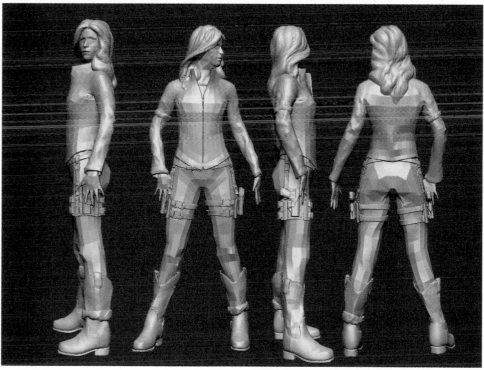

Project: Posing Fingers

Fingers can be painful to pose. When you feel frustrated, just remember that it's just the Valley of the Suck. You've been there before. You're going to be there again. It's our collective burden to trudge through the Valley of the Suck every now and then. The only thing we can do is to outlast it. Don't let it win.

1. Mask the ring finger at the knuckle. Drag an action line out along the top of the finger. Click the action line at the tip of the finger and rotate the ring finger toward the middle finger. Do the same with the pinky finger.

> You may have to click Move on the shelf and reposition the finger at the knuckle to get it to look right. I did.

When done, your model should look like Figure 8.17.

2. Pose each finger by dragging out a topological mask along the finger toward each knuckle. Sharpen the mask each time you do this by pressing Ctrl and clicking on the mesh. I usually sharpen the mask twice. Repeat for each digit. When done, your pinky should look something like Figure 8.18.

   When posing each finger, you'll find it useful to place the action line along the top of the finger, as shown in Figure 8.19. Doing so helps the finger rotate correctly. Also, as mentioned in the previous step, sharpen your mask each time you draw it.

3. To move the thumb, make a Mask Lasso selection around the thumb, as shown in Figure 8.20. Then invert that mask and draw out an action line that corresponds to metacarpal for the thumb.

4. When you are done posing your fingers with Transpose, the results might not look pretty. Figure 8.21 illustrates the result I had. This is par for the course and just requires a little resculpting, as shown in Figure 8.22. Pay special attention to the bony areas of the knuckles.

Figure 8.17
Moving fingers inward

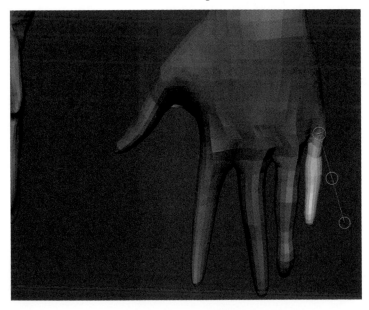

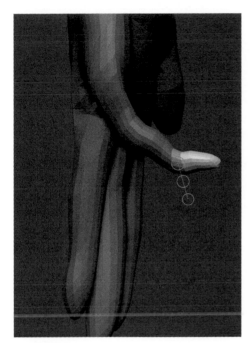

Figure 8.18
Bending a finger

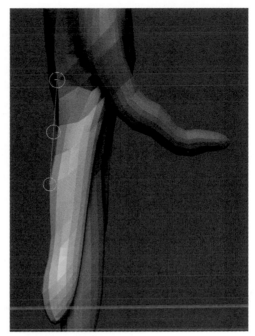

Figure 8.19
Placing the action line

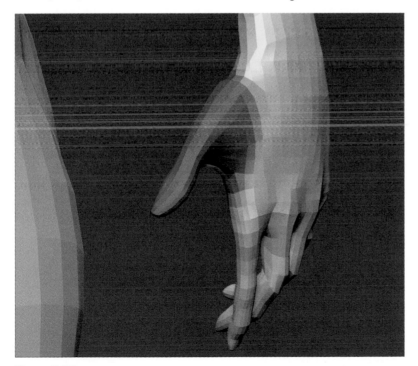

Figure 8.20
The mask for the thumb

Figure 8.21

Before resculpting

Figure 8.21

Before resculpting

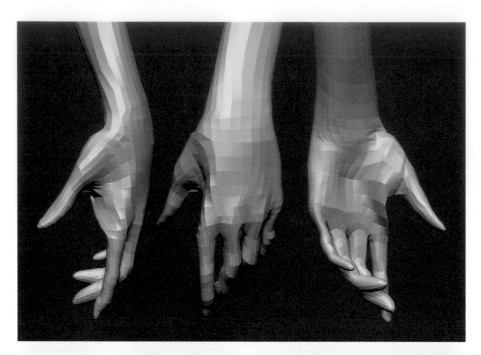

Figure 8.22

After resculpting

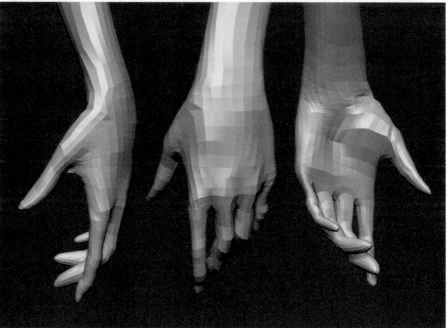

Final Sculpt

It is common, if not essential, to resculpt after posing. You must resculpt the form. Do not depend on Transpose to create the correct forms.

The tools I use the most are the Inflate brush to inflate areas that are compressed and the Clay brush to build out those areas. The Move brush is also an important tool, as you can press Alt and move the surface along its normal. Doing so lets you shrink wrap subtools to each other with relative ease.

Remember, this is the final pose before you start rendering, so spend some time here to get it right. It will really help sell the model in her Tpose if she looks great posed here. Our key, too, is to give the character life, not to obey the laws of anatomy. Push the form a little bit. Give her some attitude. Figure 8.23 illustrates our final pose.

Figure 8.23

Final model

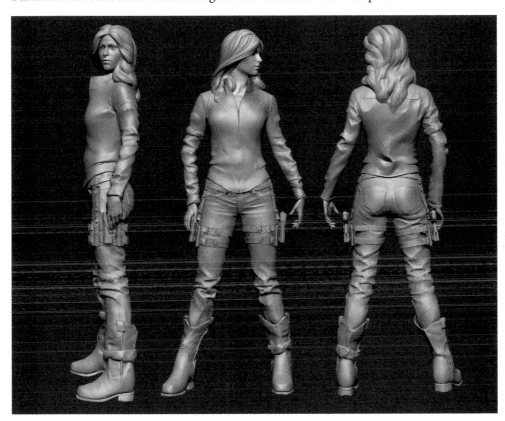

Project: Creating the Base

Creating a base for your model is not a complex task and it can be a lot of fun. You want something that will symbolize your character without taking too much of your attention. In our case, your character is a soldier type so you'll keep the base simple but engrave it with an American seal.

1. Load Shadowbox_128.ZTL from Lightbox.

2. Select the Mask Circle brush and draw out a circular mask from the top view. Do your best to keep it centered, as shown in Figure 8.24.

3. Select the Mask Rectangle brush and draw out a rectangular mask from the front view as seen in Figure 8.25.

4. Click ShadowBox in the SubTool subpalette to drop out of ShadowBox.

5. Select the ClipCenterCircle brush. Press and hold Ctrl+Shift and drag out a selection like Figure 8.26. This will clip everything outside of the circle and create very clean edges.

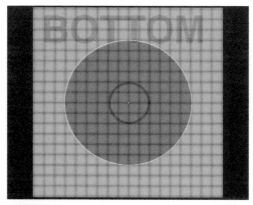

Figure 8.24
Masking with MaskCircle

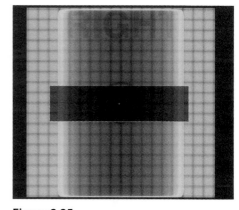

Figure 8.25
Masking with Mask Rectangle

Figure 8.26
Using ClipCircleCenter

6. Select the ClipCurve brush. Press and hold Ctrl+Shift and drag out a curve from left to right along the top of the base, as seen in Figure 8.27.

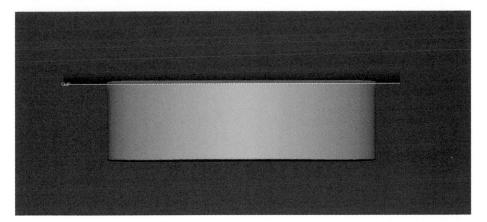

Figure 8.27

Using ClipCurve

7. Duplicate the subtool and use Transpose to lift it above the previous one; make it much thinner, as shown in Figure 8.28.

Figure 8.28

Duplicating and scaling the top part

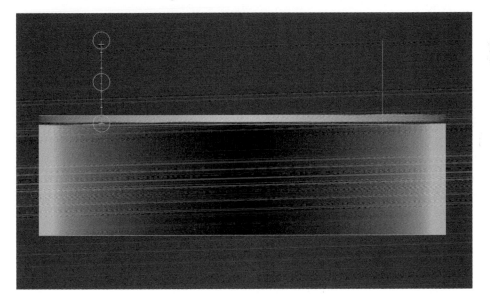

8. Divide this thinner part to at least 1 million polygons.

9. Load chapter7_americanSeal.jpg from the resource files of the DVD.

10. With the image selected, click Load To Spotlight in the Texture palette. Figure 8.29 demonstrates your progress at this point.

Figure 8.29

The American seal

11. Using Spotlight, position the image so it is in the middle of the thin part of the base as shown.

12. Press Z to turn off the controls and use the Standard brush to engrave the surface so that it resembles Figure 8.30. I brush over the surface lightly to get this effect.

13. Select the larger base in the SubTool subpalette.

14. Click Radial Symmetry in the Transform palette and set RadialCount to 24.

Figure 8.30

Sculpting the seal onto the mesh

15. Select the Trim Dynamic brush and round the upper edges of the base, as shown in Figure 8.31.

Figure 8.31

Using Radial Symmetry

16. Select Trim Front and brush directly in the center to create a faceted base for the lower portion here (see Figure 8.32).

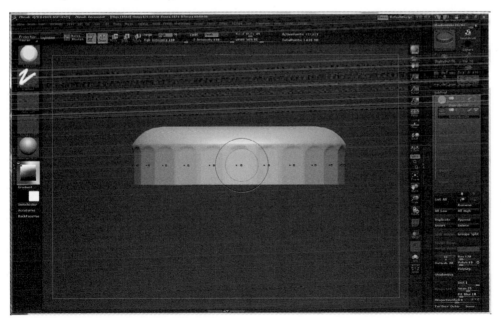

Figure 8.32

Using Trim Front

17. Select the Standard brush and set Draw Size to 10. Make sure Zadd is on. Then draw a thin line above the faceted bottom to help create a separation of the space, as shown in Figure 8.33.

Figure 8.33

Adding a line

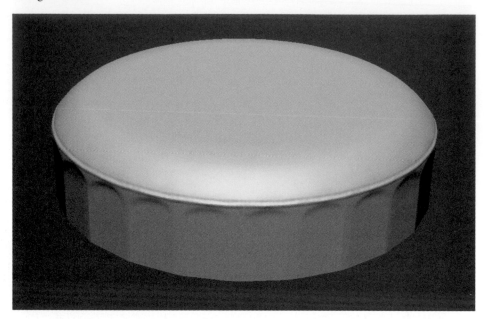

18. Adjust the thin upper layer to make sure that it rests on the lower layer and is correctly sized for your needs. Figure 8.34 illustrates the completed base.

Figure 8.34

Final base

Project: Damaging the Base

Once you have sculpted the base, it's time to add some life to it. Because the character is a soldier type, you'll want to create an impression of urban warfare. To achieve that goal, you can sculpt some thin cracks across the top and a large crack in the side of the base.

1. Select the thin top subtool. Position it so you are looking at the top of it.

2. Press Ctrl+Shift and select the ClipCurve brush.

3. Still holding Ctrl+Shift, drag out a triangular shape in one side of the model, as shown in Figure 8.35. Once you have started drawing out the curve, you can release the Shift button. Doing so will allow you more freedom when moving the curve around. Make sure to double-tap Alt every now and then to create a sharp edge.

Figure 8.35

Using ClipCurve to cut out a chunk

4. Select the Slash1 brush and set ZIntensity down to 15. At the very apex of the triangle you just cut out, you can begin to draw your cracks throughout the model, as shown in Figure 8.36.

5. Select the larger base subtool. Select the Clay brush and start to carve out the surface a bit.

6. While Trim Dynamic and Trim Adaptive help you create hard edges inside the crack, the most important brush may be the Planar Flatten brush with one modification. In the Stroke palette, turn on Stroke → Lazy Mouse → Backtrack → Line. Figure 8.37 shows the final base with damage.

7. Now it's time to put it all together: the pose model and the base. Chances are your base does not have a lot of polygons to it. Mine had about 2 million polygons.

Figure 8.36

Using Slash1 to cut lines

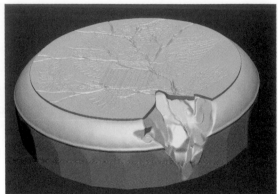

Figure 8.37

Sculpting the lower part of the base

Click Merge Visible in the SubTool subpalette to combine everything into one mesh. Then select your posed sculpt and simply append the base to it. You may need to move the model and adjust its scale. You can click Move on the shelf to reposition the model. Increase Size in the Deformation subpalette of the Tool palette to increase its size. Figure 8.38 shows the final pose with the base.

Figure 8.38

Final model with the base

Project: Shadows and Ambient Occlusion

Best Preview Render gives you two very important tools for rendering our models in ZBrush: ray-cast shadows and ambient occlusion.

Follow these steps to continue:

1. The first step to setting up your render is to turn off the polypainting so you can see the effects of the shadow without the distraction of texture. To do this, simply click the Polypaint icon until it's grayed out for each subtool.

2. Open the Document palette and make a note of the width of your document.

3. Click Shadows in the Render palette.

4. Open the Bpr Shadows subpalette in the Render palette, shown in Figure 8.39. Set Resolution to twice what your document's width was. For example, if you document was 1200 pixels wide, then set Resolution to 2400.

5. Select the MatCap_Gray material.

6. Click BPR or press Shift+R to begin rendering in Best Preview Render mode.

7. By default the shadows should be too overpowering. Let's get a look at what the shadows are doing. Select the Flat Color material and click BPR to render again.

8. Most likely you'll note that the shadows are also modeling some of the form, as shown on the left in Figure 8.40. This is most likely not something you want it to do.

9. Set Blur to 3 and VDepth to -5 and click BPR again. This time the shadows will behave more like shadows. You might need to adjust VDepth for your individual project, but this is a great starting point. The model on the right of Figure 8.40 illustrates the shadows.

Figure 8.39

Bpr Shadow subpalette

Figure 8.40

Shadow comparison

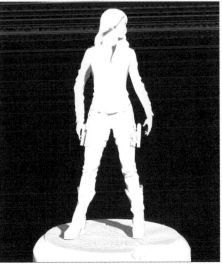

Figure 8.41

Render palette with just AO Selected

10. Turn off the shadows and then click AOcclusion so you can begin setting up Ambient Occlusion. Keep the Flat Color material active. Figure 8.41 illustrates what your Render palette should look like.

11. Click BPR or press Shift+R to begin rendering. AO takes longer to render. You may want to set your SPix to 1. This setting is directly below the BPR button.

12. Now adjust your settings in the Bpr AO subpalette, as shown in Figure 8.42, and click BPR to render. Figure 8.42 illustrates the AO render with the Flat Color material.

13. Turn Shadows back on and click BPR to see a render. For the best results, you want the render settings to help define form without defining it too much. You have to leave something for the material to do.

14. Set SPix to 3. Then select MatCap Gray from the Material palette and click BPR again. Figure 8.43 shows you what the final render looks like. I added some color to the S. Color swatch in the Shadow subpalette.

Figure 8.42

Rendered with AO

Figure 8.43

Rendered with Shadows, AO, and Material

Project: Using Render Passes

ZBrush can create render passes very easily. The advantages of a render pass is that you can do all of your compositing inside of an image editor like Photoshop and have more control.

Let's begin by following the steps below:.

1. Make sure that Shadow and AOcclusion are all enabled in the Render palette. If they aren't, then simply click the button to enable them (see Figure 8.44).

2. Set SPix to 3 at the top of the Render palette (see Figure 8.45). This setting will determine the quality of the render. The higher the value, the better the quality. However, a high setting will cause your image to take longer to render.

3. Click Create Maps to enable render passes. The advantage of render passes is that you can export them to Photoshop and create a layered composition.

4. Press Shift+R or click the BPR button to render the image.

5. Click each of the render passes and save them to your hard drive. Note that you have to click each image to export it.

6. Open Photoshop and load each of the render passes.

7. Copy and paste all of the render passes into the Diffuse pass. You will have to convert the mode of both the Shadow and AO pass from Multi-Channel to either Grayscale or RGB before you can paste them into the Diffuse pass.

8. Set the shadow pass's blending mode to Multiply. Set the AO pass to Multiply but lower the AO's opacity about 50%. Figure 8.46 demonstrates the layer setup in Photoshop.

9. Use the ZDepth pass for the lens blur filter. You have to select the entire ZDepth layer in your Photoshop document and copy it. In the Channels window, choose the New Channel button. Select the new channel and paste the ZDepth layer into it. Then choose the RGB channel to exit that mode.

Figure 8.44

Shadow and AOcclusion

Figure 8.45

Render passes

Figure 8.46

Photoshop Layer setup

10. In the Layers menu, choose Merge Visible.

11. In the Filters menu, choose Blur → Lens Blur.

12. Set Source to be the ZDepth channel you created in step 9. Adjust Blur Focal Distance and Radius, as shown in Figure 8.47, to get the effect you want. Click OK when you're done.

You can do more, and we simplified some steps here, but at this point you should have a basic gray render with some lens blur. That is a good thing. Figure 8.48 shows the result of the render.

Figure 8.47

Lens Blur filter

Figure 8.48

Rendered with Lens Blur

Project: Plastic Maquette Material

You've set up the new render features to give you some sharp shadows and make good use of ambient occlusion. Now you need to use a cooler material than MatCap Gray.

1. Select BasicMaterial from the Material palette.

2. Open the Modifiers subpalette (see Figure 8.49) in the Material palette and set Ambient to 0.

3. Open the Specular Curve and set it as shown in Figure 8.50. You want that curve to be very tight in the lower right-corner.

4. Set PhongBlinn Specular to .9. This will spread your specular highlight out a bit. Once you've done this, check your Specular setting and adjust it to get the highlight you want. In my case, I set it to 12.

5. In the light palette, seen in Figure 8.51, set Ambient to 0.

6. Double-click the third light to turn it on. This is your rim light. Its effects should be immediately noticeable. It's important to note that the color swatch has no effect with Best Preview Render so there's no need to adjust that.

7. Open the Intensity Curve for the third light and adjust it to look like Figure 8.52. It's important to get the rim light effect only along the rim. I also adjusted my Intensity to .6 for that light.

  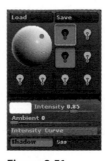 

Figure 8.49
Material palette

Figure 8.50
Specular curve

Figure 8.51
Light palette

Figure 8.52
Intensity curve

8. Click the first light in the palette to select it. Then click and drag on the large shader ball and adjust the position of the light to where you want it. In this case I adjusted it to come from the upper right.

   You may also want to adjust the position of the rim light once you know where the main light is coming from.

9. As a side note, you can also create a fill light by clicking the second light. Its default settings are already set up for a fill light. You only need to position it opposite the main light.

10. Click BPR to render the model (see Figure 8.53).

11. If you like the material you set up, then export it from the Material palette. Materials, though, often rely on light setups for much of their effect. It would be good to

just save the project. That way, you get all of your material and the light. You will, though, have to export the material if you wish to import it into a new scene.

12. To continue working on the material I recommend that you experiment with the following features:

- Anistropic Diffuse
- Anistropic Specularity
- Diffuse Curve
- Specular Curve

Also don't forget to adjust the light settings. It goes without saying that you can get most of your drama from adjusting the light positions and their intensity curves.

Figure 8.53

Rendered plastic maquette material

Project: Adding Some SSS

SSS does more for your render than simply add some subsurface scattering effects. It can go a long way toward adding another level of realism to your render. In fact, I use it more for the overall feel it gives my models than for its SSS.

1. With the Plastic Maquette material selected, click CopySH (Figure 8.54) in the Modifiers subpalette.

2. Select the Trishader material from the Material palette.

3. Then click PasteSH in the modifiers. This will paste all of the attributes from our Plastic Maquette material into this shader channel.

4. Click the circle next to S3 to disable the third shader channel. If you don't do this step, the lighting will be overpowered on your model. Figure 8.55 demonstrates what your shader channels should look like.

5. From the Material palette, select the FresnelOverlay material.

6. Select Trishader again and click S2 to make that the active shader channel. Then click PasteSH to paste into the material.

7. Open the ShaderMixer subpalette, shown in Figure 8.56, located directly above the modifiers, and set SSS to 60.

8. Also in the Shader Mixer, click BlendMode and set it to Overlay, as shown in Figure 8.57. It's important to have S2 selected for this step. These settings are different for each shader channel.

9. Click the Inner Blend color swatch and set it to an orange color.

10. Click the Outer Blend color swatch and set it to a reddish color. Figure 8.58 shows the settings used for the render coming up in a couple of steps.

11. Set the Outer Blend slider to .6.

12. In the Render palette, click SSS to enable subsurface scattering.

13. Click SSS Across SubTools to make sure that all of your subtools are treated equally.

14. Click BPR to render the model with SSS. If there are any problems, check that the last light in the Light palette has SSS enabled for it. Figure 8.59 illustrates the final render.

15. I have left my render at the default settings, but if you wish to decrease the effects of SSS you can do a couple of different things. You can increase Resolution in the Bpr SSS subpalette. You can also increase the S Exp setting in the Shader Mixer subpalette (Material palette).

Figure 8.54
Shader channels

Figure 8.55
S3 Shader channel disabled

Figure 8.56
Shader Mixer subpalette

Figure 8.57
Blending modes

Figure 8.58
Fresnel Overlay settings

Figure 8.59

SSS Render with close-up

If you wish to increase the effects of SSS, you can lower your S Exp factor to .5 or lower. Its default settings will work well to get you hooked. Other settings to adjust are the BlendMode for S2 and the Outer Blend slider.

Project: Timeline Turntable

Timeline is a new feature for ZBrush 4. It allows you to create turntables as well as animated schematic views of your model. Using ZBrush's Movie palette, you can even export movies as a MOV file, which you can edit in another application or just upload.

First you will enable the timeline along the top of the canvas:

1. Click Show in the Timeline subpalette of the Movie palette, shown in Figure 8.60.

Figure 8.60

The Movie palette

If you are new to the timeline, you'll want to be aware of where to find Help before you begin. Press Ctrl and hover over the Show button to see the pop-up help for almost all of the features regarding the timeline. You can always come back to this pop-up help if you forget how to delete a timeline marker.

2. Position the model so it is facing you and turn Perspective on.

3. Click in the timeline and drag the slider all the way to the left, as shown in Figure 8.61. This should place a marker at the very beginning of the timeline. If you make a mistake and want to delete the marker, just click on it and drag it off the timeline.

Figure 8.61

Camera Track on the Timeline

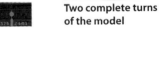

4. Rotate your model 90 degrees and place another marker about 10 units away from the beginning. The timeline has guides that help you space your markers, but this process does not lend itself to precision.

5. Rotate it another 90 degrees and click on the timeline to create another marker. Space it so that it is roughly equal distance to the others.

Figure 8.62

Turntable markers placed

6. Repeat steps 4 and 5 until the model is completely rotated around. Figure 8.62 illustrates the state of the timeline.

7. Press Shift and click underneath the timeline to play animation.

Project: XPose

XPose is a new feature in ZBrush 4 that automatically separates all of your subtools to give you an exploded view of your model. This can be very useful for helping to show off the parts of your model.

Begin by following the steps below:

1. Add another turn around to your timeline, as shown in Figure 8.63.

Figure 8.63

Two complete turns of the model

2. Click the center timeline marker where the model has just completed one turn.

3. Click Explode in the Timeline Tracks subpalette of the Movie palette, as shown in Figure 8.64.

4. Click on the timeline to set a keyframe.

5. Set XPose to 100 in the Transform palette, as shown in Figure 8.65.

Figure 8.64

Timeline Tracks subpalette

6. Click further along the timeline to store a keyframe of the model fully exploded.

7. Set XPose back to 0 and then click on the timeline further down the line to store another keyframe. Figure 8.66 illustrates the status of the XPose track.

Figure 8.65

XPose setting
and model

8. Press Shift and click underneath the timeline to preview the movie.

9. Adjust the XPose keyframes as needed. If you rotate your model note that it automatically switches back to the Camera track. You will have to click Explode in the Timeline Tracks subpalette to edit XPose's keyframes.

Figure 8.66

XPose markers on
the timeline

Project: Exporting a Movie

The settings for rendering your movie are contained in the Movie palette. Once you have a timeline created, it's time to set all the variables just the way you want them. To do so, follow these steps:

1. Dock the Movie palette, as shown in Figure 8.67, in the tray so we can more easily adjust the settings.

2. Decide if you want a movie that is the same size as the document, half the size, or one-quarter of the size. If you want the full size of the document, then choose Large in the Movie palette. If you want half the size, then choose Medium.

Figure 8.67

Movie palette

3. Press Ctrl+Shift and click under the timeline to play the whole animation.

4. Set FadeIn and FadeOut to 0 in the Title Image subpalette, as shown in Figure 8.68. This removes ZBrush's title image.

5. Choose Play Movie at the top of the Movie palette. Is it fast enough? Is it too slow?

6. To adjust the speed of playback, use the Duration setting in the Modifiers subpalette of the Movie palette, as shown in Figure 8.69. By default it is set to 30. To stretch the animation out longer, increase this number. To shorten the animation, lower this number.

7. Make sure that all of your Shadow settings, Material settings, and other Render settings are all correctly set. Then press Shift+R to use Best Preview Render.

8. Click Delete in the Movie palette to delete the movie you created previously.

9. Press Shift+R to do a Best Preview Render.

10. Press Ctrl+Shift and click underneath the timeline as shown in Figure 8.70. Since the playback was begun with BPR on, the timeline will render all the other frames with BPR. This will take longer—significantly longer.

11. Click Play Movie and make sure everything is good. If not, adjust your Timing, Material, or Render settings as needed and re-render.

> Remember, you must delete the movie before rendering a new one.

12. When you are ready to export the movie, click Export from the Movie palette. I always choose MPEG-4 Video and set the Quality to Best, as shown in Figure 8.71. I will then use QuickTime Pro to export out an H264 movie.

Figure 8.68
FadeIn and FadeOut settings

Figure 8.69
Duration setting

Figure 8.70
Where to click to render the timeline

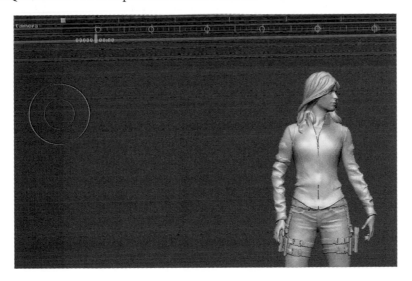

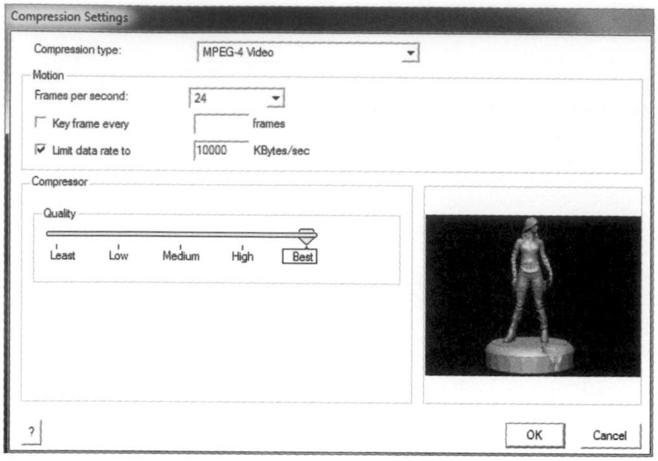

Figure 8.71

Compression settings

Summary

You might be asking yourself, "What can I do next to grow and get better?" The most important thing you can do is to continue to sculpt.

Sculpt as often as you can, and I don't mean just a head here and there. I mean, sculpt an entire character next week. You just finished this book so it's the perfect time to repeat it! Sculpt another character the following week. If you want to get better, then that is the first step.

The second step is to pay attention to the mental stuff going on. You're an athlete. Well, you're like an athlete. You might only run the 40-foot dash when the boss comes in and you're playing Xbox, but when you sit down to sculpt you are the star performer and your job is to produce so much awesomeness that the universe itself will sit up and clap.

You will not sculpt well every day, but you will sculpt well some days. As you get better you will have more good days, but you will still have bad days. Your mission, if you choose to accept it, is to sculpt every day regardless of how well it goes and then come back the next day and sculpt some more.

When you sculpt something you're proud of, send me a copy. I would love to see it.

About the Companion DVD

- ■ **What you'll find on the DVD**

- ■ **System requirements**

- ■ **Using the DVD**

- ■ **Troubleshooting**

This appendix summarizes the content you'll find on the DVD. If you need help with copying the items provided on the DVD, refer to the installation instructions in the "Using the DVD" section of this appendix.

What You'll Find on the DVD

The following sections are arranged by category and provide a summary of the content you'll find on the DVD. If you need help with installing the items provided on the DVD, refer to the installation instructions in the "Using the DVD" section of this appendix.

Chapter Files

In the Chapters directory you will find all the files for completing the tutorials and understanding the concepts in this book. Because this book is project based, you'll be expected to start at the beginning and work your way through the various projects. I've included some of the final models for you to review your progress and provide a guide for your expectations.

Workshop from ZBrushWorkshops

This DVD includes a video from ZBrushWorkshops. "Introduction to Sculpting" is designed for beginners who are just getting their hands on ZBrush and need to learn how to use the interface and get control over their sculpting.

Please also check the book's website at www.sybex.com/go/zsprealisticgame, where we'll post updates to this book should the need arise.

System Requirements

To complete the core exercises of this book, you need ZBrush version 4 or higher. Some sections also include material related to Photoshop and Maya and using these programs together with ZBrush. Hardware requirements are a PC or Mac running ZBrush with a gigabyte or more of RAM. The more RAM you have, the better results you can get with ZBrush.

> This DVD does not include the ZBrush software. You will need to have ZBrush 4 installed on your computer to complete the exercises in the book.

Make sure that your computer meets the minimum system requirements shown in the following list. If your computer doesn't match up to most of these requirements, you may have problems using the files on the companion DVD.

> Remember that a Mac license will only run on a Mac OS system and the Windows ZBrush license will only run on Windows or on the Windows partition of Boot Camp or Parallels.

- A PC running Microsoft Windows XP SP2, Windows Vista, or Windows 7. You can use ZBrush on an Intel-based Mac as well. If you are running Boot Camp or Parallels on your Mac with Windows, ZBrush will run as well on the Windows side.
  - CPU: Pentium D or newer (or equivalent such as AMD Athlon 64 X2 or newer) with optional multithreading or hyperthreading capabilities
  - RAM: 2048 MB (4096 MB for working with multimillion-polymeshes)
  - Monitor: 1280×1024 monitor resolution or higher (32 bits)
  - Minimum System Requirements: OS: Windows 2000/XP SP2 CPU: P4 or AMD Opteron or Athlon64 Processor (must have SSE2: Streaming SIMD Extensions 2)
  - RAM: 1024 MB (2048 MB recommended) Monitor: 1024×768 monitor resolution (32 bits)
- A Mac running Mac OSX 10.5 or newer
  - CPU: Intel Macintosh (must have SSE2: Streaming SIMD Extensions 2)
  - RAM: 1024 MB (2048 MB recommended for working with multimillion-polymeshes)
  - Monitor: 1024×768 monitor resolution set to Millions of Colors (recommended: 1280×1024 or higher) (You must have Streaming SIMD Extensions 2 [SSE2]).

- Your computer's processor should be a fast, Pentium 4 or newer (or equivalent such as AMD) with optional multithreading or hyperthreading capabilities
- 2048 MB of RAM (4096 MB for working with multimillion-polymeshes)
- Monitor: 1280×1024 monitor resolution or higher (32 bits)
- An Internet connection
- A DVD-ROM drive
- Apple QuickTime 7.0 or later (download from www.quicktime.com)

For the most up-to-date information, check www.pixologic.com/zbrush/system.

You should also have a Wacom tablet. While it is possible to use a mouse with ZBrush, a Wacom or other digital tablet will enable you to paint and sculpt naturally. Personally, I recommend a Wacom Cintiq. The 21-inch screen version moves the center of your sculpting action from your wrist to your elbow and shoulder. This creates a more natural sculpting environment and is the closest we get to interacting with real clay without losing the benefits of Undo.

Using the DVD

For best results, you'll want to copy the files from your DVD to your computer. To copy the items from the DVD to your hard drive, follow these steps:

1. Insert the DVD into your computer's DVD-ROM drive. The license agreement appears.

Windows users: The interface won't launch if Autorun is disabled. In that case, choose Start → Run (for Windows Vista, choose Start → All Programs → Accessories → Run). In the dialog box that appears, type *D*:\Start.exe. (Replace *D* with the proper letter if your DVD drive uses a different letter. If you don't know the letter, see how your DVD drive is listed under My Computer.) Click OK.

2. Read through the license agreement, and then click the Accept button if you want to use the DVD.

The DVD interface appears. The interface allows you to access the content with just one or two clicks. Alternately, you can access the files at the root directory of your hard drive.

Mac users: The DVD icon will appear on your desktop; double-click the icon to open the DVD, and then navigate to the files you want.

Troubleshooting

Wiley has attempted to provide programs that work on most computers with the minimum system requirements. Alas, your computer may differ, and some programs may not work properly for some reason.

The two likeliest problems are that you don't have enough memory (RAM) for the programs you want to use or that you have other programs running that are affecting the installation or running of a program. If you get an error message such as "Not enough memory" or "Setup cannot continue," try one or more of the following suggestions and then try using the software again:

Turn off any antivirus software running on your computer. Installation programs sometimes mimic virus activity and may make your computer incorrectly believe that it's being infected by a virus.

Close all running programs. The more programs you have running, the less memory is available to other programs. Installation programs typically update files and programs; so if you keep other programs running, installation may not work properly.

Add more RAM to your computer. This is, admittedly, a drastic and somewhat expensive step. However, adding more memory can really help the speed of your computer and allow more programs to run at the same time.

Customer Care

If you have trouble with the book's companion DVD, please call the Wiley Product Technical Support phone number at (800) 762-2974. Outside the United States, call +1 (317) 572-3994. You can also contact Wiley Product Technical Support at http://sybex.custhelp.com. John Wiley & Sons will provide technical support only for installation and other general quality control items. For technical support on the applications themselves, consult the program's vendor or author.

To place additional orders or to request information about other Wiley products, please call (877) 762-2974.

Index

Note to the reader: Throughout this index **boldfaced** page numbers indicate primary discussions of a topic. *Italicized* page numbers indicate illustrations.

A

abdominal muscles, *41*
action lines
    fingers, 256
    in head sculpting, *69*
    posing, 251–252
alar cartilage, in nose sculpting, 80, *81*
alar-facial junction. *See* nose, in human face sculpting
Alpha modifier, brushes, 11, 13
alphas
    for fabric wrinkles, 138, *138*, *152*
    for pore texturing, 96–98, *97*, *101*
    stitch brushes, *142*
    weapon building, 190
alveolar definition, 83
Ambient Occlusion, **267–270**, *268*
    Marmoset, *244*
    settings, *212*
    shadows, *269*
anatomy. *See also* filling in the anatomy, in body sculpting; painting in the anatomy, in body sculpting
    body sculpting considerations, 38
    painting in, **45–52**
Anatomy Tools, 2, *2*
Anatomy Tool's Male Anatomy Figure, 45
Apply to Mesh button, *98*
arms, body sculpting of, *23–26*, *26*
    filling in the anatomy, 56–57, *57–58*
    forearms, 49, *50*
    gesture, *29*
    hands, 42, *44*
    muscles, 48, *50–51*
    refinement, *29*
    splitting of, *30*
    volume and massing, 42, *44*

B

back vertices adjustment, 27
Backface Masking, 92
BackTrack
    modifier, brushes, 11
    Subpalette, *190*
Baker, Rick, 96–98, *97*, *101*
barrel, in weapon building, *182*
base coats, in painting in texture, **105–107**, *107*
    Color Picker, 106
    SkinShade4 material, 105–106, *106*
    Surface Noise settings, 106, *107*
base creation, **260–266**
    of American seal, *262*
    Clay brush, 265
    ClipCenterCircle brush, 260, *260*
    ClipCurve brush, *261*, *261*, 265, *265*
    damage, 265–266
    Deformation subpalette, 266
    Draw Size settings, 264
    finishing, *264*
    Mask Rectangle brush, 260, *260*
    MaskCircle brush, 260, *260*
    polygon count, 261
    Slash1 brush, 265, *266*
    Spotlight, 261–262
    Standard brush, 262, 264
    SubTool palette, 262
    Symmetry palette, 262, *263*
    Trim Adaptive brush, 265
    Trim Dynamic brush, 265
    Trim Front bush, *264*

blending
    crosshatching, *103*
    for eye cavities, 75
    rendering, 273, *273*
Blob brushes, 11
Blur slider, 111
body sculpting, **21–63**. *See also* bony landmarks,
    body sculpting; filling in the anatomy, in body
    sculpting; Maya, body sculpting in; painting
    in the anatomy, in body sculpting
    anatomical considerations for, 38
    anatomy painting, **45–52**
    bony landmarks, **34–38**
    combination of parts in, 167–169, *168–169*
    filling in the anatomy, **52–63**
    gesture, 21
    hair, **169–172**
    in Maya, **22–34**
    muscles, 38
    painting in the anatomy, **45–52**
    proportions, **21–22**
    volume and massing, **38–44**
bony landmarks, body sculpting, **34–38**
    acromion process, 35
    clavicle, *36–37*
    establishment of, *34*
    model division, 34
    patella, *38*
    pit of the neck, 34–35, *35*
    RGB sliders, 34
    spine of scapula, *37*
    Standard brush, 34
    for sternum, 35
    Transpose feature, 34, *35*, 169, *169*
boots, **159–167**
    cavity masking, 164, *165–166*
    Extract settings, 163, *163–164*
    finishing, *167*
    GoZ app, 159, *160*
    leather painting, *167*
    leather wrinkles, *162*
    Maya, 160

    mesh extraction, **159–162**, *161*
    in model topology, 218–220, *219–220*
    Pen A brush, 165
    photo references, 162
    RGB sliders, 166
    soles, *162*
    Standard brush, 166
    texturing, 162–166, *164–166*
    vamp masking, 163, *163*, *219–220*
breasts, body sculpting of, 62–63, *63*
brow area, 73–75, *73–75*, *91*
    glabella, 73–74
    landscape outlines, 73
brush algorithm, **11**
brush modifiers, **18**
brushes. *See also* Clay brush; H Polish brush;
    Move brush; Standard brush; stitch brushes;
    Trim Adaptive brush; Trim Dynamic brush
    algorithm, **11**
    Alpha modifier, 11, 13
    BackTrack modifier, 11
    Blob, 11
    clay, 4–5, *5*, 9, **11–13**
    ClipCircleCenter, 182
    Dam_Standard, 6, 10, **18**
    Depth Imbed modifier, 11
    dry brushing, 157, *157*
    Flatten, 9
    H Polish, **18**, 179
    Inflate, 104
    Lasso Mask, 254, *255*
    Mask Pen, 131
    Mask Rectangle, 145–146, 260, *260*
    MaskCircle, 260, *260*
    modifiers, **18**
    Morph, 92–93, *93*
    Move, 3, 4, 7, 9
    M_Polish, 150
    Pen A, 151, 165
    Planar, 11
    Polish, *9*, 9–10
    Samples modifier, 11, 13, **13–15**

Skin, 13
Slash1, 265, *266*
Smooth, 9
Smooth Subdiv, 104
Standard, 6, *7*
stitch, **142–144**
Stroke type modifier, 11, 13
Tablet Pressure modifier, 11, 13
Topological, 132, 143
Trim, *8*
Trim Adaptive, 7, 10, **15–17**
Trim Dynamic brush, 5–7, *6*, 10, **14**
Trim Front, *198*, *264*
types, in sculpting spectrum, 11
ZProject, 198, *198*
buckles, **202**, *209*
female component, *202*
male component, *203*
side views, *202*
straps, *208*
Buildup, 15
Bump Map node, *232*
Bump Value, 232
buttocks
Clay brush, 40
vertices adjustment, 27
buttons
Apply to Mesh, *98*
DelHidden, *217*
edit, *89*
Make Adaptive Skin, *89*
polygroups, *227*
Radius, 153
Unwrap, 118
Unwrap All, 227
ZAppLink, 114

C

Camera Track, *275*
Canderle, Damien, 6
canine eminence, 83
Carpeaux, Jean-Baptiste, 1–2

cavity masking
boots, 164, *165–166*
crosshatching, 102
jacket texturing, *141*
makeup, in texture painting, 111, *112*
chambers, in weapon building, *183*, 184
extraction, *185*
Transpose feature, *185*
Channel Mode, 242, *242*
character sheets, for posing, 249, *249*
chest, body sculpting of
breasts, 62–63, *63*
filling in the anatomy, 56, *56*
Chunks list, 239, *241*
clavicle, body sculpting of, *36–37*
filling in the anatomy, 53, *54*
Clay brush, **11–13**
algorithm, 11–13
base creation, 265
buttocks, 40
depth feature, 12–13
Draw Size feature, 12
eye cavities, 77
fabric wrinkles, 149
filling in the anatomy, 57, 60
fingers, 259
holsters, 195
human face sculpting, 4–5, *5*, 9, 11–13
mesh extraction, for boots, 161
volume and massing, 39–40
ClipCircleCenter brush, 182
base creation, 260, *260*
ClipCurve brush, 179
base creation, 261, *261*, 265, *265*
weapon building, 179, *180*
clones, 250
clothing, sculpting of. *See also* zippers
boots, **159–167**
combination of parts in, 167–169, *168–169*
jackets, **130–147**
jeans, **147–159**
Color node, 232

color palette, *105*, **105**
    saturation, 105
Color Picker, 106
Color Spray, 104, *104*
Color swatches, 243
color zones, in texture painting, *108–109*,
    108–109
columella junction, 81–82, *82*
compression areas, *135*
compression folds
    jackets, 130
    jeans, 149–152, *150–151*
    in model topology, 215
Compression settings, *278*
Constant Sample, 15
Cont Ori option, 16
crosshatching, **102–103**
    blending, *103*
    cavity masking, 102
    Standard brush, 102

D

Dacol, Cesar, 38
damage, to bases, 265–266
Dam_Standard brush, 6, 10, **18**
Decimation Master, *223*, **223**, *229*
    platform, *230*
Dedecker, Mark, 238
Deformation palette, 169, *192*
    base creation, 266
    holsters, *197, 200*
DelHidden button, *217*
deltoid muscles, 46, *47*, 55, *56*
Density settings, 235
Depth feature, **12–13**
    Depth Mask, 13, *13*
    Draw Size feature, 12
    effects, *12*
    functions, 12
    Skin brush, 13
    subpalette, *12*
    Z Intensity feature, 13

Depth Imbed modifier, brushes, 11
Depth Mask, 13, *13*
Diffuse pass, 269
Diffuse settings, *241*
Digital clay, 4–5
digital sculptors, 21
Displacement Map settings, *230*
Display Properties subpalette, *197*
Drag Rect stroke feature, 99
Draw Size feature, 4, 11–12
    base creation, 264
    Clay brush, 12
    human face sculpting, 4
    sculpting spectrum, 11
dry brushing, 157, *157*
Duration settings, *277*
DVD, as companion, 279–282

E

ears, in human face sculpting, *8*, *91*
Edge loops, *207*
edge loops, *90*, 236, *236*
edit buttons, *89*
Enable Control Painting, 227, *227*
exporting movies, **276–278**
    Compression settings, *278*
    Duration settings, *277*
    FadeIn settings, *277*
    FadeOut settings, *277*
    Movie palette, *276*
expressions, 65
extraction. *See also* mesh extraction, for boots;
    mesh extraction, for jackets; mesh extraction,
    for jeans
    of gun chamber, *185*
    holsters, *196, 198*
    settings, 163, *163–164*
    straps, *204*
extrusions
    fingers, 29, *31*
    mesh extraction, for boots, *160*, 160–162
    palms, *30*

straps, *205–206*
thumbs, 29, *31*
eye bags, 78, *90*
eye cavities, in human face sculpting, 4, *72*, **73–79**, *77, 79*
    blending, 75
    brow area, 73–75, *73–75*, *91*
    Clay brush, 77
    eye bags, 78, *90*
    eyeballs, *91*
    eyelids, 77
    fat in, 78
    maxilla, 75, *75*
    muscle zones, *76*, 76–78
    nasal planes, 75, *76*
    palpebral ligament, 77–78, *78*
    skull, 73
    supraorbital margins, 74
    Trim Adaptive, 77
    zygomatic bone, 74–75, *75*, 78
eyeballs, *91*
eyelids, 77
eyes, texture painting of, *112*, **112**
    photo references, 112

F

fabric wrinkles, **134–139**
    alphas, 138, *138*, *152*
    boots, leather, *162*
    Clay brush, 149
    compression areas, *135*
    compression folds, 149–152, *150–151*
    Gravity Strength feature, 149
    Inflate Balloon, *138–139*
    jeans, *149*, 149–152
    lines of action, 134–135, *135*
    Move brush, 152
    M_Polish brush, 150
    Pen A brush, 151
    PolyPaint conversion, to masks, 135–139, *136*
    sculpted, *139*
    spiral folds, *135*

Standard brush, 139, 149
supporting areas, 134, *135*
Trim Dynamic, 136, 149, 152
types, 134
UV Master, 135–136, *136–137*, 151
face sculpting. *See* human face, sculpting of
FaceMat, 241
FadeIn settings, *277*
FadeOut settings, *277*
feet, volume and massing for, *43*
filling in the anatomy, in body sculpting, **52–63**
    arms, 56–57, *57–58*
    breasts, 62–63, *63*
    chest, 56, *56*
    clavicle, 53, *54*
    Clay brush, 57, 60
    final blocking, 53
    finishing, *53*
    legs, 60–62, *60–62*
    muscles, 54, *55*, 56
    with PolyPaint, 54
    resolution adjustments, 53
    spine of scapula, 53, *54*
    Standard brush, 57, 60
    torso, 57, *57*, *59–60*
    Trim Dynamic, 57, 60
fingers, *256–258*
    action lines, 256
    Clay brush, 259
    extrusion of, 29, *31*
    Inflate brush, 259
    Lasso Mask brush, 256
    in model topology, 256
    Move brush, 259
    posing, 256–258, *256–258*
    Transpose Master, 256
finishing, **32–34**
    base creation, *264*
    boots, *167*
    head sculpting, *93*
    holsters, *201*
    makeup, in texture painting, *111*
    mouth sculpting, *87*

nose sculpting, *82*

posing fingers, 259, *259*

weapon building, *195*

Flatten brushes, 9

flattening the face, 70, *71*

forearms, 49, *50*

Free Transform's Warp, 114

Fresnel Overlay settings, *273*

G

Geometry subpalette, 218

holsters, 222

gesture, in body sculpting, 21

arms, 29

proportions, **23–26**

Goldman, Eliot, 45, 49–50, 52

GoZ app, 159, *160*, 161

GoZ interface, *204*

Gravity Strength feature, 149

Gray's Anatomy, 76

grips, in weapon building, 188–189, *188–190*, 191

gun magazine, in weapon building, *183*

guns. *See* weapons, building of

H

H Polish brush, **18**

holsters, 195

weapon building, 179

hair, sculpting of, **169–172**

curls, 224

individual strokes, 171, *171*

layering, 226

in model topology, **224**, *224–226*, **226**

Move Elastic, 226

polygon groups, *224–225*

resolution settings, 172

Split Hidden, 226, *226*

Tablet Pressure subpalette, *170*

ZSketch, 169–170, *171*

ZSpheres, 170, *170*, 172

handles, in weapon building, *181*

hands, body sculpting of, **29–31**

finger extrusion, 29, *31*

volume and massing, 42, *44*

ZSpheres, 29

hatch marks. *See* crosshatching

head, sculpting of, **65–94**. *See also* eye cavities, in human face sculpting; human face, sculpting of

action lines, *69*

color zones, in texture painting, *108–109*, **108–109**

combination of parts in, 167–169, *168–169*

ears, *8*, *91*

expressions, 65

eye cavities, 4, *72*, **73–79**, *77*, *79*

finishing, *93*

foundations of, **66–72**

masking, 67, *68–69*

Move brush, 67, *68*

neck, 72, *72*

nose, 72, *72*, **79–82**

painting in texture, by hand, *96*, **96–112**

with PolySphere, 66–67, *67*

proportions, 66, *66*

Reproject Higher Subdiv, 70, *70*

skull, 73

symmetry points, 67

texturing, **95–127**

topology creation, **87–93**

Trim Dynamic, 40

volume and massing for, 40, *40*

hip muscles, *41*

holsters, **195–209**, *213*, *221–222*

buckles, **202**, *202–203*

Clay brush, 195

Decimation Master, *223*, **223**

Deformation subpalette, *197*, *200*

depth creation for, *200*

Display Properties subpalette, *197*

extraction of, *196*, *198*

finishing, *201*

Geometry subpalette, 222

gun projections into, *198*

H Polish brush, 195
masking, *196, 198*
merged sides, *201*
in model topology, 221–222, *221–222*
Morph subpalette, 196, *197*
platform creation, 195–197, *196–197*
PolyPaint, *223*
sculpting, *199*
SourceMesh, 221, *221*
straps, **203–209**
SubTool palette, 221–222, *222*
Transpose feature, *197*, 221
with trigger, *199*
Tri-Glide fasteners, *203*
Trim Dynamic brush, 195
Trim Front brush, *198*
ZProject brush, 198, *198*
Human Anatomy for Artists (Goldman), 45, 49–50, 52, 63
human face, sculpting of, **3–10**. *See also* eye cavities, in human face sculpting
Clay brush, 4–5, *5*, 9, 11–13
color zones, in texture painting, *108–109*, **108–109**
Dam Standard brushes, 6, 10, **18**
digital clay, 4–5
Draw Size feature, 4, 11–12
ears, *8, 91*
eye cavities, 4, *72*, **73–79**, *77, 79*
Flatten brushes, *9*
flattening, 70, *71*
future applications, 18–19
geometry additions, 5
masks, *8*, 10, **18**
mouth, **82–87**
Move brush, 3, 4, 7, 9, 70
nose, 72, *72*, **79–82**
planes of, *71*
Polish brushes, *9*, 9–10
PolySphere, *3*, 3–4
proportions, 66, *66*
S curves, *4*

separation of planes, 7
Smooth brushes, 9
Standard brush, 6, *7*
Trim Adaptive, 7, 10, **15–17**
Trim brushes, *8*
Trim Dynamic, 5–7, *6*, 10, **14**, 70
Hypershade, 232

Inflate Balloon, *138–139*
Inflate brush, 104
fingers, 259
infraorbital triangle, 86, *86*
Intensity curve, *271*

jackets, **130–147**. *See also* fabric wrinkles; mesh extraction; stitch brushes
cavity masking, *141*
color interfaces, *141*
compression folds, 130
fabric wrinkles, **134–139**
final sculpt, *130*
hollowing, 133
mesh extraction, **130–134**
in model topology, *216–217*, 216–218, 237–238, *238*
opening of, *143*
Polymesh 3D, *237*
sculpting texture, *140*, **140–142**, *142*
seams, *144*
Shadowbox, **144–147**
Standard brush, 140
stitch brushes, **142–144**
jaw, in human face sculpting, 83
jeans, **147–159**. *See also* fabric wrinkles
base mesh, **147–149**, *148*
button removal, *218*
compression folds, 149–152, *150–151*
photo references, 148, *148*
pockets, *158*

resolution settings, 147

seams, 158

Spotlight, texturing with, **153**, *154–157*, **156–157**

stitching, 158, *159*

wrinkles, *149*, 149–152

K

knees, body sculpting of, 26

    volume and massing, 42, *43*

Kosta, Kris, 96–97, *97*, 100, *100*

L

Lasso Mask brush, 254, *255*

    fingers, 256

Layer masks, *123*

Layer palette, 97, *97*

leather boots. *See* boots

legs, body sculpting of, *24*

    filling in the anatomy, 60–62, *60–62*

    holster straps, *203*

    lower, *62*, 62

    muscles, 51–52, *52*

    volume and massing, 42, *42*

Lens Blur filter, *270*

life models, 1

Light palette, *271*

line work, in weapon building, **184**, **186–190**

    chambers, *183*, 184

    details as part of, 184

    grips, 188–189, *188–190*

    masks, *188*

    Move brush, 187, *187*

    Photoshop, *186*

    Save Selection dialog box, *186*

    stencils, 187, *187*

    Surface Noise settings, 188, *188*

    ZAppLink, 186, *186*

lips, 84, *84*

long pores, texturing of, 98, *99–101*, 100

M

Make Adaptive Skin buttons, *89*

makeup, in texture painting, **109–112**, *110–112*

    application of foundation, 109

    Blur slider, 111

    blush, 110

    cavity masking, 111, *112*

    evening of skin tone, 109–110, *110*

    eye liner, 110–111

    eye shadow, 110

    finishing, *111*

    pores, 111

    Standard brush, 111

Male Anatomy Figure, 52, 63

mapping

    Bump Map node, 232, *232*

    Displacement Map settings, *230*

    Mesh Export settings, 230, *230*

    in model topology, 87, *88*, *230–231*, **230–231**

    Multi Map Exporter palette, *230*, 238

    Normal Map settings, *230*

    pore texturing, **125–126**

    rendering, 269

    Specularity, 231, *231*

    UV, in texturing, **117–119**

    ZAppLink, in texturing, 120, *121*

Marmoset, **238–244**

    Ambient Occlusion settings, *244*

    Channel Mode, 242, *242*

    Chunks list, 239, *241*

    Color swatches, 243

    Diffuse settings, *241*

    documentation, 239

    FaceMat, 241

    installation, 239

    light addition, 242–243

    Material List, *240–242*

    modeling, *240*

    navigation, 240

    Open Mesh, 240

    Output settings, *244*

plugin manager, *239*
Recording Icons, *244*
Skin Environment, 242
Sky settings, 239
Specularity settings, *241*
Subdermis, 239
Turntable settings, 243, *243*
Mask Blur strength, *126*
Mask Pen brush, 131
Mask Rectangle brush, 145–146
   base creation, 260, *260*
MaskCircle, 178, *178*
MaskCircle brush, 260, *260*
masks, **18**
   cavity, 102, 111, *112*
   Depth Mask, 13, *13*
   head sculpting, 67, *68–69*
   holsters, *196*, 198
   human face sculpting, *8*, 10
   Layer, *123*
   in model topology, 218, *219*
   PolyPaint, fabric wrinkle conversion,
      135–139, *136*
   in posing, 251
   vamping, for boots, 163, *163*, *219–220*
   in weapon building, 177, *177*, *188*, 190
Master panels, in UV maps, *117*, 118, *119*
Material List, 240–242
Material palette, 268, *268*
   plastic maquette material, 271, *271*
maxilla, sculpting of, 75, *75*, 82–83, 85
Maya, body sculpting in, **22–34**. *See also*
  Marmoset
   arms, *23–26*, 26, 29, *29*
   for boots, 160
   Bump Map node, 232, *232*
   Bump Value, 232
   center of balance, *27*
   Color node, 232
   extrusions, 29, *30–31*
   gesture, **23–26**
   hands, **29–31**

Hypershade, 232
importing straps, *208*
legs, *24*
Marmoset, **238–244**
mirroring the model, **32–34**, *33*
model finishing, **32–34**, *33*
in model topology, 216, *232*, **232**
polygon modeling toolset, 22
proportions, **23–26**
reflection in, 24
resolution settings, *232*
restarting, 239
scaling in, 25
shoulders, 24, 26
side view, refining from, **26–29**, *28*
Smoothed Normals, *239*
splitting models, *32*
torso, *22–23*
volume and massing, 38–39
windows, 239, *239*
World Space, 25
Merge Vertex tool, *207*
Mesh Export settings, 230, *230*
mesh extraction, for boots, **159–162**, *161*
   Clay brush, 161
   extrusion, *160*, 160–162
   GoZ app, 159, *160*, 161
   Move brush, 161
   M_Polish brush, *161*
   sole flattening, *160*
   Trim Dynamic, 161
mesh extraction, for jackets, **130–134**
   area definition, *131*
   base creation, 130–133, *133*
   fabric panels, *134*
   functions, 130
   key features, *130*
   Mask Pen brush, 131
   model divisioning, 133
   palette, *130*
   polygons, 131
   resolution levels, 131

Standard brush, 133
SubTool palette, 132
Topological brush, 132
topology, 130
mesh extraction, for jeans, **147–149**, *148*
resolution levels, 147
mirroring, **32–34**, *33*
model topology. *See* topology, in model layouts
Morph brush, 92–93, *93*
in model topology, 233, 237
Morph Target subpalette, *92*, 92–93
holsters, 196, *197*
mouth, in human face sculpting, **82–87**
alveolar definition, 83
barrel, 83, *84*
canine eminence, 83
finishing, *87*
infraorbital triangle, 86, *86*
jaw, 83
lips, 84, *84*
lower, *83*
maxilla, 82–83, 85
muscles, 84, *84*
skeletal cutaway, *85*
zygomatic bone, 85–87, *86*
Move brush, 3, 4, 7, 9
fabric wrinkles, 152
face sculpting, 70
fingers, 259
head sculpting, 67, *68*
line work, in weapon building, 187, *187*
mesh extraction, for boots, 161
Move Elastic, 226
Movie palette, *274*, 274–275
exporting movies, *276*
M_Polish brush, 150
mesh extraction, for boots, 161
Multi Map Exporter palette, *230*, 238
muscles, body sculpting of, 38
abdominal, *41*
arms, 48, *50–51*
deltoid, 46, *47*
eye cavities, *76*, 76–78

filling in the anatomy, 54, *55*, 56
forearms, 49, *50*
hip, *41*
legs, 51–52, *52*
in mouth, 84, *84*
painting, 45–52, *45–52*
pectorals, 46, *46*
scapular, 46, *47–48*, 48
teeth, 83
torso, 48, *49*
tricep, 46, 48, *48*

N

neck, *72*
pore texturing, 101, *101*
volume and massing of, *39*
Normal Map settings, *230*
nose, in human face sculpting, 72, *72*, **79–82**
alar cartilage, 80, *81*
areas, *80*
color zones, in texture painting, *108–109*, **108–109**
columella junction, 81–82, *82*
elements, *81*
eye cavities and, 75, *76*
finishing, *82*
nostrils, 81
philtrum, 82
planes, *80*

O

OBJ file exports, 252
OilMask layer, 124, *124–125*
Once Ori option, 16–17, *17*
OnSurface, 15
Open Mesh, 240
Output settings, *244*

P

painting in texture, of head, *96*, **96–112**
base coats, **105–107**, *107*
color palette, *105*, **105**

Color Spray, 104, *104*

eyes, *112*, **112**

makeup, **109–112**, *110–112*

pores, **96–103**, *98–102*

wrinkles, *103–104*, **103–104**

zones, *108–109*, **108–109**

painting in the anatomy, in body sculpting, **45–52**

muscles, 45–52, *45–52*

terms, definitions of, 45

palpebral ligament, 77–78, *78*

patella, body sculpting of, *38*

pectoral muscles, 46, *46*

Pen A brush, 151, 165

philtrum, 82

photo references, **112–116**, *113*

boots, 162

eyes, in texture painting, 112

jeans, 148, *148*

wrinkle texturing, *126*

Photoshop

line work, in weapon building, *186*

posing, 249

render passes, *269*

ZAppLink texturing, 115–116, *115–116*, 121

Picker Palette, 16–18

Cont Ori option, 16

Once Ori option, 16–17, *17*

Select Orientation, 16–17, *17*

pins, in weapon building, *194*

pit of the neck, 34–35, *35*

Pixologic, 247

Download Center, 254

Planar brushes, 11

planes, in sculpting, 1–2, *1–2*

facial area, *71*

life models, 1

nose, *80*

organization, 2

Trim Dynamic, 5–7, *6*, 10, **14**

plastic maquette material, 270–272, *272*

Intensity curve, *271*

Light palette, *271*

light settings, 272

Material palette, 271, *271*

Specularity curve, *271*

pockets, on jeans, 158

Polish brushes, 9, 9–10

PolyCube, 192, *192*

polygon modeling, 22

hair groups, *224–225*

holster straps, *205*

removal of, in topology, **216–218**

topology, 87

polygons

base creation, 261

mesh extraction, for jackets, 131

in model topology, **216–218**

straps, *205*

in texturing pores, 97

polygroups, 217, *218*, 238

SubTool palette, 220

UV Master panels, *227*

PolyMesh 3D

jackets, *237*

posing, 254

PolyPaint. *See also* painting in texture, of head; painting in the anatomy, in body sculpting

fabric wrinkles, *135–139*, *136*

filling in the anatomy, 54

holsters, *223*

in model topology, 217, **223**

shadows, *267*

subpalettes, *137*

UV Master panels, 229

ZAppLink, 122

PolySphere, *3*, 3–4

for head sculpting, 66–67, *67*

pores, in texturing, **96–103**, *98–102*

alphas for, 96–98, *97*, *101*

Apply to Mesh button, *98*

crosshatching, **102–103**

Drag Rect stroke feature, 99

intensity set, *98*

Layer palette, 97, *97*

long, 98, *99–101*, 100

makeup, 111

mapping, **125–126**

neck, 101, *101*

polygon count, 97

pore-base layers, 97, *97*

Standard brush, 99

stretching, 100

Surface Noise settings, 97, *97–98*

variations, 98–101, *101*

Zadd/Zsub feature, 98

zones, *99*

posing, *247–248*, **247–259**

action lines, 251–252

body rotation, 248, *251–253*, 252

character sheets, 249, *249*

clones, 250

copying images, 249

establishment, 250–254

fingers, 256–258, *256–258*

finishing, 259, *259*

Lasso Mask brush, 254, *255*

loading the mannequin, *247*

multiple objects, 254–259

OBJ file exports, 252

Photoshop, 249

Pixologic, 247

PolyMesh 3D, 254

resolution settings, 250

shortlisted, *249*

topological mask, 251

Transpose Master, 254, *254–255*

ZSphere, 248

Preserve Edge, 15, **18**

proportions, in body sculpting, **21–26**

charts, 21, *22*

gesture, **23–26**

for head, 66, *66*

Radius button, 153

receiver, in weapon building, *177*, 179

Recording Icons, *244*

render passes, 268–269, *269*

Diffuse, 269

Lens Blur filter, *270*

Photoshop, *269*

rendering, **267–274**

Ambient Occlusion, **267–270**

blending, 273, *273*

maps, 269

Material palette, 268, *268*

palette, *268*

plastic maquette material, 270–272, *272*

shadows, **267–270**

SSS, **273–274**

Timeline, *277*

Reproject Higher Subdiv, 70, *70*

topology, *92*

resolution settings

filling in the anatomy, 53

hair, sculpting of, 172

in Maya, *232*

mesh extraction, for jackets, 131

mesh extraction, for jeans, 147, *148*

in model topology, 215

posing, 250

Shadowbox, 144–145

RGB sliders

bony landmarks, 34

boot texturing, 166

in model topology, 219

rib cage, volume for, *41*

Rigging subpalette, *88*

S curves, *4*

Sample Radius, 15

Samples modifier, brushes, 11, **13–15**

area for, *14*

Sample Radius, 15

subpalette, *14*

scapular muscles, 46, *47–48*, 48

scattering, subdermis depth, scatter smoothing
(SSS), *273*, **273–274**

close-ups, *274*

R

S

sculpting, **1–19**. *See also* body sculpting;
    clothing, sculpting of; hair, sculpting of; Maya,
    body sculpting in
      Anatomy Tools, *2*
      base creation, **260–266**
      human faces, **3–10**
      jackets, with texture, *140*, **140–142**, *142*
      planes, 1–2
      posing, *247–248*, **247–259**
      spectrum, *10*, **10–11**
      weapon forms, 179–183, *180–183*
sculpting spectrum, *10*, **10–11**
    brush types, 11
    Draw Size feature, 11
    Z Intensity feature, 11
    Zadd/Zsub feature, 11, 13
seams
    on jackets, *144*
    on jeans, 158
Select Orientation, 16–17, *17*
shader channels, *273*
Shader Mixer subpalette, *273*
Shadowbox, **144–147**
    duplications with, 176–177
    loading, 144
    painting images into, *176*
    resolution settings, 144–145
    smoothness setting, 145
    tools, *145*
    weapon building, 175–179, *176*
    zipper's slider body, 145–147, *145–147*
shadows, **267–270**
    Ambient Occlusion, *269*
    comparisons, *267*
    Material palette, 268, *268*
    PolyPaint, 267
    subpalette, 267, *267*
shortlisted posing, *249*
shoulders, body sculpting of, 24, 26
side views
    buckles, *202*
    knees, 26
    refining body sculpting from, **26–29**, *28*

vertices adjustment, 27
    weapon building, 176, *193*
Skin brush, 13
Skin Environment, 242
SkinShade4 material, 105–106, *106*
skull, sculpting of, 73
Slash1 brush, 265, *266*
slider body, in zippers, 145–147, *145–147*
slides, in weapon building, *180*, *191–193*, 191–194
Smooth brush, 9
    volume and massing, 39
Smooth Subdiv brush, 104
Smoothed Normals, *239*
SourceMesh, 221, *221*
Specularity curve, *210*
    plastic maquette material, *271*
Specularity map, 231, *231*
    Marmoset, *241*
spine of scapula, body sculpting of, *37*
    filling in the anatomy, 53, *54*
Split Hidden, 226, *226*
Spotlight, texturing with, **153, 156–157**
    base creation, 261–262
    Controller, *154*
    dry brushing, 157, *157*
    painting with, *155*
    placements, *156*
    positioning references, *154*
    Radius button, 153
    spot-fixed areas, *156*
    subpalette masking, *157*
    Symmetry palette, 156
    weapons, 176
SSS. *See* scattering, subdermis depth, scatter
    smoothing
Stabilize Direction, 15
Stabilize Orientation, 15
stairstepping, *126*
Standard brush, 6, *7*. *See also* Dam_Standard
    brush
    base creation, 262, 264
    bony landmarks, body sculpting for, 34
    boots, 166

crosshatching, 102

fabric wrinkles, 139, 149

filling in the anatomy, 57, 60

jacket texturing, 140

makeup in texture painting, 111

mesh extraction, for jackets, 133

in model topology, 234

pore texturing, 99

volume and massing, 39

stencils, 184, *184*, 187, *187*, 190

sternum, body sculpting of, 35, *37*

stitch brushes, **142–144**

    alphas, *142*

    straight, 142

    Stroke settings, *143*

    Topological, 143

    zipper pockets, 142

stitching, on jeans, 158, *159*

straight stitches, 142

straps, **203–209**

    buckles, *208*

    duplications, 206

    Edge loops, *207*

    extraction, *204*

    extrusion, *205–206*, 206

    GoZ interface, *204*

    on hips, *209*

    leg shapes, *203*

    Maya, importing into, *208*

    Merge Vertex tool, *207*

    platform, *208*

    polygons, *205*

    scaling, *204*

stretching pores, in texturing, 100

Stroke settings, *143*

Stroke type modifier, brushes, 11, 13

Subdermis, 239

SubTool palette, 132

    base creation, 262

    holsters, 221–222

    lists, *222*

    in model topology, 219–220

polygroups, 220

UV Master panels, 227

weapon building, 179

Surface Noise settings

    for base coats, in texture painting, 106, *107*

    pores, in texturing, 97, *97–98*

    in weapon building, 188, *188*

Symmetry palette

    base creation, 262, *263*

    in model topology, 89, 235

    points, in head sculpting, 67

    Spotlight texturing, 156

T

Tablet Pressure

    modifier, 11, 13

    subpalette, *170*

teeth, 83

Texture subpalette, 229

texturing, in sculpting. *See also* makeup, in texture painting; painting in texture, of head; pores, in texturing; wrinkles, in texturing; ZAppLink, in texturing

    boots, 162–166, *164–166*

    of head, **95–127**

    jackets, *140*, **140–142**, *142*

    mapping, **125–126**

    painting by hand, **96–112**

    photo references for, **112–116**, *113*, *126*

    with Spotlight, for jeans, **153**, *154–157*, **156–157**

    stairstepping, *126*

    texture maps, **125–126**

    weapon building, **210–212**

    ZAppLink, **113–125**

thumbs, extrusion of, 29, *31*

Timeline, **274–275**

    Camera Track, *275*

    Movie palette, *274*, 274–275

    rendering, *277*

    Tracks subpalette, 275, *275*

Turntable markers, *275*
 Xpose markers, *276*
Topological brush, 132
 stitch brushes, 143
topology, in model layouts, **87–93, 215–245**. *See also* Marmoset
 access, **233–236**
 adjustments, 221
 Backface Masking, 92
 boots, 218–220, *219–220*
 compression folds, 215
 Decimation Master, *223*, **223**, *229*
 DelHidden button, *217*
 Density settings, 235
 Displacement Map settings, *230*
 edge loops, *90*, 236, *236*
 face deletion, 236
 fingers, 256
 Geometry subpalette, 218
 hair, **224**, *224–226*, **226**
 hard-coding, 233
 holsters, 221–222, *221–222*
 importing, *92*
 jackets, *216–217*, 216–218, 237–238, *238*
 lines, *235*
 low resolution, 215
 Make Adaptive Skin buttons, *89*
 maps, 87, *88*, *230–231*, **230–231**
 Marmoset, **238–244**
 mask inversion, 218, *219*
 in Maya, 216, *232*, **232**
 Mesh Export settings, 230, *230*
 mesh extraction, 130
 model division, *234*
 Morph brush, 233, 237
 Morph Target subpalette, *92*, 92–93
 Move Elastic, 226
 Multi Map Exporter palette, *230*, 238
 new, *89*
 Normal Map settings, *230*
 optimization, 234–236
 parts combination, 218–220

platforms, *228*, **228–230**
 polygons, 87, **216–218**
 polygroups, 217, *218*, 238
 PolyMesh 3D, *237*
 PolyPaint, 217, **223**
 posing, 251
 Reproject Higher Subdiv, *92*
 RGB sliders, 219
 Rigging subpalette, *88*
 as rigging system, 215
 SourceMesh, 221, *221*
 Specularity map, 231, *231*
 Split Hidden, 226, *226*
 Standard brush, 234
 subdivision levels, 217
 SubTool palette, 219–220, *222*
 Symmetry palette, 89, 235
 Transpose feature, 221
 UV Master, *227–228*, **227–229**
 vamp masking, *163*, 163, *219–220*
 vertices merging, *237*
 wrinkles, 215
 ZSphere, 235, *236*
torso, body sculpting for, *22*
 filling in the anatomy, 57, *57*, *59–60*
 muscles, 48, *49*
Tracks subpalette, 275, *275*
Transpose feature
 body sculpting, 34, *35*, 169, *169*
 fingers, 256
 holsters, *197*, 221
 posing, 254, *254–255*
 weapon building, *181*, *185*, *189*
Transpose Master. *See* Transpose feature
tricep muscles, 46, 48, *48*
trigger, in weapon building, 178, 183
 holsters with, *199*
Tri-Glide fasteners, *203*
Trim Adaptive brush, 7, 10, **15–17**
 base creation, 265
 eye cavities, 77
 functions, 15
 Picker Palette, *16*, 16–18

Trim Dynamic brush, 5–7, *6*, 10, **14**
    base creation, 265
    fabric wrinkles, 136, 149, 152
    face sculpting, 70
    filling in the anatomy, 57, 60
    head volume, 40
    holsters, 195
    mesh extraction, for boots, 161
    wrinkle texturing, 104
Trim Front brush, *198*, *264*
Turntable settings, 243, *243*

U

Unwrap All button, 227
Unwrap button, 118
UV maps, **117–119**
    border painting, *118*
    models, *119*
    polygroups, *118*
    2D texturing, 117
    Unwrap button, 118
UV Master panels, *117*, 118, *119*
    Enable Control Painting, 227, *227*
    fabric wrinkles, 135–136, *136–137*, 151
    in model topology, *227–228*, **227–229**
    polygroups button, *227*
    PolyPaint, 229
    SubTool subpalette, 227
    Texture subpalette, 229
    Unwrap All button, 227

V

vamp masking, 163, *163*, *219–220*
vertices adjustment, 27
volume and massing, in body sculpting, **38–44**
    abdominal muscles, *41*
    arms, 42, *44*
    base mesh, *39*
    Clay brush, 39–40
    feet, *43*
    finished version, *44*
    hands, 42, *44*
    head, 40, *40*
    hip muscles, *41*
    knees, 42, *43*
    legs, 42, *42*
    in Maya, 38–39
    neck, *39*
    rib cage, *41*
    Smooth brush, 39
    Standard brush, 39

W

weapons, building of, **175–213**. *See also* holsters;
    line work, in weapon building
    alphas, 190
    Ambient Occlusion settings, *212*
    Backtrack Subpalette, *190*
    barrel, *182*
    base color, *211*
    chambers, *183*, 184
    ClipCircleCenter brush, 182
    ClipCurve, 179, *180*
    Deformation palette, *192*
    duplications, 176–177
    final block-in, *179*
    finishing, *195*
    form sculpting, 179–183, *180–183*
    grips, 188–189, *188–190*, *191*
    gun magazine, *183*
    H Polish brush, 179
    handles, *181*
    hard-surface models, 175
    holsters, **195–209**, *213*, *221–222*
    line work, **184**, **186–190**
    MaskCircle, 178, *178*
    masking in, 177, *177*, *188*, 190
    pins, *194*
    PolyCube, 192, *192*
    receivers, *177*, 179
    ShadowBox, 175–179, *176*
    side views, 176, *193*
    slides, *180*, *191–193*, 191–194

cularity curve, *210*
potlight paint mode, 176
stencils, 184, *184*, 187, *187*, 190
SubTool palette, 179
texturing, **210–212**
Transpose feature, *181*, *189*
trigger, 178, 183
Trim Dynamic brush, 179
wrinkles, in texturing, *103–104*, **103–104**.
   See also fabric wrinkles
   for fabric, **134–139**
   Inflate brush, 104
   in model topology, 215
   photo references, *126*
   Smooth Subdiv brush, 104
   Trim Dynamic brush, 104

X

Xpose, **275–276**
   model setting, *276*
   timeline markers, *276*

Z

Z Intensity feature, 11
   Depth feature, 13
Zadd/Zsub feature, 11, 13
   pore texturing, 98
ZAppLink, in texturing, **113–125**
   document size, 114
   Free Transform's Warp, 114

Layer masks, *123*
Link buttons, 114
maps, **120**
OilMask layer, 124, *124–125*
with photo references, **113–126**
in Photoshop, 115–116, *115–116*, 121
PolyPaint, 122
properties, *113*, 113–114
spot fixing, 121–122, *122*
UV maps, **117–119**
views, *121*
in weapon building, 186, *186*
Zbrush
   customer care, 282
   license agreement, 281
   for Macs, 280–281
   system requirements, 280–281
   troubleshooting, 282
   for Windows, 280–281
zippers
   pockets, 142
   slider body, 145–147, *145–147*
ZProject brush, 198, *198*
ZSketch feature, 169–170, *171*
ZSpheres, 29
   hair sculpting, 170, *170*, *172*
   in model topology, 235, *236*
   posing, 248
zygomatic bone, 74, 75, *75*, 78
   in mouth, 85–87, *86*